Guido Schryen

Anti-Spam Measures

Analysis and Design

With 50 Figures and 23 Tables

 Springer

Guido Schryen

Templergraben 64
52062 Aachen
Germany
schryen@gmx.net

ISBN 978-3-642-09087-5   e-ISBN 978-3-540-71750-8

Springer is a part of Springer Science+Business Media

springer.com

© Springer-Verlag Berlin Heidelberg 2010

Cover design: KünkelLopka Werbeagentur, Heidelberg

Printed on acid-free paper   45/3142/YL - 5 4 3 2 1 0

To my parents

Preface

I am not sure about the meaning of a preface, neither about its convenience or needlessness nor about the addressees. However, I suppose that it is expected to tell a (part of the) "story behind the story" and that it is read by at least two types of readers: The first group consists of friends, colleagues, and all others who have contributed to the "opus" in any way. Presumably, most of them like being named in the preface, and I think they deserve this attention because they have accompanied the road to the opus and are, thus, part of the whole. The second group comprises those academic fellows who are in the same boot as I am in terms of preparing or having even finished their doctoral or habilitation thesis. All others – be it that they generally like reading prefaces or expect hints with regard to the reading of this book – are likewise welcome to reading this preface.

This book contains most parts of my habilitation thesis, which was accepted by the Faculty of Business and Economics of the RWTH Aachen University, Germany. Unfortunately, to avoid possible copyright violation, I had to omit some paragraphs of the proposed infrastructure framework presented in Chapt. 6. If you are interested in the full version of this specific chapter, please contact me (schryen@gmx.net) and I will be happy to provide you an electronic copy. Usually, a thesis represents a (loosely-coupled) collection of published papers (cumulative thesis) or a classic monograph. However, this thesis is a hybrid insofar that the presentation mainly follows a thread but also contains parts that can be read isolated and that do not need to be read to "get the whole picture". Figure 1.1 (p. 5) sheds light on this issue.

Since many parts of this book have been published elsewhere (conferences, journals etc.) I got familiar with the time-consuming and sometimes frustrating process of publishing research papers. For example, I found referees who did not accept or follow argumentations while others stressed the strength of just these parts. Some found the research framework not very interesting while others appreciated it. These heterogeneous attitudes are often related to different point of views and although it is tempting to shift the blame on them when a paper is rejected I (maybe naïvely) believe that most referees try to be objective and that a good paper will be accepted sooner or later. And it is definitely the author, not the referee, who affects the quality of a paper. However, this is sometimes hard to accept.

Retrospectively, I find an amazing number of players who supported my work. I benefited from numerous discussions about technological issues with "The Caribbean explorer" (Reimar Hoven), "The broker" (Stephan Hoppe) and "Grisu" (Wilhelm Schwieren), all of who also proofread large parts of the manuscript and supported me in the set-up and maintenance of our e-mail honeypot. Further attentive proofreaders were "The girl scout" (Judith Dahmen), "Locke" (Jan Herstell), "The Leichlingen Dragon" (Thomas Wagner), and "Criens" (Rudolf Jansen). Many thanks go to Christine Stibbe and Katrin Ungeheuer, who did a great job with linguistic proofreading. Very helpful technical support was provided by Arne Böttcher, who created a lot of figures and tables, and by Agata Dura, who created the LATEX index. They both suffered from laborious work. I would also like to thank the referees of my habilitation thesis, namely Prof. Michael Bastian, Prof. Felix Freiling, and Prof. Kai Reimers for their efforts and for their feedback that helps much to improve the manuscript. Finally, I would like to mention the involved Springer staff for their very kind and very cooperative support.

I hope that this book provides detailed insights into (the meaning of) spam e-mails, that it ignites fertile discussions, and that it triggers effective anti-spam activities.

Aachen,
March 2007   *Guido Schryen*

Contents

List of Figures

List of Tables

Abbreviations

ABNF .... Augmented Backus-Naur Form
ADB .... Abuse Database
AOTs .... Address Obscuring/Obfuscating Techniques
ASTA .... Anti-Spam Technical Alliance
BATV .... Bounce Address Tag Validation
BGB .... Bürgerliches Gesetzbuch (German Civil Code)
BLOB .... Binary Large Object
CAPTCHA .... Completely Automated Public Turing Test to Tell Computers and Humans Apart
CDB .... Counter Database
CGI .... Common Gateway Interface
CMAA .... Counter Managing & Abuse Authority
CO .... Central Organization
DDoS .... Distributed Denial of Service
DFA .... Deterministic Finite Automaton
DKIM .... DomainKeys Identified Mail
DNS .... Domain Name System
DNSBLs .... Domain Name System Blacklists
DNSWLs .... Domain Name System Whitelists
DoD .... Department of Defense
DOLR .... Decentralized Object Location and Routing System
DoS .... Denial of Service
ERDs .... Entity Relationship Diagrams
ESP .... E-mail Service Provider
EU .... European Union
FQDN .... Fully Qualified Domain Name
FTC .... Federal Trade Commission
HTTP .... Hypertext Transfer Protocol
IAB .... Internet Architecture Board
IANA .... Internet Assigned Numbers Authority
ICANN .... Internet Corporation for Assigned Names and Numbers

IESG	Internet Engineering Steering Group
IETF	Internet Engineering Task Force
IMAP	Internet Message Access Protocol
IP	Internet Protocol
IRC	Internet Relay Chat
ISOC	Internet Society
ISP	Internet Service Provider
ITU	International Telecommunication Union
LCP	Lightweight Currency Protocol
LDA	Local Delivery Agent
LMAP	Lightweight Message Authentication Protocol
LMTP	Local Mail Transfer Protocol
MASS	Message Authentication Signature Standards
MDA	Mail Delivery Agent
MIME	Multipurpose Internet Mail Extensions
MoU	Memorandum of Understanding
MSA	Message Submission Agent
MTA	Mail Transfer Agent
MUA	Mail User Agent
NAT	Network Address Translation
ODB	Organization Database
OECD	Organisation for Economic Co-operation and Development
P2P	Peer-to-Peer
PEM	Privacy Enhancement for Internet Electronic Mail
PGP	Open Pretty Good Privacy
PKI	Public Key Infrastructure
POP	Post Office Protocol
RFC	Request for Comments
RO	Receiving Organization
S/MIME	Secure MIME
SASL	Simple Authentication and Security Layer
SAVE	Sender Address Verification Extension
SLD	Second Level Domain
SMTP	Simple Mail Transfer Protocol
SMTP-AUTH	SMTP Service Extension for Authentication
SO	Sending Organization
SOAP	Simple Object Access Protocol
SPA	Single-Purpose Address
SPAB	SPA block
SPABEE	SPA block encoded and encrypted
StGB	Strafgesetzbuch (German Criminal Code)
sTLD	sponsored Top Level Domain
TCP	Transmission Control Protocol

TKG .... Telekommunikationsgesetz (Austrian Law of Telecommunications)
TLD .... Top Level Domain
TMDA .... Tagged Message Delivery Agent
UBE .... Unsolicited Bulk E-mail
UCE .... Unsolicited Commercial E-mail
UML .... Unified Modeling Language
URI .... Uniform Resource Identifier
UWG .... Gesetz gegen den unlauteren Wettbewerb (German Law against Unfair Competition)
XBL .... Exploits Block List

1

Introduction

This work is about spam e-mails, which are just one type of spam we face in electronic communication. Other types are related to SMS, chats, or Internet phone (Spam over IP Telephony). However, issues relating to these are beyond the scope of this work. In this introduction, we describe the problem that (e-mail) spam causes, and its history. We also define the goals of this work, how they are addressed (methodology), and how this work is structured (architecture).

1.1 The problem

Most of us using the Internet e-mail service face almost daily unwanted messages in our mailboxes. We have never asked for these e-mails, and often do not know the sender, and puzzle about where the sender got our e-mail address from. The types of those messages vary: some contain advertisements, others provide winning notifications, and sometimes we get messages with executable files, which finally emerge as malicious codes, such as viruses and Trojan horses. Apparently, the Internet e-mail infrastructure is widely used, as well as misused, as an efficient medium for information distribution. Senders of bulk e-mail benefit from the anonymity that is inherent to the e-mail infrastructure: sender data can be easily spoofed, and remotely controlled PCs can be used for sending e-mails. The design principles of the e-mail infrastructure, which were originally intended to provide simplicity and flexibility, have become ambivalent characteristics.

There are a number of methods in use for managing unsolicited bulk e-mail, which is termed "spam". Many organizations employ filtering technology and construct elaborate rules that determine which senders are allowed to connect or deliver e-mail to their networks and which are to be blocked. However, even with good filters, which are the most deployed type of technological anti-spam measures, we have merely heuristics on hand, that sometimes misclassify e-mails: whereas a spam e-mail in our mailbox might not seem bad, an e-mail that has been erroneously classified as spam and remains, therefore, unnoticed, does. In such a case, an anti-spam measure is even counterproductive. Although policies and technology measures can be effective under certain conditions and help to maintain Internet e-mail a usable service, over time, their effectiveness degrades due to increasingly innovative spammer tactics. It is humbling to note that, for many years, statistics have shown that the number of spam e-mails is higher than the number of "regular" e-mails (ham e-mails).

Today, spam has even crossed the borderline between simply being annoying for private users and causing economic harm. For example, companies invest money in anti-spam software and IT staff, and they lose productivity of employees when these spend time in opening, reading, classifying e-mails as spam, and deleting them. Private users lose money due to fraud e-mails including phishing attacks. The worldwide economic harm caused by spam is estimated at hundreds of billion USD per year. This huge economic relevance of spam has motivated the national authorities of both many countries and federal states to address spam by legislation. However, despite some spammers being prosecuted, the effectiveness is limited, because e-mail messages today do not contain enough reliable information to trace them back to their true senders.

Beside technological and legislative anti-spam measures, organizational and behavioral measures have been proposed. However, many of these approaches still fail to address the root problems: first, sending bulk e-mail is a profitable business for spammers; and second, e-mail messages today do not contain enough reliable information to enable recipients to consistently decide whether messages are legitimate or forged [9]. Moreover, today's deployment of anti-spam measures resembles a (still open-ended) arms race between the anti-spam community and spammers. Even worse, we, generally, allocate resources of the recipients of e-mails to fight spam, instead of increasing the senders' need for resources.

What is currently lacking is the development and deployment of long-term, effective anti-spam measures, which keep Internet e-mail alive as a reliable, cost-effective, and flexible service. However, it is not necessary to "reinvent the wheel", the analysis of the combined application of already proposed solutions may also help in this regard.

1.2 The history

The etymology of the word "spam" is, usually, explained by using an old skit from Monty Python's Flying Circus comedy program (for example, see Merriam-Webster's Collegiate Dictionary): In the sketch in question, a restaurant serves all its food with lots of Spam, which is canned meat and an acronym for "**S**houlder of **P**ork and H**am**". The waitress repeats the word several times in describing how much Spam is in the dishes on the menu. When she does this, a group of Vikings in the corner start singing a chorus of "SPAM, SPAM,

SPAM..." at increasing volumes in an attempt to drown out other conversations. As "unsolicited bulk e-mail" disturbs Internet communication likewise, it was termed "spam".

In the literature, unwanted e-mail messages were being recognized as a problem in an Internet Request for Comments as early as 1975 ([134]) and in the pages of *Communications of the ACM* as early as 1982 ([41]).

Possibly the first spam ever was a message from a DEC marketing representative to every Arpanet (the predecessor of the Internet) address on the west coast, or at least the attempt to do so ([173]). In April of 1994, the term "spam" had not yet been born, but it did jump forward a great deal in popularity when two lawyers from Phoenix, named Canter and Siegel, posted a message advertising their fairly useless services in an upcoming U.S. "green card" lottery [20]. This was not the first such abusive posting, nor the first mass posting to be called a spam, but it was the first deliberate mass posting to commonly receive that name. Some more examples of early spam attacks are presented by Templeton [172].

1.3 Goals, methodology, and architecture

The still existing occurrence of spam e-mails in bulk proves that currently deployed anti-spam measures are low effective. However, this does not necessarily imply their inappropriateness as a matter of principle. One primary goal of this work is the methodical analysis of anti-spam measures in terms of their potentials, limitations, advantages, and drawbacks. These determine to which extent the measures can contribute to the reduction of spam in the long run. The range of considered anti-spam measures includes legislative, organizational, behavioral, and technological ones.

Legislative measures As legislative measures can vary in many regards, we provide a classification scheme for them. This scheme is based on attributes, whose instantiations determine the effectiveness of the particular legislative measure. We describe this determination on an abstract level and then analyze the anti-spam legislation of many countries with regard to the classification scheme (microscopic view). From a macroscopic point of view, we assess today's overall legislation landscape in terms of effectiveness, we identify currently unsolved problems, and we indicate means by which some limitations might be overcome.

Organizational measures We subsume abuse systems and (types of) international cooperation under organizational measures. This part is mainly descriptive, but it also shows the possible types of cooperation between national authorities, other non-profit organizations, companies, and users.

Behavioral measures Behavioral measures aim at e-mail users' procedures in using and distributing their e-mail addresses (ex ante behavior) and dealing with any spam e-mails which they receive (ex post behavior). With regard to the ex ante behavior, we identify locations where e-mail addresses can be harvested from. In order to support the empirical analysis of spammers' behavior concerning the collection and the usage of e-mail addresses, we provide the conceptualization and prototypic implementation of a honeypot. The evaluation of the honeypot data reflects the present behavior of spammers. We present mechanisms that allow for protecting e-mail addresses from being automatically collected. Concerning the ex post behavior, we provide a description and an analysis of options that the users have, once spam e-mails have found their way into their e-mail boxes. The findings of the analysis of behavioral measures can be used for the development of e-mail user guidelines. However, this issue is beyond the scope of this work.

Technological measures The vast majority of proposed anti-spam measures is technological-oriented. In order to maintain an overview of the methods, we propose several classification schemes. We describe technological anti-spam measures by following the functional classification. For the analysis of the effectiveness of anti-spam measures, we use the classification according to whether their application only refers to particular delivery routes that e-mails take or whether the measures are applicable independently of delivery routes. Whereas the former group of measures are analyzed informally, the latter are assessed formally: we provide a formal (graph) model of the Internet e-mail infrastructure, use automata theory to derive and categorize all possible delivery routes a spam e-mail may take (spamming options) and which any holistic anti-spam measures would need to cover. Finally, the effectiveness of (route-specific) anti-spam measures is analyzed relative to covering the identified spamming options.

The analysis of the various anti-spam measures shows that no single measure is the "silver bullet" against spam, and it is doubtful whether any single, simple solution will ever be able to reduce or stop spam. Rather, it seems appropriate to look for solutions that provide a complementary application of several anti-spam measures. The second primary goal of this work is, therefore, the conceptual development and analysis of an infrastructural e-mail framework, which features such a complementary application. After the presentation of the technological and organizational facets, the framework is analyzed twofold: its theoretical effectiveness is assessed with the aid of the formal model mentioned above, its storage and traffic requirements are analyzed quantitatively. We further consider deployment issues, as the framework would have to be integrated in both the technological and the organizational Internet infrastructure.

A graphical overview of the different parts of this work and their dependencies is given in Fig. 1.1. As the description of the empirical analysis of address abuse does not need necessarily to be read in order to follow the thread of this work, we put it at the end of the book. Besides the contents described above, this work first addresses two elementary issues: (1) It provides an introduction to spam and a motivation for addressing spam scientifically. (2) It explains the technological facet of the Internet e-mail delivery process and its susceptibility to spam.

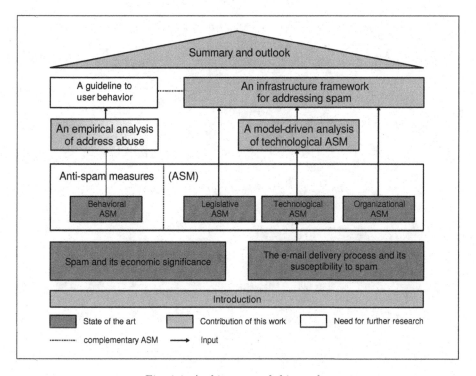

Fig. 1.1: Architecture of this work

2

Spam and its economic significance

Although "spam" is a buzzword in today's scientific and other media press, no homogeneous understanding exists of what precisely spam is. We address this definition issue by presenting and discussing prevalent definitions (Sect. 2.1), and we explain the understanding of "spam" that this work follows. Similar to the heterogeneity in defining spam, there are also no consistent empirical findings regarding the extent and the composition of spam. We explain the main reasons for this diversity, and we present statistics of "leading" market research organizations (Sect. 2.2). These numbers are useful for both the illustration of diversity and the provision of "dimensions". We then categorize spam (Sect. 2.3) with examples, in order to support the addressing of the economic harm and the economic benefit that spam can cause (Sects. 2.4 and 2.5).

2.1 Definition

Although a definition of "spam" would be useful, there does not appear to be a widely agreed and workable definition at present [123, 87]. A well accepted definition of spam could lead to a better comparability of spam statistics and to a homogenization of worldwide anti-spam legislation. However, a comprehensive definition might need to incorporate a diverse set of elements related to commercial behavior, recipient psychology, the broader legal context, economic considerations, and technical issues.

Besides various legislative understandings in different countries, the diversity with which spam is defined is well illustrated by the following definitions:

> "In France, the Commission Nationale de l'Informatique et des Libertés (National Data Processing and Liberties Commission) refers to 'spamming' or 'spam' as the practice of sending unsolicited e-mails, in large numbers, and in some cases repeatedly, to individuals with whom the sender has no previous contact, and whose e-mail address was harvested improperly."[123, p. 6]

> *"Spam is generally understood to mean the repeated mass mailing of un-solicited commercial messages by a sender who disguises or forges his identity."* [70]
>
> *"[...] spam is defined as unsolicited electronic messaging, regardless of its content. This definition takes into account the characteristics of bulk e-mail [...]".* [119, p. 7]

The OECD [123] classifies the characteristics of spam definitions as either primary or secondary. The primary characteristics include unsolicited electronic commercial messages, sent in bulk. Many would consider a message containing these primary characteristics to be spam. The remaining characteristics identified in many definitions are described as secondary characteristics which are frequently associated with spam, but not necessarily so. Table 2.1 shows this classification.

Table 2.1: Primary and secondary characteristics of spam [123]

Primary characteristics	Secondary characteristics
Electronic message	Uses addresses collected without prior consent or knowledge
Sent in bulk	Unwanted
Unsolicited	Repetitive
Commercial	Untargeted and indiscriminate
	Unstoppable
	Anonymous and/or disguised
	Illegal or offensive content
	Deceptive or fraudulent content

Despite the confusion and disagreement on a precise definition, there is fairly widespread agreement that spam exhibits certain general characteristics [87]:

1. Spam is an electronic message.[1]
2. Spam is unsolicited. If the recipient has agreed to accept a message, it is not spam. However, how and when such consent is given may not be clear, especially when a relationship between the sender and the recipient preexists.
3. Spam is sent in bulk. This implies that the sender distributes a large number of essentially identical messages and that recipients are chosen indiscriminately.

---

[1] For most purposes, this may be restricted to e-mail, but other methods of delivering spam do exist, including the Short Messaging Service, or SMS, Voice over IP, mobile phone multimedia messaging services, instant messaging services.

These three traits define Unsolicited Bulk E-mail (UBE); this also matches the definition by Spamhaus [165]. This work follows this understanding of spam. If a fourth is added – that spam must be of a commercial nature – the resulting class of messages is referred to as Unsolicited Commercial E-mail (UCE).

2.2 Spam statistics

Numerous statistics on different spam issues have been published by many organizations, such as Internet Service Provider (ISP)s, market research companies, universities, and supplier of security products. Although most studies share the findings that spam amounts to more than 50% of all worldwide e-mails, that most spam is relayed by hosts residing in the US or in Asia and that most spam is commercial advertising, they differ with regard to their figures. Two main reasons may be responsible for these differences[122]:

☐ The measurement of spam is closely linked to how spam is defined (see Sect. 2.1).
☐ Different methodologies are being used to measure and analyze spam: Three main approaches are being used for this: a survey (sampling-based) approach; a report-based approach; and a technical tool-based approach. Table 2.2 summarizes the characteristics of these approaches.

◇ Survey approach
The survey approach is closely tied to sample size as well as to the attitudes of the participants surveyed. In this context, it is important that the people surveyed are selected so as to be representative of the population being surveyed. Compared to technical tools, this approach is less costly, and can be set-up and undertaken in a relatively short time period. An example of a survey-based study is the survey of AOL and DoubleClick [44], an e-mail marketing solution provider. The questionnaire addressed 2,300 people, and the objective of the survey was to determine what triggers off consumer complaints, the process of reporting spam to AOL, or the process of unsubscribing to an e-mail.

◇ Report-based approach
The report-based approach is dependent on spam recipients themselves reporting the data, which are then analyzed. The main purpose of this approach is to analyze the contents of spam in detail and to identify the types of fraudulent or illegal spam, the spammers and the characteristics of spamming, on the basis of an analysis of the spam reported, rather than trying to measure the volume of spam or identifying the percentage of e-mail which is spam. With this approach, data is collected on a voluntary basis from users and, thus, the definition of spam (i.e. what has been reported as such) is subjective, based on the perception of the individual recipient. Various anti-spam organizations,

ISPs, E-mail Service Provider (ESP)s and organizations for data or privacy protection receive reports from the public or their subscribers and customers. For example, SpamCop (www.spamcop.net) and Abuse.net (www.abuse.net) have been operating a reporting service and provide complaint-based blacklists.

◇ Technical tool-based approach
The technical tool-based approach usually does not require the active participation of users. Generally, this means that this approach is more accurate and objective in that it does not require a subjective interpretation of users compared to the other two approaches. On the other hand, however, this approach is limited in that it cannot assess subjective reactions to spam, such as what type of action was taken by users to reduce spam or reactions to fraudulent or illegal types of spam. The technical tool-based approach is dependent on the accuracy of its technical methods, which require constant updating in order to recognize new forms of spam as they develop. Technical tools do not guarantee 100% accuracy, so that false-positive (non-spam that is mistakenly classified as spam) and false negative (spam that is mistakenly not classified as spam) results impact on the accuracy of any spam measurement using the technical tool-based approach.

In the following, we are interested in those types of statistics that are "best" created by the usage of technical tool-based approaches, such as the total amount of spam, the type or content of spam messages, or the geographic origins of spam. Organizations that collect huge data and provide such statistics are Symantec, MessageLabs, Ironport, Sophos, and Commtouch. The Symantec Probe Network consists of millions of decoy e-mail addresses that are configured to attract a stream of spam traffic that is representative of spam activity across the Internet as a whole [169]. MessageLabs collects data taken from its global network of control towers that scan millions of e-mails daily [122, p. 10]. Ironport uses the *SenderBase* traffic monitoring network and claims that this network samples 25% percent of the world's e-mail [84]. Sophos uses spam traps in its global network and analyzes millions of e-mails each day to determine whether they are spam or not [162].

The following statistics are not only affected by the intrinsic elements mentioned above, but also by some other, extrinsic factors, as Table 2.3 shows. Furthermore, the statistics focus on three issues of spam: (1) portions and trends in the development of spam categories, (2) categories of spam, and (3) origin of spam.

Figure 2.1 shows the development of spam over almost 2 years, as recorded by MessageLabs and Symantec. However, data on the spam portion in 2006 have not yet been provided by Symantec. Although the development of the spam portion is similar, the levels differ quite considerably. The figure indicates that the spam portion decreases; however, the numbers do not neces-

Table 2.2: *Comparison among approaches for spam measurement [122]*

Criteria	Survey-based approach	Report-based approach	Technical tool-based approach
Main target	Sample of (limited number of) users selected by the surveying company	Public (all e-mail recipients can report)	Subscribers or customers of certain companies or organisations
Major purpose (or focus of measurement)	Identifying types of spam or trends	Analyzing spam contents, identify spammers, etc.	Volume of spam and trends (types, origin of spam, etc.)
User action required	Active user action required	More active user action or involvement required	Almost no action of user required
Use of technical tools	Fewer technical tools used	Fewer technical tools used	Technical tools such as antispam solutions used
Accuracy	Depending on the sampling or survey methodology	Depending on the views or attitudes of users towards spam	Depending on the accuracy of technical tools
Major surveyor	Research Institution, privacy protection organisation, government, etc.	ISPs, Government, Public organisation, etc.	ISPs, Anti-spam solution providers, etc.
Resources and Period to measure	Relatively short period of time; not resource intensive	Relatively longer period of time and more resources required	Continuous relationship with subscribers and relatively more resources required

sarily signify any decrease in spam attack attempts on Internet e-mail users. Symantec [169] points out that, *"[...] as was the case during the first six months of 2005, this decline is likely due to the fact that network and security administrators are using IP filtering and traffic shaping to control spam. [...] If a message is blocked using these methods, it will not be detected by the Symantec Probe Network, and will thus not contribute to statistics gathered."*

According to Ironport, a study shows that in aggregate global e-mail is made up of 20% legitimate messages, spam makes up 67% percent, misdirected bounces make up 9 percent, viruses make up 3 percent and phishing e-mails make up less than 1 percent. Figure 2.1 show these numbers graphically.[2] Figure 2.2 gives the global e-mail composition of the Ironport company.

According to the studies of Sophos [163] and Commtouch [29], in the first quarter of 2006, most spam was sent from hosts in the United States, followed by China and South Korea. However, the portions vary considerably between these studies. It is difficult, if not impossible, to technically determine the origin of spam because spammers can use proxies or bots, which hide the

---

[2] The figure was taken from Ironport's whitepaper; however, it contains an error: phishing e-mails do not amount to more than 1%, but less.

Table 2.3: Elements affecting the variance of spam data [122]

Types of elements	Examples of Elements
Intrinsic elements	<ul><li>Definition of spam / Recipient's understanding of spam</li><li>Methodology / Organization</li><li>False negative or false positive (in technical tool-based approach)</li></ul>
Extrinsic elements	<ul><li>Network development</li><li>Severity of regulation / Effectiveness of law enforcement</li><li>Culture / Self regulatory rules</li><li>Time (period) and place (region) of measurement</li></ul>
Other temporary extrinsic elements	<ul><li>Spam virus</li><li>Activities of some high-volume spammers</li></ul>

spammer's location. The receiving e-mail server can only determine (reliably) the host that delivered (relayed) the e-mail. The numbers in Figs. 2.3, 2.4, and 2.5 are believed to refer to the relaying hosts; no precise information about the methods used is provided.

Figure 2.5 indicates that most spam is sent from hosts residing in North America, followed by hosts in Asia and hosts in Europe. The numbers refer to March 2005; however, the numbers of January and February 2006 are almost identical to these. We can therefore approximate the numbers of the first quarter with the numbers of March. [3]

2.3 Spam categories

Spam can be categorized according to the spammer's goal. Many spammers send out their bulk e-mail for advertising reasons, for example, they send commercial ads or participate in political campaigns, whereas others have some kind of criminal fraud in mind or distribute malicious software, such as viruses or Trojan horses. This section presents the most common types of spam and gives statistics, where available.

---

[3] In order to precisely determine the numbers of the first quarter, the numbers of the three months would have to be weighted with the portion of spam e-mails sent in that particular month. However, these data are not available.

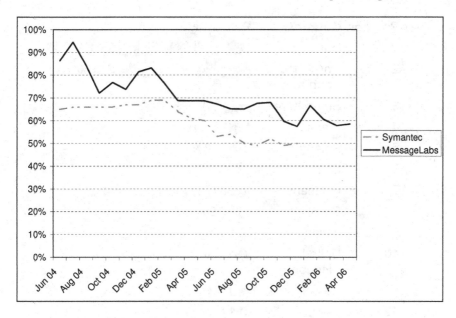

Fig. 2.1: Average global ratio of spam in e-mail [104, 169]

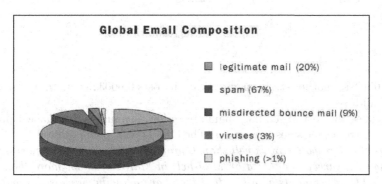

Fig. 2.2: Global e-mail composition [84]

2.3.1 Commercial advertising

Spam that follows any commercial intention is denoted as UCE (see Subsect. 2.1). Mostly, UCE is a kind of direct marketing and is viewed by companies as an important tool to approach (potential) customers, because e-mail provide a cheap and easy way to contact a large group of customers. However, most UCEs are not sent by the advertising companies themselves, but by spammers, who receive commissions from these companies [18, p. 14]. According to [123], a study estimates that the cost of sending a single e-mail is between 0.01 US$

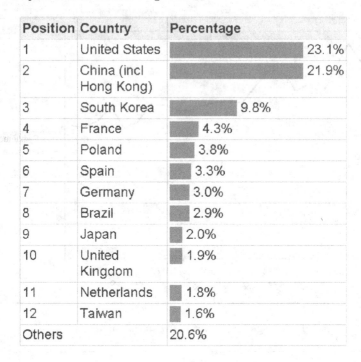

Position	Country	Percentage	
1	United States		23.1%
2	China (incl Hong Kong)		21.9%
3	South Korea		9.8%
4	France		4.3%
5	Poland		3.8%
6	Spain		3.3%
7	Germany		3.0%
8	Brazil		2.9%
9	Japan		2.0%
10	United Kingdom		1.9%
11	Netherlands		1.8%
12	Taiwan		1.6%
Others		20.6%	

Fig. 2.3: Spam relaying countries [163]

and 0.05US$, another study suggests that it costs 0.00032 cents to obtain one e-mail address.

Because the cost of sending spam are so low, spammers can make a profit despite extremely low response rates. The OECD [123, p. 9] points out: " *With low costs, low response rates will show a profit through spam nonetheless. According to a survey conducted by Mailshell in March of 2003, more than 8% of the 1,118 respondents admitted that they have actually purchased a product promoted via spam. A study by the Wall Street Journal in 2002 showed that a return rate as low as 0.001% can be profitable when using e-mail. In one case cited, a mailing of 3.5 million messages resulted in 81 sales in the first week, a rate of 0.0023%. Each sale was worth USD 19 to the marketing company, resulting in USD 1,500 in the first week. The cost to send the messages was minimal, probably less than USD 100 per million messages. The study estimated that by the time the marketing company had reached all of the 100 million addresses it had on file, it would probably have pocketed more than USD 25,000 on the project.* " As long as spammers can take in more money than it costs them, they will probably continue to spam. This is "rational" behavior in the economic sense.

Figure 2.6 shows a pharmaceutical UCE. Beside direct marketing, another type of UCE is spam e-mails that are indirectly commercial. An example

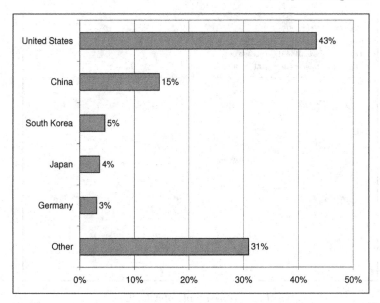

Fig. 2.4: Spam relaying countries (Commtouch) [29]

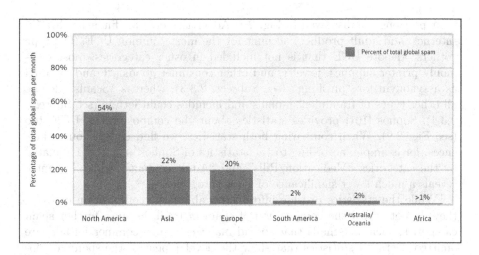

Fig. 2.5: Spam relaying continents (Symantec) [169]

would be the recommendation to purchase a particular stock, in order to affect the stock's price. Figure 2.7 displays such an UCE. Böhme and Holz [15] conducted an empirical study and showed that, in the short run, stock spam has a significant impact on both traded volume and market valuation.

According to statistics of Symantec [169], in the last year, UCE continuously amounted to about 80% of all spam e-mails. The product categories and

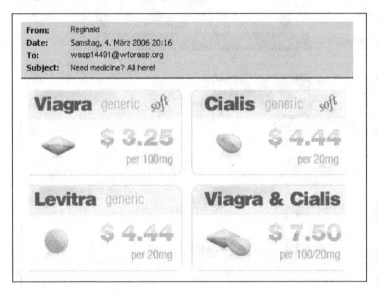

Fig. 2.6: Example of a UCE

their portions are displayed in Fig. 2.8. Advertisements for financial, health, Internet, and adult products account for the most common UCE. The type "others" denote UCE that is not included in other categories; most commonly printer supplies, jewelry, and other consumer goods. "Fraud" is used as a synonym for "phishing" (see Subsect. 2.3.3), whereas "Scams" denote all other types of fraudulent e-mails and includes chain letters (see Subsect. 2.3.4). Sophos [161] provides statistics about the composition of UCE, too (see Fig. 2.9). When comparing both statistics, we find conspicuous differences, for example, according to the statistics of Sophos, spam is dominated by the categories "Medication/Pills" and "Adult content", while Symantec reveals a much lower significance of these categories.

While the statistics provide information about the composition of UCE, they do not reveal the composition of spam in total, because further spam categories, such as e-mails that spread malware or non-commercial ads, are omitted. Detailed statistics that show the development of the spam components could not be found.

2.3.2 Non-commercial advertising

Advertising e-mails need not to be commercial-oriented. They can also propagate political, cultural, or religious ideas and/or organizations. For example, in 2003, members of the US Congress were sending out hundreds of thousands of unsolicited messages to constituents [176].

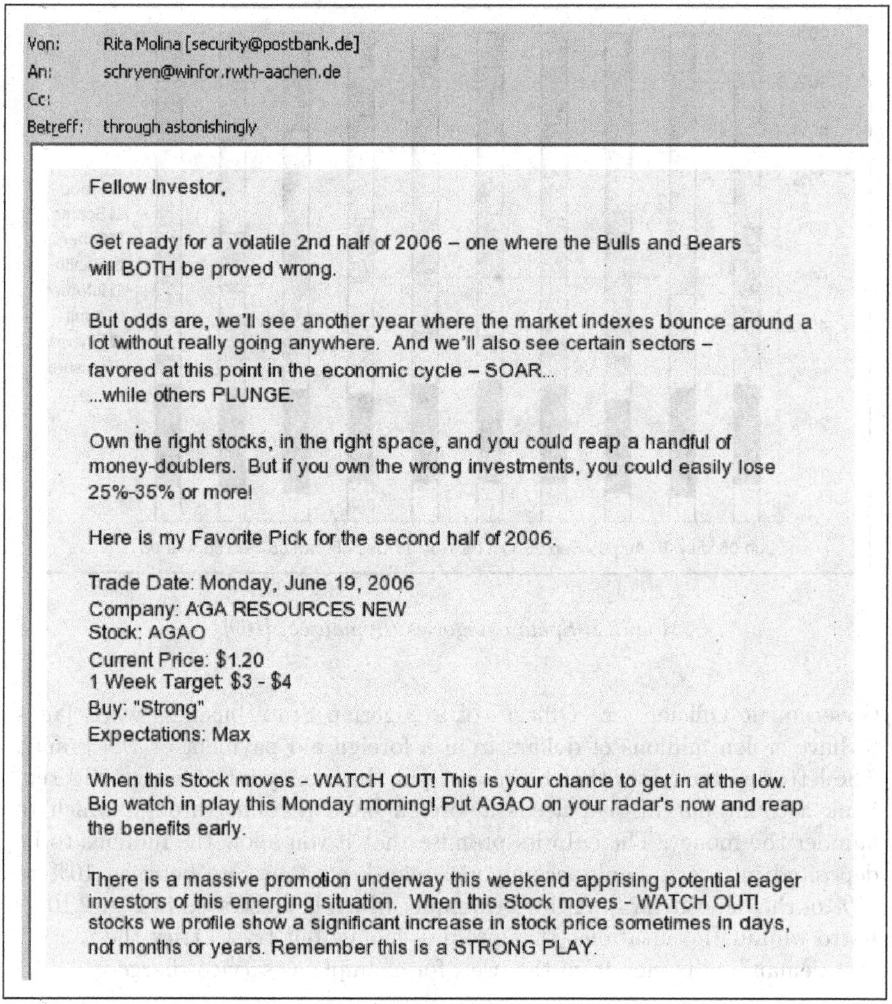

Von: Rita Molina [security@postbank.de]
An: schryen@winfor.rwth-aachen.de
Cc:
Betreff: through astonishingly

Fellow Investor,

Get ready for a volatile 2nd half of 2006 – one where the Bulls and Bears
will BOTH be proved wrong.

But odds are, we'll see another year where the market indexes bounce around a
lot without really going anywhere. And we'll also see certain sectors –
favored at this point in the economic cycle – SOAR...
...while others PLUNGE.

Own the right stocks, in the right space, and you could reap a handful of
money-doublers. But if you own the wrong investments, you could easily lose
25%-35% or more!

Here is my Favorite Pick for the second half of 2006.

Trade Date: Monday, June 19, 2006
Company: AGA RESOURCES NEW
Stock: AGAO
Current Price: $1.20
1 Week Target: $3 - $4
Buy: "Strong"
Expectations: Max

When this Stock moves - WATCH OUT! This is your chance to get in at the low.
Big watch in play this Monday morning! Put AGAO on your radar's now and reap
the benefits early.

There is a massive promotion underway this weekend apprising potential eager
investors of this emerging situation. When this Stock moves - WATCH OUT!
stocks we profile show a significant increase in stock price sometimes in days,
not months or years. Remember this is a STRONG PLAY.

Fig. 2.7: Example of an "indirect" UCE

2.3.3 Fraud and phishing

Some spammers send e-mails that are fraudulent, intentionally misguiding, or
known to result in fraudulent activity on the part of the sender. E-mails that
are fraudulent in nature are also denoted as "scam". Examples of fraudulent
messages are those that pretend to collect money for victims suffering from a
personal stroke of fate or for victims of a natural disaster. Another example
is the Nigerian money transfer fraud, Nigerian scam or 419 scam after the
relevant section of the Nigerian Criminal Code that it violates: People all
around the world have received letters from Nigeria, ostensibly from a "Senior

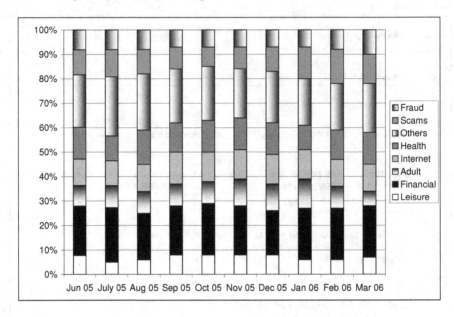

Fig. 2.8: Spam categories (Symantec) [169]

Government Official" or "Officer" of a Nigerian State business who claims to have stolen millions of dollars from a foreign aid payment or UN grants. The letter writer states that he cannot put the money into his own Nigerian bank account but instead needs a foreign bank account through which to launder the money. The culprits promise that if you allow the millions to be deposited into your bank account you may keep anywhere between 10% to 30% of the deposit [174]. A third example, which is illustrated in Fig. 2.10, is Lotto winning notifications, that promise money but try to trick the user by first demanding money from the user, for example as service charge.

A particular type of fraud is phishing e-mails that appear to be from a well-known company, but are not. Also known as "brand spoofing", these messages are often used to trick users into revealing personal information, such as e-mail address, financial information and passwords. Examples are account notification, credit card verification, and billing updates. Figure 2.11 shows an e-mail that pretends to be from the HSCB bank, but is not. If the user clicks a hyperlink to access his or her online banking account, the user is led to a web page, the design of which is that of the HSCB bank, but that is under the control of a third party. Similarly, the phishing e-mail shown in Fig. 2.12 tries to grab the data of eBay users. Current data about phishing attacks are provided by the *Anti-Phishing Working Group* (http://www.antiphishing.org).

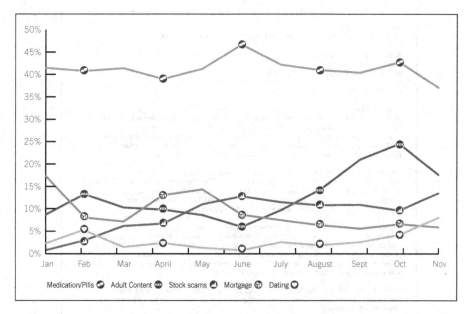

Fig. 2.9: Spam categories (Sophos) [161]

2.3.4 Hoaxes and chain e-mails

A hoax is an attempt to trick an audience into believing that something
false is real, mostly combined with a recommendation to forward the hoax
to as many people as possible. Many e-mail warn the users against viruses,
worms, or Trojan horses, some misinform about political or social events,
while others are charity hoaxes, joke hoaxes, or commercially oriented, for
example by offering free gift vouchers. A list of virus hoaxes is provided on
the web page *http://www.symantec.com/avcenter/hoax.html*; the web page
http://www.hoax-slayer.com/ provides even more types of hoaxes. Figure 2.13
shows a joke hoax. A hoax can also be used to distribute malicious software
(see Subsect. 2.3.6) by tricking a user to visit a web page that installs malware.

Chain e-mail is a term used to describe e-mails that encourage you to
forward them on to someone else, the Internet versions of chain letters.

2.3.5 Joe jobs

"Joe job" is the Internet term for forged e-mail which appears to have been
sent by one party, but has actually been forged by someone else with the
intent of generating complaints about, and damaging the reputation of, an
innocent victim. For example, a "joe jobber" might spam a message containing
child pornography to thousands of people using a forged return address of
"alan.stone@xyzcompany.com" in order to outrage the recipients and provoke

TICKET NUMBER: 46939894427
LOTTO NL. INTERNATIONAL PROMOTIONS/PRIZE AWARD DEPARTMENT

Koningen Julianaplein 21, 2391 BD
Denhaag, The Netherlands
RESULTS FOR CATEGORY "A" DRAWS

Dear Sir/Madam,

Congratulations to you as we bring to your notice, the results of the Second Category draws
of THE LOTT NL.PROMO INT. We are happy to inform you that you have emerged as a winner under
the First Category, which is part of our promotional draws. The results of the draws hve been
officially announced . Participants were selected through a computer ballot system drawn from
2,500,000 email addresses of individuals and companies from Africa, America, Asia,Australia,
Europe, Middle East, and Oceania as part of our International Promotions Program.

Your e-mail address, attached to ticket number 46939,with serial number 472- 9768 and
lucky number W-91237-H?67/B4 consequently won in the First Category. You have therefore been
awarded a lump sumpay out of 1,000,000 (One Million Euros), which is the winning payout for
Category A winners. This is from a total cash prize of ?10,000,000.00 (Ten Million Euros)
shared amongst the first Ten (10) lucky winners in this category.

In your best interest to avoid mix up of numbers and names of any kind, we request that you
keep the entire details of your award strictly from public notice until the process of transferring
your claims has been completed, and your funds remitted to your account. This is part of our security
protocol to avoid double claiming or unscrupulous acts by Participants/nonparticipants of this program.
Please contact our paying bank (leed capital Bank) immediately for due processing and remittance of
your prize money to a designated account of your choice:

NOTE: For easy reference and identification, find below your Reference and Batch numbers.
Remember to quote these numbers in your correspondence with your paying bank.Also give them the
following informations
Name
Age
Address
Occupation
REF Number:
NM/BC921245/KY14
BATCH No: NM/207161/WOP.
CONGRATULATIONS!!!
Your fund
is now deposited with the paying Bank. To begin your claims, kindly
contact the paying bank with the below information:
****
Contact person:Mr
Patrick Rowley
E-mail: Leedcaptlb@netscape.net
Tel: 00 31 633 701 450.
Fax: 00 31 847 570 900.
****
NOTE: All claims are nultified after 10 working days from today if unclaimed
Congratulations once again from all our staffs, and thank you for being
part of our promotions program.

Yours Sincerely,
Mrs. Evlyn Bakker
(Lottery Coordinator).

Fig. 2.10: Fraudulent e-mail

them into flooding John Smith's mailbox with complaints, or to tarnish the
reputation of the XYZ company.

The name "joe job" was first used to describe such a scheme directed at
Joe Doll, who offered space for free web pages. One user had his account
removed for advertising through spam; in retaliation, he sent another spam
to several million innocent victims, but with the "reply-to" headers forged
to make it appear to be from Joe Doll. He describes the victims' answers as

| Von: | HSBC Bank [service@hsbc.co.uk] <se | An: | schryen@winfor.rwth-aachen.de |
| Betreff: | *****SPAM***** Your account acce | Cc: | |

Dear online banking customer,

Thank you for using the HSBC Bank Online Transfer® - service.

In order to provide final approval for your transaction, we need additional information. Please access your **online banking account** to verify the information is correct and complete your enrollment.

If we do not hear from you within the next 24 hours, we will cancel your Online Transfer® service.

Click here for online banking

Your Promotional Code for Online Transfer® Service is: 905855815
Please use this number if needed.

If you have questions, please visit our website at www.hsbc.co.uk/contact/.

Thank you for using © HSBC Bank plc!

DO NOT REPLY TO THIS EMAIL. IF YOU HAVE QUESTIONS PLEASE CONTACT US

Fig. 2.11: Example 1 of a phishing e-mail

follows: *"The response was swift, massive and ugly. It included threats, forged messages to spam lists, and mail bombs. Enraged victims have mounted mail, ping, syn, and other attacks on joes.com, incited to vigilante justice by the forger."* [43]

2.3.6 Malware

Malware is software designed to infiltrate or damage a computer system. It is commonly taken to include computer viruses, worms, Trojan horses, spyware and adware. This type of software is often sent as an unsuspicious a-mail attachment. When the user opens the file, the malware installs itself. An interdependence between spam e-mails and malware has evolved [124]: Spam e-mails spread malware, malware is used to infect a host so that the host can be remotely controlled and used for the sending of more spam e-mails. Such infected hosts are denoted as "zombie PCs". Many people believe that most spam is sent via botnets, which are a network of zombie PCs; however, it is difficult to prove this assumption.

2.3.7 Bounce messages

Bounce messages are undeliverable e-mail messages that are returned to their sender. When a receiving e-mail server gets a message with an undeliverable address, it will generate a new "bounce" message back to the purported sender notifying that user that the e-mail was undeliverable". According to a study

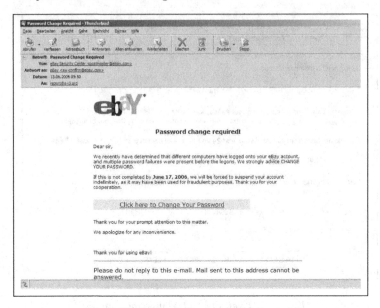

Fig. 2.12: Example 2 of a phishing e-mail

by Ironport [84], bounce e-mails that are due to undeliverable spam e-mails with forged return address and, therefore "misdirected" or returned to an innocent third party, amount to about 9% of all e-mail traffic (see Fig. 2.2) or 1.67 billion bounce e-mails every day, according to [52]. Bounce messages are not themselves spam e-mails; however, they amount to a significant part of the e-mail traffic that is due to spam.

2.4 Economic harm

Many organizations have made calculations and predictions of the economic harm that spam causes. For example,

❑   according to Ferris Research [56], in 2005, spam costs organizations world-wide USD 50 billion, of this, USD 17 billion were lost by U.S. organizations,
❑   according to a study by Sophos [123], statistics show that, in 2004, global spam had reached at least 3 trillion messages with an estimated cost of USD 131 billion, and
❑   a European Union study [70] estimates that the worldwide cost to Internet subscribers of spam is in the vicinity of EUR 10 billion a year.

However, these numbers are difficult to compare, because they include different types of spam harm, use different prediction and computation methods, and make different assumptions about economic data, such as the purchase

Subject: FW: ***WARNING*** TO ALL DOG OWNERS!!!!!

WARNING TO ALL DOG OWNERS

Warning to all dog owners: Watch your dog!

The State Highway Patrol in conjunction with the FBI has issued a warning advising all dog owners to keep their dogs indoors until further notice. Dogs are being picked off one at a time on an almost continual basis throughout the city. They are falling in great numbers. Police in the city advise all dog owners not to walk their dogs - KEEP THEM INDOORS UNTIL FURTHER NOTICE!

Fig. 2.13: Joke hoax [26]

cost of anti-spam products and the lost productivity per employee per year. In the following, we try to qualify and categorize the harm that spam can cause in order to support further quantitative analysis of total spam costs.

Figure 2.4 gives an overview of the types of harm and the participants that are affected. We denote spam's economic harm as "direct" if it is caused by the fact that spam e-mails occur. An example is the costs for increased network bandwidth. Costs are categorized as indirect if the harm emerges from actions or missing actions that result from spam e-mails. Examples are costs due to fraud and loss of profit respectively. Regarding the participants, we distinguish between ESPs/ISPs, other organizations, and private users.

According to a study by Nucleus Research [120], no evidence of any economies of scale in managing spam has been found, so large companies will have substantial costs with which to contend.

Table 2.4: Categories of economic harm caused by spam

Type of economic harm	affected participants	ISPs/ ESPs	(other) organizations	private users
Direct economic harm	Loss of productivity		X	
	Staff costs	X	X	
	Infrastructure costs	X	X	X
	Download costs		X	X
Indirect economic harm	Harm through (execution of) malicious payload			X
	Legal fees	X	X	
	Opportunity costs		X	
	Loss of reputation	X	X	
	Communication and marketing costs		X	
	Harm through fraud		X	X

We now consider the categories of economic harm caused by spam in more detail:

❑ Loss of productivity
When employees receive spam e-mails, which were able to outwit spam filters and other anti-spam procedures, they spend time opening, reading, classifying them as spam, and then deleting them. As with the estimation of the total costs caused by spam, several studies show different findings:

◇ The Australian National Office for the Information Economy estimates that the cost of time spent in opening and reading spam in the workplace averages AUD 960 (approximately USD 620) per employee each year [118].

◇ According to a study by Brightmail [17], it is assumed that 10% of the total e-mail is spam and that each employee spends 30 seconds per day deleting such. Based on theses assumptions, the study estimates that the annual costs of spam to a 10,000-person company is USD 675,000.

◇ To analyze the impact of spam on employee productivity, Nucleus [120] conducted interviews with employees and IT administrators at different US companies to learn about their experiences with spam. Key findings included that the average employee receives 13.3 spam messages per day and that time spent per person managing spam ranges from 90 minutes to 1 minute per day, with an average of 6.5 minutes. The resulting average lost productivity per employee per year is 1.4% (6.5 minutes/day divided by 480 total minutes/day). The average costs of spam per employee per year are USD 874 (1.4% times 2080 hours at an average fully loaded cost of USD 30/hour).

❑ Staff costs

Spam-related staff is needed in many regards. First, IT employees have to maintain the anti-spam infrastructure. This comprises, for example, the maintenance of anti-spam software, blacklists and whitelists and the integration of new hardware. According to Nucleus Research, for every 690 employees, a full-time IT staff person will be needed just to manage spam [120].[4] Second, help desk staff is necessary: users call central help desks from time to time, to seek help in dealing with spam issues. This element covers the costs of providing the help-desk service. Third, training for all messaging administrators and help desk staff may occur [177].

❑ Infrastructure costs

Spam e-mails burden the IT infrastructure of Organizations, especially ESPs and ISPs, in many ways: anti-spam software and probably hardware are acquired and maintained, processing power for the anti-spam software is needed, bandwidth is consumed, and storage for the spam e-mails must be provided. Assumed that one 500 KB message (with a virus attached) is sent to 10,000 users with their mailboxes at one ESP host, that means an unsolicited, unexpected, storage of 5 GB. A "state of the art" 80 GB disk can take 16 such message floods before it is filled. It is almost impossible to plan ahead for such "storms".

❑ Download costs

It costs real money for the receivers to download their e-mails: Since many receivers still pay for the time to transfer the mailbox from the (dialup) ISP to their computer, they are paying in reality for doing so.

❑ Harm through malicious payload

Many spam e-mails contain malicious code, such as viruses, Trojan horses, worms, spyware, and key loggers. The economic harm that results from the execution of malicious software has not yet been quantified.

❑ Legal fees

When organizations aim at prosecuting spammers, legal fees including costs for lawyers emerge [123].

❑ Opportunity costs

Spam e-mail can result in some types of opportunity costs:

⬦ If an e-mail system does not work properly or at all due to spam floods, it may happen that order e-mails from customers are lost (direct loss of revenue).

⬦ Legitimate business messages may be erroneously blocked or filtered out as spam ("false-positives") and do not reach their intended recipients, who often do not know that their ISP or company has stopped

---

[4] The study mentions that " Administrators spend an average of .7 minutes per employee per week managing spam and spam-related issues." However, if we multiply .7 minutes by 690, we get 483 minutes or 8,05 hours. This seems to be the working time per day, not per week. Consequently, we would need a full-time IT staff person for about $5 * 690 = 3450$ employees.

the message. As a result, legitimate e-mail marketers may lose both existing customers and the opportunity to obtain new customers [123].

◇ An indirect loss of revenue may occur, if customers lose their general confidence in e-mail marketing due to many dubious spam e-mails.

❑ Loss of reputation
If e-mail systems of organizations are not available due to spam attacks or customer inquiries are not answered, because they are "false-positives" (opportunity costs), the reputation of the organization may be reduced. In the case where a spammer pretends to send e-mails on behalf of a particular organization – joe jobs and phishing e-mails are examples of what is denoted as "identity theft" –, a loss of reputation may occur. Legitimate e-mail marketers, i.e. those marketers that send e-mails only to recipients who have opted in, may lose their reputations if they are associated with spamming activities. The loss of reputation is difficult to quantify.
ESPs can lose their reputations if their anti-spam systems do not work properly, i.e. if the false-positive and/or false-negative rates are too high. On the other hand, ESPs can gain a good reputation by providing effective anti-spam systems.

❑ Communication and marketing costs
Legitimate e-mail marketers suffer from spam (filters). They are burdened with adjusting and readjusting their business practices to comply with filters and changing regulations [87, p. 7]. Even worse, if organizations decide to switch (marketing) communication to fax or mail, communication costs will increase.

❑ Harm through fraud
Fraud, including phishing, is an indirect harm that spam can cause. In 2003, the accumulated economic impact of phishing attacks was estimated at USD 222 billion with an average profit to the "phisher" of USD 5000 per successful transaction [124].

2.5 Economic benefit

Beside the economic harm that spam causes to ISPs/ESPs, other organizations, and private users, some people and organizations profit economically from spam. Table 2.5 shows who profits from which type.

Although some studies exist regarding spammers' profit when sending UCE (see Subsect. 2.3.1), the economic benefit resulting from spam has hardly been quantified yet. The quantification of both economic harm and economic benefit is necessary in order to assess the economic impact of spam. Further (empirical) research is required in this area. However, a profound analysis of economic harm and economic benefit would require the availability of comprehensive empirical data on both senders and receivers of spam. Data on both types of parties are difficult to obtain because the participants tend to

Table 2.5: *Types of profit through spam*

Type of profit	Profiteer
Sale of advertised products and services	Advertising companies
Participation in sales	Spammers
Address pools	Collectors and harvesters of addresses
Sale of anti-spam and anti-virus software	Companies offering IT security products
Sale of bandwidth	Offerer of telecommunication infrastructures, for example telecommunication companies
Sale of juristic services	Lawyers
Competitive advantage due to successful anti-spam detection and prevention	E-mail service providers

be incommunicative with regard to the provision of such. The collection of these data and, consequently, any further analysis are beyond the scope of this work.

3

The e-mail delivery process and its susceptibility to spam

Spammers continue to exploit the technological e-mail infrastructure which was not originally designed to tackle security issues like authentication, integrity, secrecy and a mass of unsolicited e-mails. Section 3.1 presents the basics of the e-mail delivery process with a particular focus on the Simple Mail Transfer Protocol (SMTP), which is the core protocol used in Internet e-mail delivery. In Sect. 3.2, the insecurity of SMTP and its susceptibility to spam is discussed. The detailed insight into the technological processes given in this chapter is essential to the discussion of technological anti-spam measures and their limitations which are presented in Sect. 4.4.

3.1 The e-mail delivery process

Figure 3.1 provides a sketch of a typical Internet e-mail delivery process.

The sender uses a Mail User Agent (MUA) to compose a message which is then sent to a local SMTP client. This client is often integrated in the MUA. The SMTP client introduces the new message into the Mail Transfer Agent (MTA) routing network [93], including all Internet Assigned Numbers Authority (IANA)-registered SMTP service extensions, formerly also referred to as ESMTP [92]. Examples of SMTP service extensions are *Deliver By SMTP Service Extension* [117], *SMTP Service Extension for Returning Enhanced Error* [58], *SMTP Service Extension for Secure SMTP over Transport Layer Security* [78] and SMTP Service Extension for Authentication (SMTP-AUTH) [114] whereby – with all of these service extensions – an SMTP client may indicate an authentication mechanism to the server, perform an authentication protocol exchange, and optionally negotiate a security layer for subsequent protocol interactions.[1] Other authentication methods have been applied. These include

---

[1] See *www.iana.org/assignments/mail-parameters* for a list of SMTP service extensions. The implementation of SMTP service extensions is not mandatory and must not be assumed.

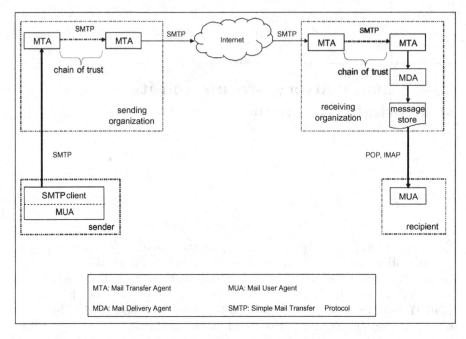

Fig. 3.1: A sketch of the e-mail delivery process

Internet Protocol (IP) address restrictions, secure IP, and prior Post Office Protocol (POP) authentication. If Transmission Control Protocol (TCP) port 587 is used, this part of the e-mail delivery process is denoted as "message submission" [72]. Once an MTA of the Sending Organization (SO), e.g. the e-mail provider or the employer's organization, has received a message, it might be SMTP-passed sequentially to some other MTAs inside the SO. Because all these MTAs belong to the same organization, this part of the communication is trustworthy. The last MTA of the SO may SMTP-connect to an MTA of the Receiving Organization (RO) or may SMTP-connect to another SMTP server on the Internet. This server can work as an intermediate relay (that is, it may assume the role of an SMTP client after receiving the message) like all the other preceding MTAs, or as a gateway (that is, it may transport the message further using some protocol other than SMTP). Once a relay or gateway on the Internet is used, many more relays and gateways may follow before the message arrives at an MTA of the RO. The RO may involve some other MTAs, analogously to the SO. The final delivery MTA hands over the e-mail to a Mail Delivery Agent (MDA), which deposits the message in a message store. The recipient uses an MUA that usually has facilities for receiving messages via POP [115] or the Internet Message Access Protocol (IMAP) [32], both of which are, in contrast to SMTP, which is a "push-based" protocol, "pull-based" protocols. E-mail access can also be Hypertext Transfer Protocol (HTTP)-based [73].

SMTP in particular has to be addressed if the vast majority of Internet (spam) messages are to be managed and controlled. Protocols other than SMTP-related ones have to make their own provisions for SMTP-compliant interfaces. If technological anti-spam approaches are to be successful, they have to accommodate the wide deployment of SMTP and its weaknesses. Consequently, the SMTP delivery process is inspected here in more detail. The specification of SMTP can be found in RFC 2821 [93], which subsumes the original SMTP specification of RFC 821 [135], the domain name system requirements and implications for e-mail transport from RFC 1035 [108] and RFC 974 [133], the requirements for Internet hosts in RFC 1123 [108], and material drawn from the SMTP extension mechanisms [92]. In order to get a more comprehensible overview of the protocol and its security weaknesses, the textual representation is modeled with a diagram. Unified Modeling Language (UML) provides activity diagrams and sequence diagrams, both of which are appropriate. However, as the information flows between the communicating MTAs are relevant, a sequence diagram is used. Figure 3.2 shows a UML (2.0) sequence diagram modeling SMTP.

When an SMTP client has a message to transmit, it establishes a two-way transmission channel to an SMTP server. The responsibility of an SMTP client is to transfer e-mail messages to one or more SMTP servers, or report its failure to do so. The server responds to each command with a reply; replies may indicate that the command was accepted, that additional commands are expected, or that a temporary or permanent error condition exists. The server response consists of a number and a text represented by the attributes *code* and *text*. Commands specifying the sender or recipients may include server-permitted SMTP service extension requests. The dialog is purposely lock-step, one-at-a-time, although this can be modified by mutually-agreed extension requests, such as command pipelining [59], which is not modeled here. Regarding the reply codes, the limited set offered by SMTP is used, even though RFC 1893 [185] provides enhanced Mail System Status Codes. These are not necessary for use in this modeling context.

The SMTP procedure contains four phases: the session initiation, the client initiation, the e-mail transactions, and the session termination. An SMTP session is initiated when a client opens a connection to a server and the server responds with opening information. The SMTP server is allowed to reject a transaction by giving a 554 response. A server taking this approach must still wait for the client to send a *quit* before closing the connection. Once the server has sent the welcoming message and the client has received it, the latter normally sends the *EHLO* command to the server, indicating the client's identity, which is also denoted as the Fully Qualified Domain Name (FQDN), e.g. *darth-vader.winfor.rwth-aachen.de*. In addition to opening the session, the use of *EHLO* indicates that the client is able to process service extensions and the client then requests that the server provide a list of the extensions which the server supports; each service extension contains a keyword and a parameter list. Older SMTP systems, which are unable to support service

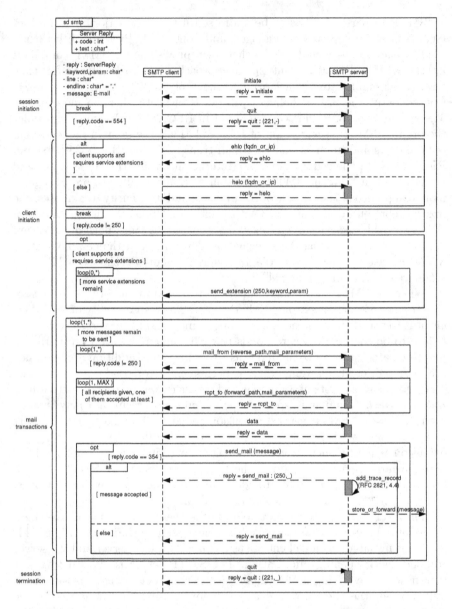

Fig. 3.2: UML sequence diagram modeling SMTP

extensions, and contemporary clients, which do not require service extensions
in the e-mail session to be initiated, may use *HELO* instead of *EHLO*. If the
server does not accept the command for some reason, the return code is not
250 and the session is terminated.

Each SMTP e-mail transaction basically consists of three steps: The transaction starts with a *MAIL FROM* command which provides sender identification. A series of one or more *RCPT TO* commands follows, providing receiver information. Subsequently, a *DATA* command initiates transfer of the e-mail data.

1. The first step in the procedure is the *MAIL FROM* command with a *reverse-path* as mandatory argument and a parameter list as optional argument. This command tells the SMTP receiver that a new e-mail transaction is starting and that it has to reset its state tables and buffers, including any recipients or mail data. The *reverse-path* contains the source mailbox, which can be used to report errors. The optional list of parameters is associated with negotiated SMTP service extensions. The SMTP client needs to repeat sending the *MAIL FROM* command until it is accepted by the SMTP server returning a 250 OK reply. If the mailbox specification is not acceptable for some reason, the server must return a reply, indicating whether the failure is permanent or temporary (i.e., the address might be accepted were the client to try again later).

2. The second step in the procedure is the *RCPT TO* command. The first or only argument to this command includes a *forward-path* (normally a mailbox and domain) identifying one recipient. If this is accepted, the SMTP server returns a 250 OK reply and stores the *forward-path*. If the recipient is known to be a non-deliverable address, the SMTP server usually returns a 550 reply. This step in the procedure can be repeated theoretically any number of times[2], but does not end until at least one *forward-path* has been accepted. The optional list of parameters is associated with negotiated SMTP service extensions.

3. The third step in the procedure is the *DATA command*. If this is accepted, the SMTP server returns a 354 Intermediate reply and considers all succeeding lines up to but not including the end of mail data indicator (usually a line only consisting of a ".") to be the message text. This procedure is subsumed with the method *send_mail*. When the end of text has been successfully received, the SMTP receiver sends a 250 OK reply, adds a trace record (see below) and stores, forwards, or relays the message. Message data must not be sent unless a 354 reply has been received.

Steps 1 to 3 are repeated until no message remains to be sent. Finally, the session is terminated by the SMTP client sending the *QUIT* command. This command specifies that the receiver must send an OK reply, and then close the transmission channel. A typical SMTP transaction scenario is shown in Fig. 3.3.

---

[2] An MTA can limit the number of recipients, but the minimum total number of recipients that must be buffered is 100 recipients.

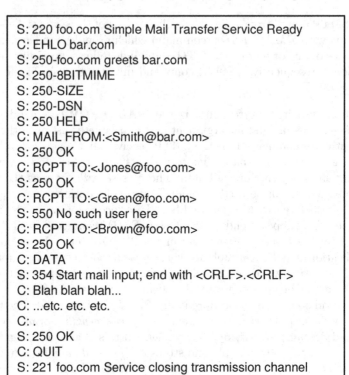

```
S: 220 foo.com Simple Mail Transfer Service Ready
C: EHLO bar.com
S: 250-foo.com greets bar.com
S: 250-8BITMIME
S: 250-SIZE
S: 250-DSN
S: 250 HELP
C: MAIL FROM:<Smith@bar.com>
S: 250 OK
C: RCPT TO:<Jones@foo.com>
S: 250 OK
C: RCPT TO:<Green@foo.com>
S: 550 No such user here
C: RCPT TO:<Brown@foo.com>
S: 250 OK
C: DATA
S: 354 Start mail input; end with <CRLF>.<CRLF>
C: Blah blah blah...
C: ...etc. etc. etc.
C: .
S: 250 OK
C: QUIT
S: 221 foo.com Service closing transmission channel
```

Fig. 3.3: A typical SMTP transaction scenario [93]

Regarding the SMTP delivery process some further issues are mentioned here which are either not modeled in detail or not at all in Fig. 3.2 in order to keep the model clear:

❑ There are circumstances in which the acceptability of the *reverse-path* (in *MAIL FROM* command) may not be determined until one or more *forward-path* (in *RCPT TO* commands) can be examined. In those cases, the server may reasonably accept the *reverse-path* (with a 250 reply) and then report problems after the forward-paths have been received and examined.

❑ Further SMTP commands exist (*VRFY, EXPN, HELP, NOOP,* and *RSET*). They are only additives in sending an e-mail and can be used at any time during a session, or without previously initializing a session.

❑ The QUIT command may also be issued by the SMTP client at any time.

❑ Mail parameters are optional and associated with negotiated SMTP service extensions.

❑ Once an SMTP client lexically identifies a domain to which mail will be delivered for processing, a Domain Name System (DNS) [107, 108] lookup

MUST be performed to resolve the domain name. RFC 2821 [93, p. 59f] describes this procedure in detail: *"The names are expected to be FQDNs. The lookup first attempts to locate an MX record associated with the name. If a CNAME[3] record is found instead, the resulting name is processed as if it were the initial name. If no MX records are found, but an A RR is found, the A RR is treated as if it was associated with an implicit MX RR, with a preference of 0, pointing to that host. If one or more MX RRs are found for a given name, SMTP systems MUST NOT utilize any A RRs associated with that name unless they are located using the MX RRs; the 'implicit MX' rule above applies only if there are no MX records present. If MX records are present, but none of them are usable, this situation MUST be reported as an error. When the lookup succeeds, the mapping can result in a list of alternative delivery addresses rather than a single address, because of multiple MX records, multihoming, or both. To provide reliable mail transmission, the SMTP client MUST be able to try (and retry) each of the relevant addresses in this list in order, until a delivery attempt succeeds. However, there MAY also be a configurable limit on the number of alternate addresses that can be tried. In any case, the SMTP client SHOULD try at least two addresses."*

❑ An SMTP server may close the connection after detecting the need to shut down the SMTP service. Then the server returns a 421 response code.

❑ Commands may not be sent in an arbitrary order if the restrictions on sequences, as indicated in Fig. 3.2, are violated, e.g. if an RCPT command appears without a previous MAIL command, the server must return a 503 "Bad sequence of commands" response.

❑ When the SMTP server accepts a message either for relaying or for final delivery, it inserts a trace record (also referred to as a *Received* entry) at the top of the mail data. This trace record indicates the identity of the host that sent the message, the identity of the host that received the message, and the date and time the message was received. Relayed messages will have multiple time stamp lines. The trace information must contain

◇ the *FROM* field – this should contain both the name of the source host, as presented in the *HELO/EHLO* command, and an address literal containing the IP address of the source, determined using the TCP connection –,

◇ the *ID* field, and

◇ the *FOR* field which may contain a list of path entries when multiple RCPT commands have been given.

However, many SMTP implementations do not add all the fields required, as the (real e-mail) example in Fig. 3.4 shows.

An Internet mail program must not change a *Received* entry that was previously added to the message header. SMTP servers must prepend *Re-*

---

[3] A CNAME (canonical name) Resource Record defines an alias for a DNS name.

ceived entries to messages; they MUST NOT change the order of existing entries or insert *Received* entries in any other location.

Each *Received* entry corresponds to an SMTP server which adds its trace record at the beginning of the header which it receives. Therefore, the delivery route of an e-mail consists of the *Received* part from bottom to top.

Figure 3.4 shows an example of the *Received* part (trace records) of an e-mail, which was first received by *mail4.ing-diba.de*, then sequentially passed to *mx0.gmx.net*, followed by two internal delivery steps, *relay2.rwth-aachen.de*, *circe* and *ms-dienst.rz.rwth-aachen.de*.

```
Received: from circe (circe.rz.RWTH-Aachen.DE [134.130.3.36])
   by ms-dienst.rz.rwth-aachen.de
   (iPlanet Messaging Server 5.2 HotFix 1.12 (built Feb 13 2003))
   with ESMTP id <0IEL00CLZ3NMDN@ms-dienst.rz.rwth-aachen.de> for
   gs062356@ims-ms-daemon; Thu, 07 Apr 2005 18:11:47 +0200 (MEST)
Received: from relay2.rwth-aachen.de ([134.130.3.6])
   by circe (MailMonitor for SMTP v1.2.2 ) ; Thu,
   07 Apr 2005 18:11:46 +0200 (MEST)
Received: from mx0.gmx.net (mx0.gmx.de [213.165.64.100])
   by relay2.rwth-aachen.de (8.13.0/8.13.0/1) with SMTP id j37GBieU019246
   for <schryen@winfor.rwth-aachen.de>; Thu, 07 Apr 2005 18:11:44 +0200
   (MEST)
Received: (qmail 27154 invoked by alias); Thu, 07 Apr 2005 16:11:39
   +0000
Received: (qmail invoked by alias); Thu, 07 Apr 2005 16:11:34 +0000
Received: from mail4.ing-diba.de (EHLO mail1.ing-diba.de)
   62.157.215.141] by mx0.gmx.net (mx062) with SMTP; Thu,
   07 Apr 2005 18:11:34 +0200
```

Fig. 3.4: *Example of the RECEIVED part of an e-mail*

All data sent before the *DATA* command are denoted as envelope. The data sent after this command are the content, consisting of the header and the body. Figure 3.5 shows an example of an e-mail and its parts as well as the analogy between a paper-based mail and an e-mail.

3.2 SMTP's susceptibility to spam

SMTP is a protocol which is highly susceptible to spam. This is mainly rooted in two facts: (1) in contrast to (paper-based) mail the sending of e-mails is (almost) free of charge. Usually, only fees for the spammers' data connection to the Internet provider apply, and these are based on time, volume or both. Increasingly more time- and/or volume-independent flat rates are available. This makes it hard to estimate the cost for spammers to send their e-mails,

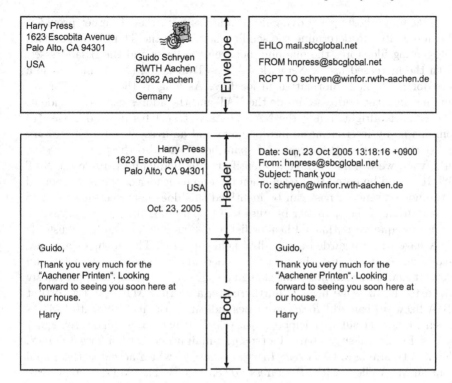

Fig. 3.5: Analogy between a paper-based mail and an e-mail

but the costs are likely to decrease further. For example, an OECD report [123, p. 9] mentions a 2002 survey in which it is estimated that the cost of sending a single e-mail averages USD 0.05. In 2005, the German Federal Office for Information Security (BSI) has published a report which assumes that 1,000,000 e-mails cost 100 Euro (0.0001 cent/e-mail) [18, p. 17]. Independent of the exact cost, it seems legitimate to denote this cost as "negligibly low". (2) SMTP was designed to work in an environment which is not susceptible to security attacks, such as are common and manifold on today's Internet. In particular, the lack of accountability is a major technical reason as to why spam is such a problem. The security problems of SMTP which affect spamming are discussed here in more detail.

SMTP allows the spoofing of an addresser's data and thereby allows anonymity, which makes it hard or even impossible for a recipient to detect the real sender: the host, acting as client, sends its FQDN with the *HELO/EHLO* command, this host name is often believed to be the real name and accepted for the *Received* entry by the SMTP server. Although an address literal containing the IP address of the source, determined using the TCP connection, is also added, often no plausibility check is performed. Less probably, but not totally improbably, the IP address might be spoofed (IP spoofing). Furthermore, as many hosts get a dynamic IP address from their Internet provider, it is impossible to determine the sending host after the TCP/IP connection unless a log file stores the mapping between the hosts and the IP addresses. With the increased use of Network Address Translation (NAT) may come a need for additional information in log files. As long as there is a 1:1 mapping between the addresses inside the NAT and the addresses used outside it, everything is alright, but if the NAT box also translates port addresses (to combine many internal hosts into one external address) it will be necessary to log not only the IP addresses of spam hosts but also the port addresses. Otherwise, we will not be able to identify the individual host inside the NAT [98]. It should be noted that even when the e-mail header contains no spoofed data and the sending host can be identified this does not necessarily lead to identification of the spammer because many spamming hosts are hijacked.

A consequence is that all header fields not inserted by the last trustable MTA have to be regarded as possibly being spoofed. This includes any malicious violation against the rule mentioned above, according to which an Internet mail program must not change a *Received* entry that was previously added to the message header. Furthermore, a corrupt MTA (and a corrupt MUA likewise) can add *Received* entries indicating the involvement of MTAs which did not actually participate in the e-mail delivery or it can delete regular entries. Figure 3.6 shows part of a (spam) e-mail header with a forged FQDN. The last trustable MTA is *relay1.rwth-aachen.de*, which accepted the e-mail from an MTA client with IP address *202.83.175.98*. This MTA pretended to have *winfinity.com* as its FQDN. However, a manually performed DNS reverse lookup exposes the MTA as having the FQDN *ntc.net.pk*. Whether any other MTA has been involved in the delivery is undetermined. Missing host authentication and data integrity makes any tracing back to the sending host difficult or even impossible.

SMTP does also not guard against spoofing of the sender's e-mail address. Spammers exploit this to make it harder to determine who the responsible party is, and to make it harder to know whom to complain to. Spammers also evade filters, either by pretending to be a sender on a recipient's whitelist, or by pretending not to be a sender on a recipient's blacklist. The common use of forged *MAIL FROM* in the envelope and *From* in the header puts the blame on innocent persons, hosts, or organizations. In addition, there is no inherent relationship between either "reverse" (from *MAIL* command) or "forward" (from *RCPT TO* command) address in the SMTP envelope and the addresses in the headers. As SMTP is not designed to validate any data, this makes it difficult to trace spammers. While these issues address missing authentication and missing data integrity SMTP also faces the problem of missing data privacy.

Although SMTP allows the use of "message submission", SMTP-AUTH and some more security procedures like SMTP after POP, these extensions are mostly restricted to the dialog between the user's e-mail client and an SMTP server (SMTP-AUTH is an exception to this). Their drawbacks and

```
Received: from ue2501 (ue250-1.rz.RWTH-Aachen.DE [134.130.3.33])
    by ms-dienst.rz.rwth-aachen.de
    (iPlanet Messaging Server 5.2HotFix 1.12 (built Feb 13 2003))
    with ESMTP id <0IEL00FMH9K3HX@msdienst.rz.rwth-
    aachen.de>; Thu,07 Apr 2005 20:19:17 +0200 (MEST)
Received: from relay1.rwthaachen.de ([134.130.3.3])
    by ue250-1 (MailMonitor for SMTP v1.2.2 ) ; Thu,
    07 Apr 2005 20:19:14 +0200 (MEST)
Received: from winfinity.com ([202.83.175.98])
    by relay1.rwthaachen.de (8.13.0/8.13.0/1) with  SMTP id j37IHPJ5013445;
    Thu,07 Apr 2005 20:19:06 +0200 (MEST)

                          spoofedFQDN
```

Fig. 3.6: Example of (part of) a spoofed e-mail header

limitations include low flexibility and a low security level, because user passwords stored on their computers do not seem to be very effective in today's security environment. Security features on an end-to-end level are missing. Klensin [93, p. 63] says: *"Real mail security lies only in end-to-end methods involving the message bodies, such as those which use digital signatures [...] and, e.g., PGP [...] or S/MIME [...]."*

RFC 2920 allows command pipelining which means using a single TCP send operation for multiple commands to improve SMTP performance significantly (see Sect. 3.1). If "turned on", this feature supports the sending of bulk e-mails and is thus susceptible to spamming.

Unfortunately, beside the communication-based security problems, SMTP displays three more weaknesses regarding a server's functionality:

❏ SMTP includes the commands *VRFY* and *EXPN*. They provide means for a potential spammer to test whether the addresses on his or her list are valid (*VRFY*) and to even procure more addresses (*EXPN*).
❏ The e-mail infrastructure and SMTP were designed to be flexible and to protect against breakdowns of e-mail nodes. Therefore, the concept of MTA relays was included in the infrastructure. An MTA relay is usually the target of a DNS MX record that designates it, rather than designating the final delivery system. The relay server may accept or reject the task of relaying the mail in the same way it accepts or rejects mail for a local user. If it accepts the task, it then becomes an SMTP client, establishes a transmission channel to the next SMTP server specified in the DNS, and sends it the mail. If it declines to relay e-mail to a particular address for policy reasons, a 550 response should be returned. An open relay does not restrict e-mail traffic. The former occurs when an e-mail server processes a message where neither the sender nor the recipient is a local user. It

can be used by spammers as an intermediate MTA to spread spam e-mails via a spotless MTA. As soon as an MTA is known to send spam e-mails, it will be quickly included in publicly available IP (black)lists, excluding it from all (outgoing) e-mail traffic by the use of blocking mechanisms (see Subsect. 4.4.1). Third party mail relaying was a useful SMTP-based procedure in the past, but these days, open e-mail relays pose a significant threat to the usefulness of e-mail and should be avoided.

❑ The *SMTP Service Extension for Remote Message Queue Starting* [37] provides the SMTP command *ETRN*. It means that the MTA will re-run its mail queue, which may be quite costly and susceptible to Denial of Service (DoS) attacks.

In 1999, many weaknesses had already been identified and "Anti-Spam Recommendations for SMTP MTAs" [98] were proposed as a "best current practice" RFC. Although they have not helped very much in fighting spamming, some ideas have been picked up by anti-spam measures, as discussed in Chap. 4. The recommendations include the following ideas:

❑ The MTA must be able to restrict unauthorized use as e-mail relay. The suggested algorithm is:

  ◇ If the *RCPT TO* argument is one of the MTA's domains, a local domain or a domain that the MTA accepts to forward to (alternate MX), then the message should be accepted and relayed.
  ◇ If the SMTP client's IP or FQDN is trustable, then the message should be accepted and relayed.
  ◇ Otherwise, the message should be refused.

Many open relays have already been fixed by implementing this algorithm or a similar one. However, the algorithm has a big drawback: if an authorized user is abroad and, thus, probably using a dynamic IP – which is assigned by a provider, hotel etc., – wants to use his or her home MTA for sending an e-mail to a recipient outside his or her organization, the e-mail is very likely to be refused.

Although another recommendation, i.e. to verify the *MAIL FROM* argument so that the sender name is a real user or an existing alias, would help to address this problem, at the same time it opens the door to spammers because it is not difficult to identify user names and their addresses.

❑ In order to improve traceability and accountability, MTAs must be able to provide *Received* entries with enough information to make it possible to trace the e-mail path, despite the spammers' use of forged host names in *HELO/EHLO* statements. Each *Received* entry must contain the IP address of the SMTP client and *date-time* information as described in RFC 2822 [142]. It also should contain the FQDN corresponding to the SMTP client's IP address, the argument given in the *HELO/EHLO* statement, and authentication information if an authenticated connection was used for the transmission or submission.

Any information that can help to trace the message should be added to the *Received* entry. It is true, even when the initial submission is non-SMTP, for example submission via a web-based e-mail client where HTTP is used between the web client and server, a *Received* entry can be used to identify that connection stating what IP address was used when connecting to the HTTP server where the e-mail was created.

These recommendations try to ensure that an e-mail sent directly from a spammer's host to a recipient can be traced with enough accuracy; a typical example is when a spammer uses a dial-up account and the ISP needs to have his or her IP address at the *date-time* to be able to take action against that person.

Organizations with a policy of hiding their internal network structure must still be allowed and able to do so. They usually make their internal MTAs prepend *Received* entries with a limited amount of information, or prepend none at all. Then they send out the e-mail through some kind of firewall/gateway device, which may even remove all the internal MTAs' *Received* entries before it prepends its own *Received* entry. By doing so, organizations take on the full responsibility of tracing spammers that send from inside their organization or they accept being held responsible for those spammer activities. It is required that the information provided in an organization's outgoing e-mail is sufficient for them to perform any necessary tracings. In the case of incoming e-mail to an organization, the *Received* entries must be kept intact to ensure that users receiving e-mail on the inside can give information needed to trace incoming messages back to their origin. Generally speaking, a gateway should not change or delete *Received* entries unless it is a security requirement that it does so. Changing the content of existing *Received* entries to make sure they "make sense" when passing an e-mail gateway of some kind most often destroys and deletes information needed to make a message traceable. Care must be taken to preserve the information in *Received* entries, either in the message itself, the e-mail that the receiver gets, or if that is impossible, in log files. Even if all these recommendations for traceability and accountability are followed, they do not effectively address the specific scenario where spam is sent out from infected computers of innocent users. Then, the user's computer would be identified as a spam source, leading to this particular computer being fixed, but not to the real spammer being identified.

❑ In order to protect local users from receiving spam e-mails, MTAs should be able to refuse e-mails from a particular host or a group of hosts. This decision can be based upon the IP address or the FQDN.

❑ An MTA should protect local e-mail addresses and thus be able to control who is allowed to issue the commands *VRFY* and *EXPN*. This may be "on/off" or access lists may be used. An MTA that also has the ability to handle mailing lists and to expand them to a number of recipients, needs to be able to authorize senders and protect its lists from spam.

❑ The MTA should control who is allowed to issue the *ETRN* command in order to protect against DoS attacks. This may be " on/off" or access lists may be used. Default should be "off".

Some procedures included in the "Anti-spam recommendations for SMTP MTAs" (and also in modern authentication methods, see Subsect. 4.4.4) rely on the availability and correctness of the DNS. For example, one of the recommendations is about verifying *MAIL FROM* domains with the DNS (assure that appropriate DNS information exists for the domain). When making use of this capability, there are two things to consider [98]: There is an increased amount of DNS queries, which might result in problems for the DNS server itself in coping with the load. This itself can result in a DoS attack against the DNS server. It should also be noted that forged DNS responses can be used to impede e-mail communication. For example, if a site is known to implement a FQDN validity check on addresses in *MAIL FROM* commands, an attacker may be able to use negative DNS responses to effectively block acceptance of e-mails from one or more origins. Therefore, one should carefully check the DNS server in use. SMTP's susceptibility to spam can and should be reduced by following the MTA implementation recommendations. However, to reduce spam effectively, more sophisticated technological means had to be designed and deployed. They are presented and discussed in Chap. 4.

The Anti-Spam Technical Alliance proposed further anti-spam recommendations for ISPs [9] which are, to a certain extent, being implemented by today's technological anti-spam measures and which are taken up in Sect. 4.4.

4

Anti-spam measures

Many different anti-spam measures have evolved and are currently deployed. Laws and regulations, organizational approaches implementing different kinds of cooperation, behavioral measures, economic measures, and technological measures provide today's most important anti-spam leverages. They address three conditions: motivation, capability, and permission. Motivation and capability are mandatory for bulk e-mailers. The third condition refers to the legal permission some bulk mailers are grasping at in order to avoid litigation. Figure 4.1 illustrates the relationship between anti-spam measures and both the intrinsic as well as the extrinsic factors for the sending of bulk e-mail (which is legally allowed).

In Sect. 4.1, legislation and regulatory frameworks are addressed. Section 4.2 focuses on organizational measures and cooperation by inspecting abuse systems and international cooperation. Behavioral measures, such as the protection of e-mail addresses and the handling of received spam e-mails, are covered in Sect. 4.3. Finally, the largest branch of anti-spam measures, the technological ones, are discussed in Sect. 4.4. These include filters, blocking, and authentication mechanisms. Economic measures are closely linked to other measures, such as technological or behavioral measures. Therefore, economic measures are not covered in a single section, but they are discussed in the related sections.

There is a broad consensus, in the literature and in practice, that the problem of spam clearly needs a multi-faceted approach and that different types of anti-spam measures should be applied complementarily rather than competitively.

4.1 Legislative measures

Given the severity and the potential damage that spam can cause, the authorities of both many countries and federal states have started to address

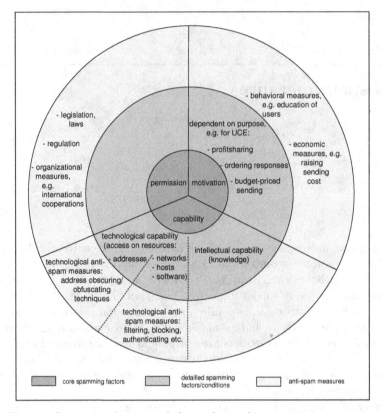

- legislation,
laws

- regulation

- organizational
measures,
e.g.
international
cooperations

- behavioral measures,
e.g. education of
users

dependent on purpose,
e.g. for UCE:

- profitsharing

- economic
measures, e.g.
raising
sending
cost

- ordering responses

permission | motivation | - budget-priced
sending

capability

technological capability
(access on resources:
- addresses, - networks
- hosts
- software)

intellectual capability
(knowledge)

technological anti-
spam measures:
address obscuring/
obfuscating
techniques

technological anti-
spam measures:
filtering, blocking,
authenticating etc.

core spamming factors   detailed spamming
factors/conditions   anti-spam measures

Fig. 4.1: Spamming factors and their relationship to anti-spam measures

spam by legislation. In addition, the European Union (EU) initiated the *Directive 2002/58/EC* [42], which had to be legislatively implemented by each EU member state by 31 October 2003. However, today's world-wide legislative coverage of unsolicited bulk e-mail is heterogeneous, and its effectiveness is controversially discussed.

Some main parameters in which anti-spam measures – if they are provided at all – can differ are discussed in Subsect. 4.1.1, whereas Subsect. 4.1.2 presents the core issues of many countries' legislative measures against spam e-mails. This section closes with the assessment of the present legislation landscape in terms of effectiveness, the identification of currently unsolved problems, and the indication of means by which some limitations might be overcome (see also Schryen [154]).

4.1.1 Parameters

Important parameters by which anti-spam legislation can vary are: the type of subscription, the scope, the sender and recipient type, and the set of possible accusers. Figure 4.2 illustrates the described parameters and their possible values.

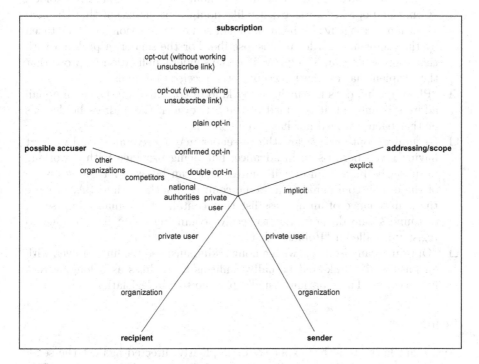

Fig. 4.2: Some parameters of anti-spam laws

Subscription

Laws can differ in the way in which a recipient can refuse to accept the receipt of e-mails, in other words, the kind of subscription. There are two families of approaches: an "opt-in" approach, which requires that the sender has the recipient's permission prior to sending, and an "opt-out" approach, which provides a mechanism for declining the receipt of further e-mails from a particular sender. These families comprise the following provisions [2], which are presented in order of decreasing restriction on the sender's options.

☐ "Double opt-in", which is sometimes also referred to as "verified opt-in" or "closed loop opt-in", requires that a subscriber takes two actions to get onto a list. The first action requests the addition of an e-mail address to a list, and the adding-on can be done, for example, via a web form or an e-mail. The owner of the list then sends a confirmation (challenge) message, which must be answered by the recipient. Only when this reply is received is the address added to the list. The reason for requiring the sender to confirm the adding-on is that someone other than the address holder could have added the address without the permission of the holder.

❑ "Confirmed opt-in" works exactly like double opt-in, except that the confirmation message has to be answered or some other action has to be taken by the recipient in order to unsubscribe. For the sender, a problem with this approach occurs if, by law, it is the sender's obligation to prove that the recipient has explicitly accepted the receipt of e-mails.

❑ "Plain opt-in" does not include any kind of confirmation. Once an e-mail address is entered, it is added to the list, even if the address holder has neither been involved nor has given consent.

❑ Generally, "opt-out" means that a sender may receive an e-mail without having given permission in advance, but being provided with a working unsubscribe link or an e-mail address that can be used for the cessation of the e-mail communication. Some countries, such as the USA, propose the maintenance of an address list that contains the e-mail addresses of consumers who do not want to receive commercial e-mails [66]. Such a registry is called a "Robinson list".

❑ "Opt-out" can also come with a nonworking unsubscribe link, or even with an unsubscribe link that actually confirms an address as belonging to a live account. These options usually play no role in legislation.

Scope

Anti-spam laws are either explicitly or implicitly directed against the sending of particular kinds of e-mails and the related harm they can cause. This kind of addressing depends on the law's scope, which can cover, for example, (bulk) e-mails explicitly, the distribution of malicious software in general, or the distribution of pornographic content. Furthermore, if (bulk) e-mails are directly addressed, many laws specify the type of e-mails covered, usually by focusing on commercial e-mails (UCE). The following examples illustrate the diversity by which laws can address the sending of (bulk) e-mails and related harm, the first three items representing an implicit coverage and the last two representing an explicit coverage:

❑ If a (spam) e-mail is fraudulent in some way, in the USA, this e-mail may be violating the *Computer Fraud and Abuse Act*, the *Racketeer Influenced and Corrupt Organizations Act (RICO)*, and the *Electronic Communications Privacy Act (ECPA)* [2].

❑ In Germany, the *Strafgesetzbuch (German Criminal Code) (StGB)* 1998 covers a broad range of delicts which may potentially be committed if spam e-mails are sent. For example, it is a violation of the *StGB* to obtain computer resources surreptitiously (§265a), to modify data (§303a), to sabotage computers (§303b), and to disturb the proper working of telecommunication systems (§317). The execution of malicious e-mail attachments, such as viruses, worms, and Trojan horses, can lead to this kind of harm. Even the content of an e-mail can offend a law, for example, pornographic content (§317) [18, p. 48f].

☐ In Germany, spamming can be regarded as an intrusion into a company's commercial activities according to §1004 *Bürgerliches Gesetzbuch (German Civil Code) (BGB)* 2002 [94, p. 30].

☐ In Austria, the sending of e-mails to more than 50 recipients with the purpose of direct marketing violates §107 *Telekommunikationsgesetz (Austrian Law of Telecommunications) (TKG)*, unless the recipient has given acceptance prior to the sending.

☐ The U.S. *CANSPAM Act of 2003* (see Subsect. 4.1.2), in principle, authorizes senders of commercial e-mails to send their UCE, unless the recipient has explicitly refused its receipt (§1037): *"(A) It is unlawful for any person to initiate the transmission of any commercial electronic mail message to a protected computer unless the message provides (i) clear and conspicuous identification that the message is an advertisement or solicitation; (ii) clear and conspicuous notice of the opportunity under paragraph (3) to decline to receive further commercial electronic mail messages from the sender; and (iii) a valid physical postal address of the sender. (B) Subparagraph (A)(i) does not apply to the transmission of a commercial electronic mail message if the recipient has given prior affirmative consent to receipt of the message."*

☐ The *Directive 2002/58/EC* [42], which had to be legislatively implemented by each EU member state by 31 October 2003, is aimed at protecting the rights of natural persons as well as the legitimate interests of legal persons. The directive regulates some kind of opt-in mechanism and requires each direct marketing e-mail to contain information on how to cease the e-mail communication [42, Article 13, 1.,4.]: *"The use of automated calling systems without human intervention (automatic calling machines), facsimile machines (fax) or electronic mail for the purposes of direct marketing may only be allowed in respect of subscribers who have given their prior consent. ... In any event, the practice of sending electronic mail for purposes of direct marketing disguising or concealing the identity of the sender on whose behalf the communication is made, or without a valid address to which the recipient may send a request that such communications cease, shall be prohibited."*

For the purpose of litigation, legislators have to precisely specify when an e-mail can be regarded as unsolicited and when, thereby, its sender is violating the corresponding law. It should be noted that anti-spam laws avoid the usage of the term "spam", because its legislative semantics have not yet been defined.

Sender and recipient

Laws can target specific types of senders and recipients to which they apply, such as private users and organizations. For example, the *Directive 2002/58/EC* [42, Article 13 5.] limits its "generic" opt-in approach to recipients who are natural persons.

Possible accuser

Laws may impose a restriction on who can sue e-mailers. Many anti-spam laws, such as the *CANSPAM Act of 2003*, do not provide legislative means for individuals, but only for state authorities and some other organizations, such as ISPs (*CANSPAM Act of 2003*, Sec. 7). Likewise, the German *Gesetz gegen den unlauteren Wettbewerb (German Law against Unfair Competition) (UWG)* 2004 opens the door to litigation for competitors, specific associations, chambers of commerce, chambers of crafts, and some more "qualified" organizations only.

Further requirements

Laws may make further requirements of e-mails. As mentioned above, the *CANSPAM Act of 2003* (§1037), for example, prohibits the use of a harvested e-mail address, requires that advertisement or solicitations are clearly and conspicuously identified, and requires that each e-mail contains a functioning return e-mail address or other Internet-based mechanism that allows the recipient to opt-out of the commercial e-mail list. This list of further possible requirements of e-mails is far from being complete.

4.1.2 Anti-spam laws

Just as the volume of spam has increased in recent years, so has the number of anti-spam laws across the world. Surveys [87, 125] carried out by the International Telecommunication Union (ITU) and the Organisation for Economic Co-operation and Development (OECD) – both organizations sent out questionnaires mainly to their member states – found both a large number of anti-spam laws and a pronounced heterogeneity of the legislation. The latter is what the world-wide legislation is assumed to be because of the high number of anti-spam laws' parameters in which the laws may vary and which were presented in the previous subsection. The studies present detailed information about the anti-spam legislation in 47 countries. Country-specific information about "Consumer protection agencies", "Data protection authorities", and "Communications regulators" with responsibility for the enforcement of laws related to spam are provided by OECD [126] and ITU [87], the latter also providing information about the international cooperation in which countries are participating (see Subsect. 4.2.2). Tables 4.1 and 4.1 summarize which state has a designated (opt-in or opt-out) anti-spam law, which countries have implemented the European Directive 2002/58/EC and when the laws were updated.

According to the studies of the ITU [87] and the OECD [125], only 31 countries – the United Nations has 191 member states, not including Vatican City [183]– confirmed that they have an explicit anti-spam legislation, most of them containing opt-in rules. No legislation information is available for large parts of the world, such as Africa, the Middle East, large parts of Asia, and Latin America. Countries with an anti-spam legislation mainly address commercial e-mails and UCE. When comparing the world-wide legislation with those countries that are responsible for more than 50% of all e-mails that were classified as spam by many market research and anti-spam companies, such as "Commtouch" [29], "Sophos" [160], and "Spamhaus" [164], we find that these countries, namely USA, China, Republic of Korea, and Russia, either have a non-restrictive law, such as an opt-out law, or have no anti-spam laws at all. Countries with opt-in rules, such as those that implemented the European Directive 2002/58/EC, were found to play only minor roles in sending spam. It is remarkable that most e-mails classified as spam still originate from the USA. This may be due to the fact that the US CANSPAM Act, that explicitly permits opt-out marketing, overrides state laws even if they are stronger [2]. Portals containing links to legislative anti-spam laws can be found on *http://www.spamlaws.com/* and *http://notebook.ifas.ufl.edu/spam/Legislation.htm*.

A study of the ITU [86] analyzed the zones of consensus and disagreement in existing legislation. According to this study, laws strongly converge in the following instances (p. V): *"... a focus on commercial content, the mandatory disclosure of sender/advertiser/routing, bans on fraudulent or misleading content, bans on automated collection or generation of recipient addresses, the permission to contact recipients where there is an existing relationship, the requirement to allow recipients to refuse future messages, and a mix of graduated civil and criminal liability."* The study also identified five key areas that are vital to a harmonized spam law but which have evaded consensus thus far (p. V): *"... a prior consent requirement for contacting recipients, a designated enforcer, label requirements for spam messages, the definition of spam (whether it is limited to e-mail communication, or includes other applications, such as SMS), and the jurisdictional reach of the system's spam laws."*

Summing up, there is no consensus on the legislative attitude towards spam and its handling. There are still many countries which have no or low-effective anti-spam laws and which, thereby, tolerate spammers, who have an incentive to locate operations in locations with less legislation and regulation.

Table 4.1: Country-specific anti-spam laws 1/2 [87, 125]

Country	Opt-in	Opt-out	Remarks	Year of last known law update
Argentina		x		2001
Armenia	no anti-spam law		Law on Personal Data deals with some aspects of spam.	
Australia	x			2004
Austria	x		(*)	2006
Belgium	x		(*)	2003
Brazil	no anti-spam law		Criminal , civil , anti competition and pro consumer laws exist, which could also be used against spam.	
Bulgaria	no anti-spam law		Some provisions of the Personal Data Protection Act deal with certain aspects of spam.	
Burkina Faso	no anti-spam law		There have been several draft laws proposed.	
Canada	no anti-spam law		Some statutes include some, although not all, of the measures that are generally available in spam-specific legislation.	
Chile		x		2004
China	no information available		The law prohibits the sending of e-mail with false or materially misleading information, the relaying of e-mails without authorization, the gathering of e-mail addresses illegally.	2006
Colombia		(x)	In 2004, the national legislator introduced a new bill to Congress, which proposes an opt-out system. No further information is currently available.	(2004)
Costa Rica	opt-in/opt-out system			2002
Cyprus	no information available		Section 06 of the Regulation of Electronic Communications and Postal Services Law of 2004 (Law 12 (I) / 2004 deals with unsolicited communications (spam).	2004
Czech Republic	x			2004
Denmark	x		(*)	2004
Estonia	x		(*)	2004
Finland	x		(*)	2004
France	x		(*)	2004
Germany	x		(*)	2004
Hong Kong		(x)	The use of personal data for sending out e-mail spam for direct marketing purposes might be regulated by section 34 of the Personal Data (Privacy) Ordinance, which requires the sender to provide the recipient with an "opt-out" choice for receiving no further marketing e-mails.	
Hungary	no information available		Art. 14, Act CVIII of 2001 on Electronic Commerce of the Hungarian law provides for restrictions regarding unsolicited commercial communication.	2001
Ireland	x		(*)	2003
Italy	x		(*) Italy has enacted a tough anti-spam law that makes spamming a criminal offence and is punishable by up to three years' imprisonment.	2003
Japan		x		2005
Republic of Korea		x		2003

Table 4.2: Country-specific anti-spam laws 2/2 [87, 125]

Country	Opt-in	Opt-out	Remarks	Year of last known law update
Latvia	x			no information available
Lithuania	x		(*)	2004
Luxembourg	no anti-spam law			
Malaysia	no anti-spam law		Act 588 provides that a person who initiates a communication using any applications service, whether continuously, repeatedly or otherwise, during which communication may or may not ensue, with or without disclosing his identity and with intent to annoy, abuse, threaten or harass any person at any number or electronic address, thereby commits an offence.	
Malta	x		(*)	2003
Mexico	no anti-spam law		The Office of the Federal Attorney for Consumer Protection reformed the Federal Law for Consumer Protection (FLCP) to add one chapter related, in general, to consumer protection in the context of electronic commerce. The amendments provide that "suppliers shall respect consumer's choice not to receive commercial advertising". These provisions could be interpreted in such a way to include spam under those articles.	
Netherlands	x		(*)	2004
New Zealand	x			2005
Norway	x			2003
Peru	x			2005
Poland	x		(*)	2002
Portugal	x		(*)	2004
Romania	x			2002
Russia	no anti-spam law			
Singapore	no anti-spam law		Legislative framework for the control of e-mail spam has been proposed.	
Spain	x		(*)	2003
Sweden	x		(*)	2004
Switzerland	no anti-spam law		Anti-spam legislation will probably enter into force in 2007 and will be similar to EU law	
Turkey	no anti-spam law			
United Kingdom	x		(*)	2003
United States		x	While many U.S. states have also passed laws addressing spam, they are pre-empted by CAN-SPAM except to the extent to which they address falsity or deception in commercial email messages.	2004

(*) in compliance with the European Directive 2002/58/EC

4.1.3 The effectiveness

The implementation of laws addressing unsolicited bulk e-mail is believed to have had some minor or spotty effects on the spam plague at the most, although the press reports almost weekly about cases where e-mailers have been sentenced for spamming. Some cases brought under a specific anti-spam law and their status and outcome were reported by the OECD [126, p. 36ff]. However, apart from partial success stories, thus far anti-spam laws could not stop the development that, today, about 2 out of 3 e-mails are classified as spam. The ITU [87, p. 9] points out: *"However, while the laws proposed to combat spam were put forth with good intentions they are not actually addressing the problem in a substantive way."*. As mentioned above, more than half of spam e-mails originate from countries with no anti-spam law or with an opt-out rule. This indicates that opt-in laws have a positive effects on spamming whereas opt-out laws are scarcely prohibitive. On the other hand, it must be conceded that opt-out laws are still useful, because they provide clear legislative guidelines for companies and recipients, thereby restricting reputable companies' uncontrolled e-mail marketing, that gets out of hand [159]. Consequently, a partially positive impact of anti-spam laws on the sending of spam can be assumed. This motivates further work on anti-spam laws and their propagation. Furthermore, if it is true that most of the spam targeted at Internet users in North America and Europe is generated by a hard-core group of known professional spammers, whose names, aliases and operations are documented in the Spamhaus' *Register Of Known Spam Operations (ROKSO)* database [164], then the prosecution of a small number of spammers would be likely to reduce spam enormously, provided that these come under an anti-spam jurisdiction. Finally, legislation can help to limit the occurrence of spam by determent through impending penalties and through successful prosecution against spammers.

A general problem of legislative measures against spam e-mails is that an international phenomenon is being addressed by national legislation. Going into detail, we find the following facts and problems:

❑ A substantial portion of received spam crosses international boundaries. An accompanying question for countries is whether they have jurisdiction over messages that originate within their borders but are being sent to a different country. Domestic provisions prohibiting the sending of spam, instituting rules for legitimate messages, or requiring the labeling of messages are likely to have little effect on messages of extra-territorial origin [127]. Another question is whether a national authority or even a private user in a foreign country B is allowed to initiate litigation against a spammer who is residing in country A.

❑ The international legislative anti-spam landscape is heterogeneous and not transparent: even if a spammer violates a national anti-spam law of his/her country and another country's entity is aware of this violation, the operational tasks involved in litigation, such as the involvement of national organizations, might be difficult to perform. Moustakas et al. [111, p.7] stress this issue even stronger: *"There can be no solution to the spam problem without some kind of worldwide 'minimum standard' of legislation. Global harmonization is a very difficult task since US and EU have opt-out / opt-in regimes."*

❑ The litigation of a person or organization presumes that the sender has been identified. Two challenges arise in this context:

(1) The sender must be localized. If a sender uses address and name spoofing – and this is very likely to be the case – and also uses instruments for hiding, such as an e-mail proxy or third party hosts, for example bots, localization is difficult, if not impossible.

(2) Like other forms of online crime, the regulation of spam and the enforcement of spam laws are complicated by difficulties associated with the collection and preservation of evidence (evidentiary burden) [127].

❑ The implementation of laws needs resources and skills, which are often not available: *"Several developing nations, such as India, have laws that prohibit hacking, stalking or harassment over the Internet etc., but even then, the implementation of these laws is in the hands of the local police or other law enforcement organizations, who may be inadequately funded, ill equipped and poorly trained to keep abreast of cyber crime trends, let alone spam-related issues."* [128, p. 14]

It is especially the OECD and the ITU that have made suggestions on how to address these problems and, therefore, how to improve worldwide anti-spam prosecution [86, 127]:

❑ The expansion of international cooperation is necessary to share information in furtherance of cross-border investigations and prosecutions involving spam. This issue includes the improvement of both the ability to cooperate and the cooperation itself with the relevant private sector entities. Subsection 4.2.2 presents some existing international cooperation and agreements.

❑ Law enforcement organizations should be funded, equipped, and trained to be capable of investigating the often complex issues associated with spam and to proceed to take action against offenders.

❑ Countries with non-restrictive laws or no anti-spam laws at all should switch to or introduce restrictive legislation respectively, so that the regions that spammers can move to without being endangered by legal prosecution are reduced or, even better, eliminated. In order to support a definition of anti-spam legislation that is both effective and relatively equal in terms of levels of enforcement – the latter would support international cooperation – the OECD [127] proposes constraints on the anti-spam policy and a checklist for the development of anti-spam regulatory approach. The ITU [86] stresses that harmonizing laws that regulate spam offer considerable benefits, insofar as a model law could assist in establishing a

framework for cross-border enforcement collaboration. Although they have
not drafted a model law, they have framed and categorized the issues that
drafters would need to take up. Supporting developing countries in introducing anti-spam legislation, we have to keep in mind that, unlike many
developed economies, developing countries often do not have supporting
institutions which are necessary to implement legislation effectively [128].

However, considering the fact that two strong economic areas – the USA
and the EU – have implemented very different types of legislation – opt-out
vs. opt-in –, it must be doubted that legislative homogeneity will be achieved
in the near future. Furthermore, the effectiveness of the USA legislation has
proven to be low, and it should be difficult to make this country move to a
more restrictive opt-in system.

4.2 Organizational measures

Organizational measures comprise abuse systems, which offer a forum for users
who want to complain about received spam e-mails. They also include different
forms of international cooperation.

4.2.1 Abuse systems

Abuse systems are intended to help the Internet community to report and
control network abuse and abusive users. Ideally, spammers are identified and
duly prosecuted. Abuse systems can be part of ESPs' infrastructures or part
of a provider-independent organization. If users are not sure whom to complain to, they can send abuse e-mails to abuse systems which help forward
complaints to system managers who can act on them. The Network Abuse
Clearinghouse and SpamCop both offer such a service. Abuse e-mails may
also be sent to national organizations, federations, and authorities, such as
regulatory authorities and consumer advice centers. For example, the Fed-
eration of German Consumer Organizations set up a spam abuse system in
September 2005, which aims at determent and prosecution. Abuse systems
can also be maintained by international or supranational organizations such
as the EU. The "Selfregulatory Plan on Tackling Spam" (SpotSpam) is a recently launched EU database project. The project's aim is to facilitate legal
action against spammers at the international level, and the project's core idea
is that spam complaints can be submitted to the SpotSpam database via national "Spamboxes". The information stored in the database will enable the
appropriate authorities to take action against spammers. Additionally, law
suits are regarded as more successful when they can be based on multiple
end-user complaints in various countries.

Related to abuse systems described above are systems that maintain blacklists (see Subsect. 4.4.1). These store IP addresses of hosts from which spam

e-mails originate. Abuse messages regarding the same host may lead to host's IP being placed on a blacklist.

4.2.2 International cooperation

In the context of international cooperation, we can differentiate between bilateral government-to-government cooperation, between private sector groups, government-to-private sector, and multilateral [124].

An example of an initially bilateral cooperation is the Memorandum of Understanding (MoU) between the UK and the USA, which was later extended to include Australia as well. The MoU provides a framework for cooperation in fighting cross-border spam affecting all three countries. Another MoU was signed by the "Korea Information Security Agency", the "Australian Communications Authority" and the "National Office for the Information Economy of Australia" [85], which agreed on a closer cooperation and the exchange of information relating to spam in accordance with the relevant laws and regulations of each country. Many more countries were involved in the multilateral "London Action Plan": On October 11 2004, government and public agencies from 27 countries responsible for enforcing laws concerning spam met in London to discuss international spam enforcement cooperation (member organizations come from Australia, Belgium, Canada, Chile, China, Denmark, Finland, Hungary, Ireland, Japan, Lithuania, Malaysia, Mexico, Republic of Korea, Spain, Sweden, Switzerland, the Netherlands, UK, and USA). The purpose of the London Action Plan is to promote international spam enforcement cooperation and address spam-related problems, such as online fraud and deception, phishing, and dissemination of viruses. It is meant to be a simple, flexible document facilitating concrete steps to start working on international spam enforcement cooperation [178]:

"The governments and public agencies intend to use their best efforts to

❑ *encourage communication and coordination among the different Agencies that have spam enforcement authority within their country [. . .],*
❑ *take part in periodic conference calls, at least quarterly, [. . .]*
❑ *encourage and support the involvement of less developed countries in spam enforcement."*

In appreciation of public-private partnerships, the cooperation is partially open to the private sector including ISPs, telecommunications companies, information security software providers, mobile operators, domain name registrars and registries, etc. Private organizations are intended to participate in segments of periodic conference calls and to assist in training sessions. The London Action Plan is also an example of government-to-private-sector cooperation.

Other instances of multilateral cooperation include particular organizations which have been set up for anti-spam or other purposes. The OECD has created the OECD Spam Task Force which arranges workshops and which is currently developing an anti-spam Toolkit, an instrument to help governments, regulators and industry players orient their policies relating to spam solutions. The ITU, the EU, the International Consumer Protection Enforcement Network (ICPEN), and the Asia-Pacific Economic Cooperation (APEC) are further examples of organizations which address spam multilaterally. For example, besides the establishing of the *Directive 2002/58/EC* [42] and the proposal of a cooperation procedure concerning the transmission of complaint information [51], the EU went a further step towards addressing spam by initiating the project "SpotSpam" (see Subect. 4.2.1).

An example of a private sector cooperation is the Anti-Spam Technical Alliance (ASTA) which was established by the Internet community and the companies AOL, British Telecom, Comcast, Earthlink, Microsoft and Yahoo!. ASTA recommends actions and policies for ISPs and ESPs and some more types of organizations including governments and online marketing organizations.

Although some more international cooperation have been set up [87], this process is still at the fledgling stage.

4.3 Behavioral measures

Behavioral measures aim at e-mail users' procedures in using and distributing their e-mail addresses and dealing with any spam e-mails that they receive. To fully understand both issues, it is necessary to detect ways for spammers to harvest e-mail addresses and to identify options for users for how to deal with spam messages in their e-mail boxes.

4.3.1 The protection of e-mail addresses

Harvesting e-mail addresses is one option for acquiring valid e-mail addresses, and harvesters sit at the beginning of the spam "value chain". Protecting e-mail addresses from being harvested reduces, it is hoped, the spam mass which would have to be addressed by technological anti-spam measures which consume resources. In principle, all locations where (many) e-mail addresses are stored are interesting for harvesters. The following belong to the most discussed ones which seem to deserve protection [140, 18]:

☐ UseNet: An empirical study alluring harvesters with spamtrap addresses in newsgroups (see Chap. 7) shows that postings are scanned for addresses which are then used by spammers.

☐ Mailing lists and newsletters: Subscribers to mailing lists and newsletters are supposed to give valid e-mail addresses. As mailing lists contain many addresses, they are especially valuable for harvesters. Schryen (2005) shows empirically that the subscribing to newsletters can lead to the receiving of spam e-mails.

❑ Web pages: Contact information is available on many web pages. Especially discussion forums, guestbooks and blogs contain many addresses which can be easily harvested. Address crawlers performing an in-depth search on the results of search engines are freely available and provide hundreds of thousands of e-mail addresses in just a few hours. Empirical studies have shown that web sites are intensely crawled. These studies are described in detail in Chap. 7.

❑ Web browsers: Some sites use various tricks to extract a surfer's e-mail address from the web browser, sometimes without the surfer noticing it. These techniques involve:

  ◇ Some browsers giving the e-mail address the user has configured into the browser as the password for the anonymous FTP account,

  ◇ The usage of JavaScript possibly making the browser send an e-mail with the e-mail address configured into the browser.

  ◇ Some browsers passing a header with the e-mail address on to every web server visited.

❑ Internet Relay Chat (IRC) and chat rooms: Chat services are suspected of revealing e-mail addresses. For example, some IRC clients will give a user's e-mail address to anyone who cares to ask for it.

❑ Finger daemons: Some finger daemons are set to be very friendly – a finger query asking for *john@host* will list login names for all people named John on that host. A query for *@host* will produce a list of all currently logged-on users.

❑ Public databases and directories: Databases such as those attached to the "whois" service, and directories, such as white and yellow pages, may prove a valuable resource for harvesters.

❑ Social engineering attacks: This method entails the harvester tricking people into giving him or her valid e-mail addresses: Chain letters, which promise a gift for every person to whom the letter is forwarded, as long as it is CC'ed to the harvester.

❑ Address book and e-mails on other people's computers: Some viruses and worms spread by e-mailing themselves to all the e-mail addresses they can find in a local e-mail address book. As some people forward jokes and other material by e-mail to their friends, some viruses and worms even scan the e-mail folders for addresses that are not in the address book.

The author is not aware of empirical studies which comprehensively inspect and compare the sources mentioned above. In Chap. 7, an empirical study is presented which explores web pages, newsletters, and the Usenet with regard to harvested addresses and their (mis)use. As mentioned above, some prior studies are considered in detail, too.

For protecting e-mail addresses from being harvested, many approaches have been proposed, including the following:

❑ An easy (ad hoc) approach would be to create throw-away e-mail aliases, distribute these, and not check e-mail sent there after a while. Apparently, such an approach is insufficient in at least two ways: (1) Over time, it leads to a vast number of unused and/or forgotten accounts and maintenance overhead, both for users as well as for providers. Users would be forced to continuously keep track of whom they have provided with which e-mail address. (2) Throw-away accounts cannot prevent spam from being delivered to them, as the spammers do not know the status of an e-mail account. If an e-mail is successfully delivered to an account, this account counts as being valid and probably in use. However, it can be useful to set up e-mail addresses for certain purposes, which could be abolished after some time when they are "bombed" with spam e-mails.

❑ Many ad hoc Address Obscuring/Obfuscating Techniques (AOTs) have been proposed which aim at preventing e-mail addresses from being harvested by programs when the addresses are published on web sites. One option is to integrate addresses into pictures in a way that humans can identify the address but machines cannot. Another one is to code e-mail links so that they are protected against harvesters. The address *anakin.skywalker@starwars.com*, for example, could be written as

anakin.skywalker-AT-starwars.com

or as

anakin.skywalkerREMOVETHIS@starwars.com

One could also use a JavaScript function supported by all modern browsers. A web page could contain the code [27]

<script>mail2("anakin.skywalker","starwars",0,"","Anakin Skywalker")</script>

When you click on the resulting hyperlinked text *"Anakin Skywalker"*, this opens a window of the local e-mail client with the address *anakin.skywalker@starwars.com* already pasted in the "To"-field.

These approaches may help obscure addresses as long as spammers' harvesters are not trained to deal with the most frequently deployed hiding techniques. However, they are of limited use where e-mail addresses cannot be obscured arbitrarily. For example, web forms for newsletter subscription and local address books depend on textual addresses, the latter even being based on unmodified addresses. AOTs, which also rely also on technological means, are presented in Subsect. 4.4.8.

4.3.2 The handling of received spam e-mails

If spam e-mails have found their way into a user's e-mail box, the user has several options for dealing with them:

❑ An argument for answering spam e-mails could be to play a trick on the spammer by consuming his or her time in the hope that the spammer will get tired of wasting time on useless dialogues, and will stop spamming. However, many recommendations advise the recipient not to reply, especially then, when an e-mail includes a "remove me" opt-out request. By replying to a spam e-mail, the sender confirms to the spammer that the address is in use, probably confirms that the ISP is not using effective spam filters, confirms that the user actually opens and reads spam e-mails, and that he or she is willing to follow the spammer's instructions, such as "click here to be removed". The sender would, therefore, be an excellent candidate for more spam.

❑ The user should check if the provider's and/or the e-mail client's spam filters are enabled. However, the user should be aware of possible misclassification and should especially take false-positives into account.

❑ Messages can be reported to spam databases which are open to the anti-spam community for research purposes.

❑ Several abuse organizations have been set up, to which complaints about spam e-mails can be directed (see Subsect. 4.2.1). Many ESPs provide an abuse e-mail address. They can analyze spam e-mails, which have been reported to this address and use them, for example, to improve filters or to take other technological measures. Abuse messages can also be directed to abuse organizations, such as Network Abuse Clearinghouse. The Anti-Phishing Working Group, for example, builds a repository of phishing scam e-mails and web sites to help people identify scamming and avoid being scammed in the future. Several countries have assigned abuse notification tasks to national authorities. In the USA, spam that is fraudulent can be sent to the US Federal Trade Commission. Spam that promotes stocks can be sent to the US Securities and Exchange Commission. Spam containing or advertising child pornography can be reported to the Federal Bureau of Investigation. In New Zealand, you can report child pornography to the Department of Internal Affairs. In Germany, spam can be reported to the Federal Network Agency. In many countries, it is up to these authorities to prosecute spammers (see Sect. 4.1).

Like laws and regulatory measures, behavioral measures are intended to be applied complementarily to technological anti-spam measures which are described in the next section.

4.4 Technological measures

Because spamming is undertaken with the usage of technological means, it is not surprising that, meanwhile, a vast set of technological anti-spam measures has been proposed and implemented. Cranor and LaMacchia [30] give a good overview of important measures, although this is slightly outdated. Schryen

[148] and Spammer-X [166] provide more updated outlines, Schryen [149] and [18] likewise in the German language.

Before presenting and discussing anti-spam measures, a classification of these may be helpful. The following taxonomies seem to be appropriate:

❑ Measures are applied at different stages of the e-mail delivery process. They can come into operation on the e-mail client, on the MTAs of the sender's ESP, on e-mail nodes outside the sender's and recipient's ESP, on the MTAs of the recipient's ESP recipient, or on the recipient's client [18, p. 85]. The first two locations enable measures to be preventive. Because the spam e-mails have not been sent through the Internet, the latter are denoted as reactive measures. It is desirable to stop spam e-mails as early as possible so as not to waste resources like bandwidth, storage and recipients' time. Therefore, preventive measures should be treated privileged. However, blocking and filter mechanisms (see Subsects. 4.4.1 and 4.4.2), which are still the most common technological anti-spam measures, are applied on the recipient's side.

❑ Spam e-mails can take different delivery routes. For example, sometimes spammers set up their own MTAs and send spam e-mails to the recipients' ESPs directly. Another option is to exploit the infrastructure of ESPs by sending e-mails via their MTAs. While some anti-spam measures, like filters, can be applied independently of the delivery route, others, like blocking outgoing TCP port 25 by ISPs (see Subsect. 4.4.3), are only applicable when spammers use "adequate" routes. The model driven analysis of measures' effectiveness presented in Chap. 5 acts on this classification by focusing on non-route-specific anti-spam measures.

❑ Anti-spam measures can be functionally classified (see Fig. 4.3).

❑ From a practice-oriented point of view, anti-spam measures may be divided into short-, medium-, and long-term ones, according to the time and effort their respective deployment takes. For example, filter and blocking mechanisms count as short-term measures as, usually, implementation can be restricted to an organization's local e-mail infrastructure with insignificant modifications. Some DNS-based measures (see Paragraph 4.4.4), which affect the structure and content of DNS entries, may take some months or even years to come into operation. Public Key Infrastructure (PKI)-based measures (see Paragraph 4.4.4) and resource-based measures (see Subsect. 4.4.6) may take even longer due to considerable modification and extension respectively of the infrastructure. However, this classification is a bit arbitrary and fuzzy because it lacks (objective) criteria for deciding whether a measure is implementable in the short-, medium-, or long-term.

Figure 4.3 shows the first three taxonomies of technological anti-spam measures; because of the disposal of the time-related classification, this particular one is omitted. The (structure of this) chapter follows the functional classification.

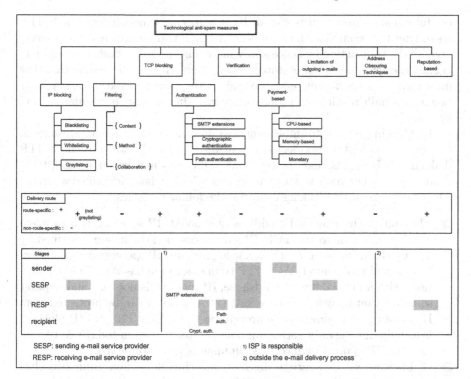

Fig. 4.3: Technological anti-spam measures

4.4.1 IP blocking

When a client initiates an SMTP connection, a TCP/IP connection with the SMTP server is established on the transport and network layers. The IP address of the sending host can be easily determined and is the first information about the client which is available to the server. On the basis of the IP address, a server can decide to accept or reject an SMTP session part. If the IP address is associated with a client who has sent spam in the past, the connection may be declined. This procedure is denoted as "blacklisting", with suspicious IP addresses being stored on blacklists. Sometimes, even whole IP ranges are elements of black lists, for example, IP ranges assigned to specific domains or to ISPs. Analogously, the IP address may belong to a trustworthy SMTP client, thus leading to an SMTP connection acceptance ("whitelisting"). The term "greylisting" is misleading and does not denote a complementary application of white- and blacklisting. Rather, it describes an approach where the IP address is part of a set of information which is used for the acceptance/rejection decision. Usually, some more envelope data, like the arguments of the *RCPT* and *MAIL FROM* command are used: each e-mail transaction is first rejected and a set of information (parameters) characterizing this preliminary unsuccessful e-mail transaction is stored. If, in a specific time-window, the SMTP client tries to accomplish the unsuccessful e-mail transaction again, the server accepts the transaction by successfully matching the transaction's parameters against the set of parameters stored. Greylisting relies on the assumption that most spam sources do not re-send e-mails – they are believed to assume that bounced e-mails result from invalid addresses – in contrast to "regular" e-mail systems.

IP blocking is easy to implement and does not consume many resources, because the accept/reject decision is made at an early stage of the SMTP dialogue. This means that the recipient MTA does not consume much CPU time and does not have to store a message which is later identified as spam. The drawbacks of IP blocking comprise the following issues:

❑ They fail if the client's IP address is spoofed. IP spoofing is a problem which is inherent to the TCP/IP suite; possible attacks are described by Tanase [170]. However, for the following reasons, IP spoofing does not seem to be a real problem: (1) As SMTP connections are based on TCP connections with an initial 3-way handshake, IP spoofing is not easy and requires some relevant knowledge and effort. (2) A network can be protected from IP spoofing with some simple prevention techniques [170]. (3) IP blocking is usually not the only anti-spam policy implemented in today's MTAs. In practice, IP spoofing aimed at spamming is rarely observed.

❑ IP blocking works heuristically and, in principle, suffers from two classification faults: if a non-spam SMTP transaction is declined, we have a "false-positive", if a spam SMTP transaction is accepted, we get a "false-negative". This problem is discussed in more detail in the context of black-, white-, and greylisting.

Some details and effects of IP blocking depend on the procedures which are used. These are briefly presented here.

Blacklisting

Blacklists can differ in many ways. Some organizations, like ISPs, maintain private blacklists without sharing them with the Internet community. Thus, many 3rd parties currently offer this service by providing either free or commercial access. They usually provide a standardized access on realtime data via the DNS. When they are DNS-based, they are called Domain Name System Blacklists (DNSBLs). The "realtime" feature is necessary, as spammers tend to change their sending hosts very frequently. The data can contain the IP addresses of hosts of known spammers, of open relays, or of illegal 3rd party exploits (Exploits Block List (XBL)). Examples of the first category include *Spamhaus block list (SBL), Arbitrary black hole list (ABL)*, and *Domain Name System Real-time Black List (DNSRBL)*, databases of the second category include *Open Relay Database (ORDB), MAPS Dial-up User List*

(MAPS-DUL), and Spam Prevention Early Warning System (SPEWS) (see page 63). Spamhaus, for example, provides an XBL including open proxies, worms/viruses with built-in spam engines, and other types of Trojan horse exploits. DECLUDE Internet Security Software [38], Email-policy.com [49], and InfoSec [81] give a comprehensive list of DNS-based blacklists.

The way the DNS is used for the distribution of blacklist entries is simple. If, for example, an SMTP server faces an incoming connection from a client with the IP address *24.2.20.42* and wants to use Spamhaus' SBL, the server requests an A record of *42.20.2.24.sbl.spamhaus.org* (the bytes of the IP address have been inverted). If the IP address *24.2.20.42* is included in the blacklist, the DNS would provide a specific A record. In the case of SBL, an A record with IP *127.0.0.2* would be returned. Otherwise, no A record for *24.2.20.42* is available, indicating that this particular IP is not blacklisted. Many lists only provide the return value *127.0.0.2* while others arrange for different return values (*127.0.0.0/8*), for example, in order to give the reason for listing a particular IP address. Some DNSBLs can even be downloaded completely to enhance response time and availability.

DNSBLs are reasonably effective at identifying the

☐ IP address ranges of networks with a history of sending abusive mail,
☐ IP addresses of specific hosts with a history of sending abusive mail, typically because they are controlled by a Trojan or other hostile software, and
☐ ranges of IP addresses assigned to hosts whose users generally send mail via their ISP's mail servers and are not expected to send mail directly.

DNSBLs can also differ in their policy, which contains information about the degree of accountability (MAPS is a company and can be found easily; SPEWS is a completely anonymously run organization), how an IP address gets on the list (some accept reports and investigate, some accept reports and immediately blacklist the address, some actively search for perceived problems), and how an address gets off the list (some have carefully published policies, while others have essentially unknown criteria) [2]. A popular method of putting IP addresses (temporarily) on a blacklist is a frequency analysis of the incoming e-mails per host. Spammers sometimes send a huge number of e-mails to a specific e-mail server during a short period, which results in an exceptionally high frequency. Hosts featuring such a behavior can be blocked, but whitelists should be used complementarily to take into account "regular" bulk e-mails like newsletters.

The main disadvantages of blacklisting are the following:

☐ Blacklists can never be exhaustive. As spammers tend to use IPs for a short time only, maybe only a few hours, blacklists may not be up-to-date, thus leading to false-negatives.

❑ Blacklists sometimes contain addresses or even an address range belonging to an ESP or ISP, because one or a few spammers have misused the providers' infrastructure. Before the providers' administrator becomes aware of this and deals with the problem, the (ham) e-mails of thousands or even millions of customers may have been blocked, leading to false-positives. This drawback generally affects all e-mail (relay) hosts which have been blocked, even though they are themselves victims of spammers and/or hackers.

❑ DNS-based blacklists lead to an increased Internet traffic and make the DNS a more critical resource, as it is vulnerable in terms of integrity and authenticity (DNS spoofing).

Variants of blacklists have evolved. "Right Hand Side Blacklists" do not store IP addresses but domain names. As domain names can be easily spoofed, this approach is not very promising. Uniform Resource Identifier (URI) Realtime Blacklists differ from "ordinary" blacklists in that they are used to detect spam based on message body URIs (usually web sites). This allows the blocking of messages that have spam hosts which are mentioned in message bodies. The measure addresses the idea that spammers have more trouble camouflaging advertised web sites than misusing IP addresses. surbl.org provides such a list. However, these measures are limited to spam e-mails with URIs and are susceptible to false-positives. They have to solve redirects and need software to parse URIs in message bodies and have to extract their hosts, and check those against a URI Realtime Blacklist; this procedure is quite a resource-consuming one. Furthermore, this blacklisting version needs to receive and parse the whole message, which involves more filtering (see Subsect. 4.4.2) than blocking.

Whitelisting

Like blacklists, whitelists can be maintained locally or be provided publicly. When they are published via DNS, they are, analogously to blacklists, denoted as Domain Name System Whitelists (DNSWLs). DECLUDE Internet Security Software [38] provides some publicly available DNSWLs. Unlike blacklists, their up-to-dateness is less critical. Whitelists alone are rarely a very effective way of dealing with e-mails, as the false-positive rate is too high (e-mails from unknown senders would be blocked); false-negatives might occur very rarely, because the sender is identifiable and accountable. They should be used complementarily to other approaches and applied as a first-level measure, meaning that e-mails from hosts which are whitelisted do not have to be checked by other anti-spam measures.

Greylisting

Greylisting has contributed to the successful protection of e-mail servers against spam. However, there are some inherent drawbacks and its long-term effectiveness seems quite limited:

☐ For each e-mail transaction, the receiving MTA usually stores a data triple consisting of IP and some other envelope data. Thus, an SMTP transaction can be neither accepted nor rejected unless all data are available. Unlike black- and whitelisting, this measure takes slightly more time to come to a decision. Furthermore, storage capacity is needed.

☐ Greylisting results in an increase of e-mail traffic as most e-mails have to be resent.

☐ The main problem with greylisting is the assumption that spammers do not implement the resume feature in order to increase their throughput. Thus, spammers can easily circumvent greylisting, especially with (high quality) lists of valid e-mail addresses. This leads to false-negatives.

☐ The abuse of regular e-mail hosts is not addressed.

☐ Not all sending hosts are conform with RFC 2821, because they do not resend messages. Thus, messages can get lost (false-positives).

☐ Large e-mail systems sometimes consist of several sending hosts (for example, for sending newsletters),which may take turns in resending rejected e-mails. Because the hosts feature different IP addresses, it may happen that an e-mail never passes the greylisting mechanism and gets lost (false-positives).

☐ Existing Internet e-mail permits the unauthorized use of addresses in the *MAIL FROM* command, which results in having notices and bounce e-mails sent to unwitting and unwilling recipients. Bounce Address Tag Validation (BATV) [97] defines an extensible mechanism for validating the *MAIL FROM* address. This mechanism permits the *MAIL FROM* target domain to distinguish between notification message addresses that are valid and those that are not. For that purpose, tracking information can be encoded in the *MAIL FROM* address which is used as *RCPT TO* argument when the e-mail has to be bounced and which allows the recipient MTA to validate the bounce e-mail. In order to address reply attacks, which means (in this context) that an attacker obtains a copy of a message containing a valid sender address and later sends one or more e-mails to this address, each e-mail gets a unique sender address, e.g. by encoding the current time as well. This, however, causes trouble with greylisting because a (temporarily) rejected message will be resent with a different *MAIL FROM* content and, thus, will be rejected (over and over) again.

4.4.2 Filtering

Filtering methods are heuristics (as are IP blocking methods) which try to classify e-mails into the two categories spam and ham. For example, a filter may look for key words or phrases such as "you are receiving" and "to un-subscribe", may look for specific structures (e.g. HTML MIME attachments) or may consider the language used (the Chinese language is often viewed as suspicious). The filters can be applied by the client's ESP, by the recipient's ESP, and by the recipient as well. Some authors treat IP blocking as specific filtering. However, in this manuscript, a sharp boundary between IP blocking and filtering is drawn because IP blocking uses different methods to those applied in what is widely understood as filtering, that is, investigating at least the header and/or the body.

Filtering methods are widely deployed and they can vary in the inspected content, in the method used, and in the form of collaboration. Some filters consider only the header or the body, while others take both. Some filters even involve envelope data as well. There is a broad range of specific filtering methods available. This is also due to the fact that, in principle, all algorithms for text classification can be applied, which is a well established field. E-mail filtering is also a task that includes the two phases "training" and "classifying". Therefore, the field of machine learning may provide appropriate algorithms, too. This subsection comprises some of the most relevant methods without making claims at completeness: filtering can be rule-based, signature-based or statistical (this field is dominated by probabilistic Bayesian filters). Filtering can also use Support Vector Machines, Boosting Trees, Artificial Neural Networks and Markov Random Field Models.

Some filters are collaborative, i.e. they are not centralized but involve many servers which share information about spam e-mails. Some collaborative signature-based systems are mentioned below.

To be effective, at least two challenging requirements have to be fulfilled:

1. Filters have to continue learning because spammers frequently change their e-mails with regard to structure and content.
2. Filters have to be trained individually, because different organizations or individuals may use different terminology. For a doctor or a hospital, the names of medical products belong to their language use and for insurance companies the terms "mortgage" and "insurance" are common, while most private users may view these suspiciously.
3. Filters have to be robust. For example, spammers are now working aggressively to evade filters, and one of the things they are doing is breaking up and misspelling words to prevent filters from recognizing them. So as spammers start using "c0ck" instead of "cock" to evade simple-minded spam filters. Furthermore, they have to address the problem that occurs when spam and ham e-mails become more and more alike.

Filtering methods share some major drawbacks which are independent of the applied filtering method:

❑ A main problem with the filter-based approach is that it is not 100% accurate in detecting spam; both false-positives and false-negatives occur (misclassification). As an example of false-negatives, Graham [76] points out: *"The other kind of spams I have trouble filtering are those from companies in e.g. Bulgaria offering contract programming services. These get through because I'm a programmer too, and the spams are full of the same words as my real mail."* Probably even worse are false-positives: in 2003, an e-mail vetting system filtered parts of the "Sexual Offences Bill" being sent to Members of Parliament belonging to the British "House of Commons". It thereby blocked discussion of the new Sexual Offences Bill [12]. Androutsopoulos et al. [7] present a game theoretic model of spam e-mailing which they propose to use to determine the optimal point (of the filter) in the tradeoff between false-positives and false-negatives.

☐ Filtering methods, especially when they inspect the body of an e-mail, are quite resource-consuming. ESPs have to reserve CPU time to inspect millions of e-mails per day, some client-based solutions may pose problems for individuals who download all of their e-mail using a modem as they still have to wait for the unwanted e-mail to download. This problem is reduced by e-mail systems that allow clients to preview e-mail headers [30, p. 78].

☐ The more spam e-mails resemble ham e-mails, the less effective are the filters. Spammers are nowadays already quite successful at generating similarity.

☐ Filtering mechanisms reduce a spam e-mail's probability of being delivered to the recipient. A big danger is that this encourages spammers to send even more e-mails in an attempt to bypass the filters. Thus, filters have the negative effect of exacerbating the problem of resource consumption originating from spam [181, p. 2].

Constructing and evading filters has led to a still open-ended arms race between the anti-spam community and spammers. It seems doubtful whether, despite various announcements, filters will ever be the silver bullet in the fight against spam.

The rest of this subsection is dedicated to the specific filtering methods and systems mentioned above without inspecting and comparing their effectiveness. Although many papers include some empirical testing, their data sets are often small and, moreover, different data sets are often used. Thus, the results have problems regarding representativeness and comparability. Androutsopoulos, Koutsias, Chandrinos and Spyropoulos [6], Androutsopoulos, Paliouras, Karkaletsis, Sakkis, Spyropoulos and Stamatopoulos [8], O'Brien and Vogel [121], Gómez Hidalgo and Maña López [74], and Provost [137] provide comparative studies of various filtering methods.

It should be noted that some filtering systems use a variety of filtering methods and aggregate the partial results to an overall result. For example, "SpamAssassin" (*http://spamassassin.apache.org/index.html*) uses text analysis, Bayesian filtering, and collaborative filtering databases, and assigns a score to each e-mail, indicating the likelihood that the e-mail is spam. Each e-mail server can be set up to apply its own threshold used to distinguish ham from spam.

Rule-based filtering

When rules are used for spam filtering, they can be created manually by users, or automatically. A simple rule may look like this:

spam ← (subject contains "VIAGRA") and (body contains "Dear Sir")

and can refer to the header and/or the body. A detailed discussion of automatic induction of e-mail filtering rules is presented by Cohen [28] and Crawford et al. [31]. A main disadvantage of rule-based filtering is that it can easily be overcome if spammers slightly change their notions, for example "V1AGRA" instead of "VIAGRA", or use verbalizations that are close to those in ham e-mails.

Signature-based filtering

Signature-based methods do not deal with whole messages or specific tokens but reduce a message to a signature. This can be done in various ways, for example by using a hash function. However, it is important for these methods' effectiveness that they are robust against minor changes in spam e-mails, such as a personalized salutation or other slight variations of the message, and are updated and possibly distributed very frequently because the contents of spam e-mails quickly change. The general procedure for screening an e-mail is to build its signature and to compare it with known spam signatures in databases.

Signature-based filtering methods differ not only in the way they build the signature; they can be client- or server-based, meaning that users or server administrators respectively identify e-mails as spam; they can be collaborative or non-collaborative; collaborative filters often use a Peer-to-Peer (P2P) network for signature distribution. Especially when users report spam e-mails, it is important to set up a threshold which the number of reports has to exceed because a single user's assessment may be shared by only a very small number of users thus leading to a high false-positive rate. Well known example systems are:

❑ Vipul's Razor (*http://razor.sourceforge.net/*) is a distributed, collaborative, spam detection and filtering network. The project description is as follows: *"Through user contribution, Razor establishes a distributed and constantly updating catalogue of spam in propagation that is consulted by e-mail clients to filter out known spam. Detection is done with statistical and randomized signatures that efficiently spot mutating spam content. User input is validated through reputation assignments based on consensus on report and revoke assertions which in turn is used for computing confidence values associated with individual signatures."*

☐ Damiani et al. [35] propose a collaborative spam filter with e-mail servers sharing information via a P2P network. For each message which has been reported as spam by users, a 256-bit digest is calculated, which is robust against typical disguising attempts. Two messages are considered to be the same if their digests differ by 74 bits at the most. The authors use a three-tier architecture consisting of a user tier, a peer tier containing e-mail servers, and a super-peer tier containing those e-mail-servers which serve as collectors and pollers of spam reports. The servers share their information (digests of spam messages) with each other by sending and receiving spam reports to/from their assigned super-peer servers. The super-peer servers share their information with each other, too. The protocol includes digital signatures of spam reports.

☐ Zhou et al. [191] use a P2P network, too. Instead of a single digest for a message, they generate a set of fingerprints for each message and distribute these through an extended Decentralized Object Location and Routing System (DOLR) .The goal is to efficiently match messages, distributed throughout the network, that share strong similarities in their content.

☐ *Distributed Checksum Clearinghouse (DCC)* (*http://www.rhyolite.com/anti-spam/dcc/*) is based on a number of open servers that maintain databases of message checksums.

Bayesian filtering

Statistical filters based on the probabilistic "Bayes theorem" were regarded as being helpful in spam detection as early as 1998 [132, 143]. They are still very popular and widely deployed and use the mathematical fact that, given an e-mail's feature vector – a feature is usually the occurrence of a typical spam token like "V1AGRA" –, the e-mail's probability of being a spam e-mail can be calculated using some other probabilities which are known. The Bayes theorem is

$$P(S|M) := \frac{P(M|S) \times P(S)}{P(M)}$$

A simple example is used to illustrate its application in a Bayesian filter. Let S be the event "message is spam" and M be the event "message contains the token 'mortgage' ". Then, $P(S|M)$ denotes the probability that a message which belongs to the historical data and which contains the token "mortgage" is categorized as spam. Furthermore, let the historical data feature the following characteristics:

☐ The number of spam e-mails is 5000. 600 of them contain the token "mortgage".

☐ The number of ham e-mails is 500. 9 of them contain the token "mortgage".

Then, $P(S|M)$ can be calculated with

$$P(S|M) = \frac{(600/5000) \times (5000/5500)}{(609/5500)} \approx 98,52\%$$

It is remarkable that the spam probability of an e-mail containing the token "mortgage" is about 98%, although it is part of only 12% of all spam e-mails in the historical data. It is important to take into account that this token occurs in less than 2% of all stored ham e-mails. The application of the Bayes theorem illustrated above is simplified due to the comprehension of its effect. In practice, it is necessary to consider many tokens in the Bayes theorem leading to

$$P(S|w_1 \wedge w_2 \wedge \ldots \wedge w_n) = \frac{P(w_1 \wedge w_2 \wedge \ldots \wedge w_n|S) \times P(S)}{P(w_1 \wedge w_2 \wedge \ldots \wedge w_n)} \tag{4.1}$$

with w_i being the event that token i is part of the e-mail currently under consideration. After some transformation of (4.1), we yield [99]

$$P(S|w_1 \wedge w_2 \wedge \ldots \wedge w_n) = \frac{\prod_i P(w_i|w_{i+1} \wedge \ldots \wedge w_n \wedge S) \times P(S)}{P(w_1 \wedge w_2 \wedge \ldots \wedge w_n)} \tag{4.2}$$

A Bayesian filter is termed "naïve" if it assumes (complete) stochastic independence of the occurrences of the tokens $w_i, i = 1, 2, \ldots, n$. Then, (4.1) can be simplified to

$$P(S|w_1 \wedge w_2 \wedge \ldots \wedge w_n) = \frac{\prod_i P(w_i|S) \times P(S)}{P(w_1 \wedge w_2 \wedge \ldots \wedge w_n)} \tag{4.3}$$

Let us assume that we have again 5000 spam e-mails and 500 ham e-mails. The number of spam e-mails containing a specific token is given in Table 4.3. Let us further assume that, in total, 8 e-mails contain all tokens listed in Table 4.3. Then, the application of (4.3) yields

Table 4.3: Tokens and their numbers of occurrence

madam	promotion	republic	shortest	sorry	supported
3000	4500	2000	3000	4500	4900

$$P(S|w_1 \wedge w_2 \wedge \ldots \wedge w_6) = \frac{\left(\frac{3000}{5000} \times \frac{4500}{5000} \times \frac{2000}{5000} \times \frac{3000}{5000} \times \frac{4500}{5000} \times \frac{4900}{5000}\right)}{\frac{8}{5500}} = 71,442\%$$

This probability seems to be too low to put up with a misclassification. This raises the question of an appropriate threshold. One option is to fix a probability as a threshold, another one is to relate $P(S|w_1 \wedge w_2 \wedge \ldots \wedge w_n)$ to $P(H|w_1 \wedge w_2 \wedge \ldots \wedge w_n)$, with H being the event "message is ham", and fix a value for this quotient.

To take changing texts and notions into account, a Bayesian filter can learn by adding a newly classified e-mail to the historical data, thus adapting probabilities.

Graham [75] gives a practical-oriented introduction to naive Bayesian filters. Graham [76] provides an improvement on them via, among other things, a more sophisticated treatment of tokens. An evaluation of naive Bayesian anti-spam filtering is provided by Androutsopoulos, Koutsias, Chandrinos, Paliouas and Vassilakis [5]. Their conclusion is *"[...] that additional safety nets are needed for the Naive Bayesian anti-spam filter to be viable in practice."* In the examples above, only the occurrence of a token is relevant, not the number of occurrences nor the order in which they appear. Schneider [146] compares naive Bayesian filters with respect to these two options – in information retrieval and text categorization the first option is denoted as "multi-variate Bernoulli model", the second one, considering numbers as well as the order, is denoted as "multinominal model". In his study, the multinominal model achieves slightly higher accuracy than the multi-variate Bernoulli model.

Other methods for text classification

Many more methods for text classification have been applied in the classifying of e-mail as spam or ham. These include Support Vector Machines [46] – Metzger et al. [105] propose collaborative filtering –, Boosting Trees [22], Artificial Neural Networks [45] and Markov Random Field Models [25]. They are implemented and tested in prototypic environments, but a long-term (comparing) study of their empirical effectiveness is unknown to the author.

4.4.3 TCP blocking

Unlike IP blocking, TCP blocking does not aim at detecting spam on the recipient's side but rather on preventing spam on the sender's side, which is preferable. Because SMTP e-mails are directed to TCP port 25, ISPs and companies often block all (outgoing) TCP traffic on this port. It is a simple option for banishing spam sent from SMTP clients directly to the MX host. This measure addresses spamming on the transmission layer and mainly addresses scenarios where spammers set up SMTP engines on their own PCs or on exploited computers. This measure is easy to implement. However, the blocking of port 25 can be problematic for ISP customers who need to run their own e-mail server or communicate with an e-mail server on a remote network to submit e-mail (such as a hosted domains e-mail server) [9]. To allow customers to reach their SMTP server, often message submission (usually using TCP port 587) and SMTP-AUTH [114] are offered as authentication mechanisms.

4.4.4 Authentication

Authentication schemes fall into three categories. The first includes SMTP extensions, the second is based on cryptographic authentication and addresses an end-to-end security. The third category comprises path authentication proposals which identify the domain of the last hop or the last MTA. This category includes protocols which are termed "Lightweight MTA Authentication Protocols".

SMTP extensions

Protocol extensions, such as SMTP-AUTH [114], "SMTP after POP" and "SMTP after IMAP", have been provided to support authentication of users or SMTP clients. SMTP-AUTH defines an SMTP service extension, whereby an SMTP client may indicate an authentication mechanism to the server, perform an authentication protocol exchange, and optionally negotiate a security layer for subsequent protocol interactions. This extension is a profile of the Simple Authentication and Security Layer (SASL) [113] and also allows e-mail users to perform an authenticated connection between their MUA and the SMTP server, for example by using a username/password pair. Both "SMTP after POP" and "SMTP after IMAP" are always based on a username/password pair and authenticate a user through a successful POP or IMAP connection. After a successful connection, the user is allowed to send e-mails for a specific period of time, for example ten minutes.

These approaches address the spoofing of sender names and/or host names and are intended to improve accountability. However, user names and passwords are generally not kept protected on users' PCs and are available to malicious code on zombie PCs. SMTP-AUTH can only serve to authenticate a user or host. If spam has already reached a server or an account has been corrupted, SMTP-AUTH is useless.

Cryptographic authentication

Cryptographic authentication approaches address e-mail spoofing in general. A digital signature is added to the message and verified by the recipient as being associated with the message sender identity. Digital signatures can be based on public-key cryptography, that uses two different keys – a private one for encryption and a public one for decryption –, or it can be based on symmetric key cryptography with the same key being used for encryption and decryption. To verify the cryptographic signature of a message, the originally signed message body is used, and the hash of that is compared to the hash of the decrypted digital signature. Approaches can also differ in the kind of identity that is verified: some are user- or address-based (signing is usually done by the MUA) while others work by verifying the domain or the ESP (signing is done by the MTA) respectively.

Public key cryptography proposals include S/MIME [139], PGP [19], META Signatures [96], IIM [55], DomainKeys [40], Microsoft Postmarks [106] and others. The IETF has set up the working group "Message Authentication Signature Standards (MASS)" to discuss such approaches submitted for standardization. With some proposals, the public key is not included in the signature and it is made available in some special record or server associated with sender identity (this is the approach taken by DomainKeys, which puts the public key in a DNS record and is the approach used by PGP with its keyserver system). Others prefer to include the public key as part of the signature itself (META, IIM, S/MIME and most other digital signature schemes), which is more advantageous as it allows the receiver to decrypt and verify the signature without any external lookup (and it can be done offline). However, such verification does not guarantee that the signature will indeed be authorized by the sender, so the final step would still involve either checking with the sender's authorized source to make sure that the public key used in signature is associated with the sender's public key, or by having the public key itself signed by a third party (the third party could be a certificate authority), whose key is known and trusted to be correct by the recipient [95].

Table 4.4 summarizes some of the most important cryptographic authentication proposals with the identity being verified, the data which are signed, the signature location and format, and some more information about the cryptography and the signature type. Recently, DomainKeys Identified Mail (DKIM) [4] has been proposed. This combines Yahoo's DomainKeys and Cisco's Identified Internet Mail. Advocates of cryptographic solutions argue that spam could be effectively addressed by these. Tompkins and Handley [179], for example, sketch an e-mail environment based on public key cryptography, where A accepts a message from B only if B's public key is in A's database, either because A and B know each other or because they share a common contact C, who has introduced B to A. Public e-mail communication has to be initiated via a form on a publicly accessible web page. However, some major limitations and drawbacks of cryptographic authentication in fighting spam emerge here:

❑ They primarily address e-mail spoofing and thus have no effect if spam e-mails do not contain spoofed data or data cannot be categorized as spoofed. This may happen when a user's private key is not sufficiently protected against unauthorized access – then the SO cannot distinguish between genuine and forged e-mails – or when spammers can readily obtain keys for a domain intended, and then used, solely for the temporary purpose of spamming.

Table 4.4: Cryptographic authentication proposals [95]

Proposal	Identity being verified	Signed data	Signature location, format	Cryptography, signature type, comment
BATV	RFC2821 MAIL FROM - entire address	RFC2821 MAIL FROM address	Signature part of RFC2821 MAIL FROM data in BATV format	Private signature, exact algorithm not specified but likely symmetric key based.
Cisco Identified Internet Mail	RFC2822 "From" (preferred) - domain or email address, RFC2822 "Sender" (possible)	Message Data (signed) and header fields (included)	Signature in message header in custom IIM-Signature header field.	Public Key Cryptography based on RSA. Public key included with signature. Authorization using public key fingerprints in dns or special KRS server.
META Signatures	RFC2822 "Sender" - domain or email AND/OR mail server name	Message Content Parts and Message Header Fields	Signature in message header using META-Signature header field. Body hash in EDigest header field.	Public Key Cryptography based on RSA. It supports several authorization methods. Public key can be included in signature.
Microsoft PostMarks	RFC2822 "From" full address	Message Content Part(s)	X.509 additional signature added into special part of S/MIME	Public Key Cryptography with X.509. Signature in non-standard part of X.509 and added by intermediate MTAs.
PGP	RFC2822 "From" - entire address	Message Content Part(s)	PGP signature in message body. Variations exist with signature as part of text data or with PGP/MIME as separate MIME body part.	Public Key Cryptography. PGP is famous for its web-of-trust model with users authorizing each other.
S/MIME	RFC2822 "From" - entire address	Message Content Part(s)	X.509 signature in message body as special MIME body part.	Public Key Cryptography with standard ITU X.509 format signature, RSA or DH.
SES	RFC2821 MAIL FROM - entire address	RFC2821 MAIL FROM (optionally Message Data)	Signature added to RFC2821 MAIL FROM data in SES format	Symmetric Key Cryptography. In some cases only part of the signature and part of the hash is included in MAILFROM.
Yahoo DomainKeys	RFC2822 "Sender" - domain only	Message Data and Message Header Fields	Signature in message header in DomainKey-Signature field.	Public Key Cryptography based on RSA, public key in DNS record and not included in the signature.

❑ On the recipient's side, either the provider's MTA or the user's MUA may detect an e-mail with spoofed data. If it is a spam e-mail, it is rejected, but this decision cannot be made prior to receiving or downloading the message completely, and to calculating the hash and comparing it to the hash from the decrypted digital signature. However, this means that many resources have already been consumed. In another case e-mail data seem to be spoofed and the message is thus rejected although no spoofing has actually occurred (see next issue).

❑ Because of the inclusion of a hash of the entire or a majority of the message data in the signature, the cryptographic signatures can have problems with signature verification for messages that come through intermediate sites, because some intermediate systems modify or transform the message (for example from one encoding to another). In the current Internet e-mail infrastructure, most vulnerability to signature survival is posed by message processing done by mail lists, as many of these do not simply retransmit the message to subscribers but also change subject header fields to add "[list]" tags, and the majority may also add a footer to the e-mail body to inform the subscriber that this message came through the list [95].

❑ Proposals which authenticate on domain level do not allow an accountability on user level. Therefore, it may be possible to blame an organization for being a spam source, but not a specific user or person on whose behalf the organization is sending these messages. This means that acceptance/rejection decisions are made on domain level, thereby probably "punishing" guileless e-mail users. Proposals which authenticate on user level require each user to apply cryptography using secure procedures and devices. This does not only mean enhanced user effort and costs, due to secure devices such as cards and card readers, but also the providing of an infrastructure for key management.

❑ In order to allow a world-wide e-mail communication, it is necessary to standardize data formats of keys and certificates, cryptographic algorithms, and infrastructural issues so that all e-mail users can communicate with each other independently of their ESP's implementation. This, however, requires at least the interoperability of different cryptographic environments. All this is a tall order: PKIs, for example, have never been successfully deployed in the context of the highly heterogeneous Internet. A successful PKI would need to be federated (so that no single provider could lock down the market), distributed, and replicated (for performance and resilience) [2]. In the context of identification and authentication Garfinkel [69] argues that another reason for the slow adoption of PKIs is that its capabilities generally do not match typical user requirements.

Path Authentication

In order to avoid cryptographic-based authentication, which needs some kind of PKI and implements an end-to-end authentication, a weaker family of (mostly DNS-based) path authentication mechanisms has been proposed. The theory of path authentication in general is that, if the destination verifies the previous hop (SMTP client) and can trust its results, and if the previous hop verifies the original sender, then the original sender of the e-mail can be considered to have been verified and authorized [95].

A (mainly DNS-based) family of path authentication methods against spam is Lightweight Message Authentication Protocol (LMAP) which is specified in an Internet Draft [39]. LMAP attacks the e-mail forgery problem by checking that the host from which the message was sent is authorized to send e-mail using the domain in the message's envelope or header. For example, it is checked whether a message that claims to be from *buffy@sunnydale.com* was actually sent from an MTA acting on behalf of the *sunnydale.com* organization. If not, the e-mail is a forgery or an intermediate MTA was used as an external e-mail relay (see the discussion of disadvantages below). LMAP is based on two concepts: publication of authentication data by a domain (mostly with DNS records) and application of that data by a recipient (MTA). It thus effects the protocols SMTP (RFC 2821) and DNS (RFC 1034).

When a message is sent via SMTP, the recipient MTA has a variety of items that it could use to authenticate the e-mail sender: IP address, HELO/EHLO argument, return path, and message headers. All of these items can be used for various kinds of authentication. This has led to many specific LMAP proposals differing in the kind of identity that is authorized, the data with which the identity is associated, the network source, and the DNS record type (if DNS is used). The most popular of these are listed in Table 4.5 [95] and comprise SPF [190], RMX [36], DMP [54], MS-Sender-ID [103, 102], CSV [33, 129], and MTAMARK [168]. A discussion and comparison of LMAP proposals is given by Leibzon [95] and Schryen and Hoven [158]. No standardization has been achieved. Moreover, the IETF working group MARID was dissolved in 2004.

The disadvantages and limitations of LMAP approaches are manifold:

❑ LMAP is primarily intended to attack some kind of spoofing and not spamming in general. Spam e-mails which do not contain spoofed data will not be detected. Therefore, LMAP proposals are not stand-alone solutions towards spam, but rather they can be used as part of a comprehensive approach.

Table 4.5: LMAP proposals [95]

Proposal	Identity Being Authorized	Identity Associated With	Network Source Verified Using	Record Type
SPF "Classic" (MAIL FROM Identity)	RFC2821 MAIL FROM	Original message sender or system acting on its behalf	IP address of SMTP client	SPF record in DNS
SPF - From	RFC2822 "Sender"	Original message sender or system acting on its behalf	IP address of SMTP client	SPF record in DNS
SPF - Sender Identity	RFC2822 "From"	Original message sender or system acting on its behalf	IP address of SMTP client	SPF record in DNS
RMX	RFC2821 MAIL FROM	Original message sender or system acting on its behalf	IP address of SMTP client	RMX record in DNS
RMX+	RFC2821 MAIL FROM	Original message sender or system acting on its behalf	IP address of SMTP client	Verification using HTTP CGI
DMP	RFC2821 MAIL FROM	Original message sender or system acting on its behalf	IP address of SMTP client	DMP style txt in-addr like record in DNS
MPR	RFC2821 MAIL FROM	Original message sender or system acting on its behalf	SMTP client HELO name	Special Use of PTR DNS records
SPF - Submit Identity	RFC2821 SUBMITTER	Identity associated with SMTP Client network site	IP address of SMTP client	SPF record in DNS
MS-Sender-ID	RFC2822-based PRA (Sender + Resent) or RFC2821 SUBMITTER	Identity associated with SMTP Client network site	IP address of SMTP client	SPF record in DNS
MS-Caller-ID	RFC2822 PRA (Sender + Resend-)	Identity associated with SMTP Client network site	IP address of SMTP client	custom XML record in DNS
SPF "Classic" (HELO Identity)	RFC2821 HELO/ EHLO	Identity of SMTP Client	IP address of SMTP client	SPF record in DNS
CSV	RFC2821 HELO/ EHLO	Identity of SMTP Client	IP address of SMTP client	Special use of SRV DNS records
SPF - PTR Identity	PTR address pointer for IP address of SMTP Client	Identity of SMTP Client	IP address of SMTP client	SPF record in DNS
MTAMARK	IP address of SMTP Client	Identity of SMTP Client	IP address of SMTP client	TXT records in INADDR dns delegation zones

❏ Message relaying and forwarding is affected by LMAP: E-mail forwarders have traditionally left the sender envelope untouched. Assume a situation where an LMAP compliant domain A sends a message to address B, which forwards the message to an LMAP compliant recipient C using the original sender address from A. If a $B \rightarrow C$ forward had been set up, A's LMAP records would be checked by C's LMAP client, and the message would be correctly rejected. If the recipient C did desire the $B \rightarrow C$ forwarding, a workaround would be necessary. One option is that B's MTA rewrites the sender address to one in B's domain; a second one is to alter the *.forward* file to apply a return path in B's domain. A third option can be implemented in C's MTA, which gets a whitelist indicating that forwarded messages are expected to arrive for C from B.

❏ Many web systems, such as greeting card systems and mail-a-link systems, offer a facility for sending e-mails from the web site to a third party, with the web user's return address. Few of these systems carry out any validation of the sender's address, although they tend to be rate-limited or inherently so slow that they are not useful for sending out spam. However, since users can enter any return address, the e-mail they send is technically indistinguishable from e-mail with forged return addresses.

❏ LMAP proposals do not prevent users from fraudulently claiming to be another user within a domain.

❏ Spammers can set up valid LMAP records for domains that are intended to be used for a short time only. After sending their bulk e-mail the domains will soon be blacklisted and become useless to spammers, so that they simply set up new domains and LMAP records.

❏ Most versions of LMAP use the DNS to distribute the data against which mail is authenticated. This makes the DNS the critical resource required by all of these proposals. Insecurities in the DNS could allow hostile parties to page forged authentication information into the DNS. Packet floods and other denial of service attacks against DNS servers could make it impossible for LMAP clients to obtain LMAP authentication data.

❏ Other, more proposal-specific drawbacks are described by Leibzon [95].

4.4.5 Verification

As spammers usually send millions of e-mails, they are believed to ignore any bounce e-mails (see Subsect. 4.4.1) which they receive. On the basis of this behavior, verification mechanisms have been applied to stop spam e-mails from being delivered. In the verification scheme, no e-mail gets through unless the sender or SO is whitelisted. If a sender tries to deliver to a protected mailbox, the message in question is held in a quarantine queue and a challenge is returned. This can be as simple as "reply to this message" to let the sender's e-mail client perform a mathematical computation or sending the user an image and asking him or her to enter the word that is included there (since the human brain is much better at visual processing than even powerful computers, this seems trivial for nonhandicapped people and hard for algorithms; these algorithms are called Completely Automated Public Turing Test to Tell Computers and Humans Apart (CAPTCHA) algorithms [186, 187]). Once the challenge is correctly solved, the sender address or the SO is added to the recipient's whitelist and the original message is delivered. Due to the fact that a recipient's challenge requires a sender's response, this procedure is also termed "challenge-response" procedure.

An example of an e-mail verification system is Sender Address Verification Extension (SAVE), as proposed by Bless et al. [14]: for each e-mail featuring a non-whitelisted sender address, the MTA of the RO generates a multipart MIME message containing at least two different puzzles: one manual puzzle solvable by a human, e.g., a picture with a number combination in it, and one automatic puzzle as a task which can be solved by a machine, e.g. breaking a hash. Manual puzzles allow SAVE unaware users to send e-mails while automatic puzzles can be solved by instances of SAVE plugins for an MUA, MDA, or MTA. Thus, SAVE does not only include CAPTCHA but also provides a resource-based approach (see Subsect. 4.4.6). This approach aims at consuming CPU resources, which leads to the increase of spammers' (computational) costs.

Challenge-response-based methods feature the following drawbacks:

❑ E-mail communication becomes more complicated.
❑ The Internet traffic increases due to the challenge e-mail and the response action.
❑ The sending of regular bulk e-mail, like newsletters, fails in practice when manual responses are necessary, because too many human resources are required or it is too expensive. As challenge response procedures have the intention of increasing the computational effort of e-mail sending to an extent which prevents or at least exacerbates spammers' mass e-mailing, these procedures hit regular mass e-mailing likewise.
❑ When an innocent party's (valid) e-mail address is misused as the sender address, then the challenge e-mail will be delivered to the ingenuous user, which results in one more useless e-mail.
❑ When the response is aligned with a CAPTCHA, its quality has to be inspected because it may fail in two different ways: a human being may have difficulties in recognizing an object if it is presented amid too much clutter – using current Turing technology may have an adverse impact on users who have visual disabilities –, on the other hand, they must not be vulnerable to intelligent recognition software. Mori and Malik [110], for example, developed efficient methods that can identify a word in EZ-Gimpsy image, used by Yahoo to set up an e-mail account, with a success rate of 92%.
❑ Responses aligned to manual tasks may suffer from a social engineering attack: suppose the spammer's task is to identify a string in a picture and to retype it in a web form. The spammer then tricks a user into visiting

a web page with the extracted picture included and to solve this problem by promising access to adult material, for example. The user retypes the string and it is at the spammer's disposal in a machine-readable format. All this can be done automatically.

4.4.6 Payment-based approaches

Payment-based approaches rely on e-mail systems to create economic disincentives to spam. To accomplish this, e-mail servers require a small payment in exchange for delivering an e-mail to the recipient's inbox or for accepting an e-mail from a user client. The payment is kept small enough to allow legitimate e-mail to pass into user inboxes, but large enough to make the sending of large numbers of e-mails unprofitable or too time-consuming [179]. However, at the same time, this poses the problem of how to deliver solicited bulk e-mail.

The mode of payment could be CPU time or memory capacity as well as real-world currencies or virtual currencies. The former are often also referred to as "proof-of-work" procedures. Microsoft's "Penny Black project" (*http://research.microsoft.com/research/sv/PennyBlack/*), for example, has comprehensively investigated several of these modes to reduce spam by making the sender pay. The following discussion investigates the different modes of payment and their limitations in detail. Payment-based systems are currently rarely deployed.

CPU-based

CPU-based approaches constitute a proof-of-work which takes a parameterizable amount of CPU work to compute for the sender. Pricing functions proposed by Dwork and Naor [48], "hashcash" stamps [10] and digital stamps of the "Camram" system [88] belong to the most considered approaches. The pricing functions are described in detail as an example of systems which also consider regular bulk e-mail.

Dwork and Naor [48] propose e-mail systems which require the sender to compute some moderately expensive, but not intractable, function ("pricing function") of the message and some additional information (note that this procedure is not a challenge-response procedure in the sense that the server provides a challenge for each message). It also may be chosen in order to have something like a trap door: given some additional information, the computation would be considerably less expensive ("shortcut"). The shortcut may be used by the resource manager to allocate cheap access to the resource by bypassing the control mechanism. This mechanism is useful, if not necessary, for sending regular bulk e-mail. Furthermore, each user can have a frequent correspondent list of senders from whom messages are accepted without verification so that friends and relatives could circumvent the system entirely. In the context of e-mails, the authors propose the use of a hash function so that the sender never applies the pricing function to a message, which may be long, but only to its hash value. Furthermore, the hash function itself is used by some pricing functions. The system requires a single pricing function f_s, with shortcut c, and a hash function h. The selection of the pricing function and the setting of usage fees are controlled by a pricing authority. All users agree to obey the authority. There can be any number of trusted agents that receive the shortcut information from the pricing authority. The functions h and f_s are known to all users, but only the pricing authority and its trusted agents know c. To send a message m at time t to destination d, the sender computes $y = f_s(h(\langle m,t,d \rangle))$ and sends $\langle y,m,t \rangle$ to d. The recipient's e-mail program verifies that $y = f_s(h(\langle m,t,d \rangle))$. If verification fails, or if t is significantly different from the current time, then the message is discarded and (optionally) the sender is notified that transmission has failed. If the verification succeeds and the message is timely, then the message is routed to the reader.

Dwork and Naor [48] propose three families of pricing functions. The simplest one is based on the extraction of square roots and is briefly sketched to enhance understanding, but has no known shortcut. A more complex one is a Fiat-Shamir based scheme with shortcut. This is sketched, too. The square root-based pricing function needs a prime p, e.g. of length 1024 bit. Then, f_p is defined by

$$f : Z_p \to Z_p, f_p(x) = \sqrt{x} \bmod p$$

The server can verify the computation as follows:

$$\text{Given } x, y, \text{ check that } y^2 = x \bmod p$$

The checking step requires only one multiplication. In contrast, no method of extracting square roots mod p is known that requires fewer than about log p multiplications. The security of the signature scheme of Fiat and Shamir [57] is based on the difficulty of factoring large numbers (or equivalently of extracting square roots modulo a composite) and a hash function whose range size is exponential in a (security) parameter. To explain the scheme, some definitions are helpful: Let $N = pq$, where p and q are primes of sufficient length to make factoring N infeasible (at least 1024 bits should be used). Let $y_1 = x_1^2, \ldots, y_k = x_k^2$ be k squares modulo N, where k is a parameter. Finally, let $h : Z_N^* \times Z_N^* \to \{0,1\}^k$ be a hash function. h can be obtained from many hash functions by taking the k least significant bits of the output. The square roots $x_1, \ldots, x_k$ are needed for the shortcut. Let us write $h(x,r^2) = b_1 \ldots b_k$, where each b_i is a single bit. Then the sender has to find a pair (z,r^2) satisfying the condition

$$z^2 = r^2 x^2 \prod_{i=1}^{k} y_i^{b_i} \bmod N.$$

Dwork and Naor [48] use the term "pricing function" loosely, because sometimes – e.g. in this case – f is a relation defined by $f_s = (z,r^2)$. A procedure for evaluating f_s without shortcut information is presented by Dwork and

Naor [48, p. 6], with 2^k being the expected number of iterations. Retrieving the shortcut $x_1 \ldots x_k$ is as hard as factoring [138]. With the shortcut at hand, one can choose an r at random, compute $h(x, r^2) = b_1 \ldots b_k$ and set $z = rx \prod_{i=1}^{k} x_i^{b_i}$. Then, we have $f_s(x) = (z, r^2)$. Using the shortcut, the computation involves only $k + 2$ multiplications and one evaluation of the hash function. On server side, given x, z, r^2, the verification can be carried out by checking $z^2 = r^2 x^2 \prod_{i=1}^{k} y_i^{b_i}$ mod N. This computation requires one evaluation of the hash function and $O(k)$ multiplications, where O is the "Big O notation" used to describe the asymptotic behavior of functions. A consideration of the efficiency of computations shows this scheme's appropriateness for imposing a "difficult" computation task on the sender while allowing a verification to perform an "easy" computation task.

Independent of the particular approach applied, CPU-based anti-spam measures display some critical characteristics:

☐ They waste the resources of senders by requiring that a meaningless computation be performed. Hijacked computers can thus suffer from a highly increased consumption of CPU time.

☐ When botnets (The Honeynet Project & Research Alliance [175] provide a good introduction to botnets) are used, the total CPU time required to send (some million) spam e-mails is distributed among many (thousand) hosts.

☐ Time requirements vary greatly across the range of CPU speeds. Therefore, it seems difficult to find a balance between preventing unsolicited mass e-mailing and allowing regular e-mailing in an adequate time range.

☐ It is necessary to update e-mail clients and to convince users to do so. Furthermore, e-mails protocols will have to be substantially changed.

☐ Most authors of CPU-based approaches suggest that, if a recipient R has previously agreed to receive e-mail from a sender S, then each e-mail from S to R is sent in the normal way. However, this requires authentication mechanisms on the user level.

Unfortunately, because of sharp disparities across computer systems, this approach may be ineffective against malicious users with high-end systems, prohibitively slow for legitimate users with low-end systems, or both. Abadi et al. [1, p. 2] envision "... *that high-end systems might evaluate memory-bound functions somewhat faster than low-end systems, perhaps even 2-10 times faster (but not 10-100 faster, as CPU disparities might imply).*"

Memory-based

Abadi et al. [1] propose a family of moderately hard, memory-bound functions. Their approach is to force the sender S to access an unpredictable sequence of locations in a large array. The size of this array is chosen so as to be significantly larger than the largest cache available. The initial ideas comprise the following issues:

- Let $F : \{0, \ldots, 2^n - 1\} \rightarrow \{0, \ldots, 2^n - 1\}$ be a function where 2^n is the number of entries in the array.
- The inverse F^{i-1} cannot be evaluated in less time than a memory access. If S has to compute F^{-1} many times, then it becomes worthwhile for S to build a table for F^{-1} and to rely on the table thereafter. The table can be computed by 2^n applications of F. Building the table also requires memory accesses, for storing the table entries. However, these memory accesses can benefit from batching, and their cost (like that of applying F) is not necessarily uniform across machines. Therefore, the cost of building the table should not be dominant in S's work in responding to R's challenge, where R is the recipient. Rather, the dominant cost should be that of performing many table lookups.

The challenge-response procedure is as follows:

- R picks an integer $x_0 \in \{0 \ldots (2^n - 1)\}$ and computes, for $i = 0 \ldots (k-1)$:

$$x_{i+1} = F(x_i) \text{ xor } i$$

and a checksum of the sequence $x_0, \ldots, x_k$. R sends x_k and this checksum to S.
- S constructs a table for F^{-1} by applying F to all integers in $0 \ldots (2^n - 1)$.
- S builds sequences $y_k, \ldots, y_0$ starting with $y_k = x_k$ and such that

$$y_i \in F^{-1}(y_{i+1} \text{ xor } i)$$

so that $y_{i+1} = F(y_i) \text{ xor } i$.
- S returns y_0 if the checksum matches.
- R checks that $y_0 = x_0$.

Dwork et al. [47] prove that, on average, the sender of a message must perform many unrelated accesses to memory, while the receiver, in order to verify the work, has to perform significantly fewer accesses.

In principle, memory-based approaches share the disadvantages and limitations of CPU-based ones, except that the former's proof-of-work requirements vary less across the range of systems.

Monetary

These proposals typically require senders of e-mails to pay a fee for each e-mail communication, usually unless the recipient has whitelisted the sender. The currency used can be real cash (bonding schemes where the sender posts a bond to a third party that the sender forfeits if it spams) or virtual/digital cash. Both types are discussed below, each of them illustrated with an example system.

In an e-cash system, e-stamps are used. These are special digital tokens issued by some form of digital money bank. In such a system, the sender puts a stamp on every piece of e-mail he or she sends, and the recipient refuses to take e-mails without an e-stamp, at least not e-mails from strangers. If strangers try to e-mail without a stamp, they get a "bounce" back, telling them that they need to put a stamp on their e-mail (or follow certain other guidelines) to get the e-mail through. When the recipient gets a stamped e-mail, he or she can forward the stamp along to their bank for redemption. The system can be made even easier to implement if sites, rather than users, take on the responsibility of putting stamps on e-mail. IBM, for example, is probably willing to take responsibility, on behalf of its employees, to stamp their e-mails or certify them as non-abusers. Templeton [171] discusses many more conceptual, implementation and deployment issues. Loder et al. [101] discuss these systems using the term "attention bond mechanisms" by introducing a formal model, with which they attempt to capture the value structure for e-mail messages for both sender and recipient. Their findings include that, in certain cases, attention bond mechanisms leave recipients better off than even an idealized or perfect filter, that costs nothing and makes no mistakes. An example system is the concept proposed by Fahmann [53] where each recipient can set his or her own price and where it is the recipient's decision whether to collect the fee or to decline payment. His solution has three parts:

1. Each e-mail account has an accept list (or whitelist) that is maintained by the owner and that consists of the owner's friends and associates. Messages from people on this list are delivered without further ado.
2. The owner of an e-mail account can create interrupt tokens and provide them to people and companies that might have some legitimate need to contact the owner in the future. An interrupt token is a numeric code that can be attached to a message, allowing it to be delivered.
3. Uninvited callers or e-mail senders must make a binding offer to pay an interrupt fee to the recipient. The fee is, in effect, held in escrow. If the call is completed and if the recipient chooses to collect the fee, the money is transferred to the recipient's bank account; if not, the fee is returned to the sender, or is perhaps never collected in the first place.

The procedure is as follows: When a message arrives at the e-mail server, it is examined. If the sender is on the recipient's accept list (possibly including senders of solicited bulk e-mail such as newsletters), the message is passed through to his or her inbox. If the message header or body contains a "Token:" field with a valid ten-digit interrupt token, it is likewise passed through to the in-box. If the message contains no valid token, the sender receives a machine-generated reply indicating that, where, and at what price, a token may be bought to realize a binding offer. Limitations, drawbacks, and challenges involved with real cash systems include the following [171]:

❑ Sender authentication is necessary to enable the recipient to reliably distinguish e-mails sent by whitelisted persons from those sent by non-whitelisted ones. As the envelope's *MAIL FROM* as well as the header's sender information may be forged (e.g. by the cunning exploitation of user address books), an additional authentication mechanism is required. Although public-key cryptography provides the algorithmic means (digital signature), this approach suffers from two main problems: (1) a PKI is necessary which provides a key pair not only for organizations, but also for individuals, and (2) each e-mail has to be downloaded completely to get and to verify the digital signature.

❑ When ordering e-stamps, (strong) authentication is mandatory because the usage of an e-stamp is aligned with a binding offer and, thus, with the user's cash. Exploitation of third party e-stamps may have significant financial consequences for the third party.

❑ A giant incentive is generated to write an e-mail virus that would cause millions of people to e-mail a dummy, offshore e-mail address, where a scammer "takes the money and runs".

❑ Fully formed, the stamp system is complex and the technological and organizational ramifications are extensive: a (world-wide) digital signature infrastructure and a digital money infrastructure (featuring low transaction cost and high availability), including digital cash, is needed. Many people have proposed such infrastructures in the past, but none have been successful. Additionally, the solution needs new software at both sender and recipient.

❑ If communication has to be possibly paid for, whereas the service was hitherto free-of-charge, people may use such an Internet e-mail service reluctantly. The danger of underutilization of e-mail is believed not to be rooted only in the fact that people simply hate the idea of paying for their e-mail [3], but also in the fact that the system is a bit user-unfriendly: if somebody unknown to you sends you an e-mail without an e-stamp, you can put it in a different folder for later scanning, or bounce it back with the request that the stamp be added. This is a big request because it means the user has to either go through a complex process, and, in the long-run, to avoid these bounces, has to get new e-mailing software or a plug-in for his or her existing one.

❑ Eventually, everyone has to bear the costs and this goes against the open Internet flavor. In general, we would prefer the e-mail service not to punish legitimate users for the misbehavior of others [90].

Turner and Havey [181] proposed an e-mail infrastructure using Lightweight Currency Protocol (LCP) [182]. The core idea is that each SMTP e-mail server will use LCP pseudo-currency to make a payment every time that it sends e-mail and will receive a payment when it receives a piece of e-mail. Each organization can issue its own currency. SO A and RO B have to agree on a currency before an e-mail can be sent. This currency can be A dollars, B dollars or even C dollars, issued by a third organization C, whose dollars are widely accepted as e-mail currency. A can either generate its own dollars or obtain other dollars by either accepting e-mails or by buying them with real-world dollars. The e-mail infrastructure is geared to a balanced proportion between the number of outgoing and incoming e-mails. This approach addresses spam as follows: when spammers send out millions of e-mails from their domains, they will not receive a commensurate level of responses. Thus, a spammer cannot acquire the lightweight currency needed to make so many deliveries. The spammer is thus forced to earn lightweight currency by selling other useful resources in the resource market – the resources are not restricted to e-mail related capabilities –, or to purchase widely-accepted currency using real-world dollars. This approach has the following limitations and disadvantages:

❑ Spammers are not barred from misusing an ESP: they can set up e-mail accounts on ESPs whose currencies are well accepted and use these accounts for sending spam e-mails.
❑ When spammers use infected computers of unsuspicious users, e-mails may be sent on behalf of the user, thus exploiting the user's ESP.
❑ Organizations which send solicited bulk e-mail, e.g. newsletters or confirmation e-mails, will get into trouble with the balance, as the number of outgoing e-mails will exceed the number of incoming e-mails.

4.4.7 Limitation of outgoing e-mails

Some ESPs have implemented rate limits on outbound e-mail traffic. Over the last few years, hackers have begun to conspire with spammers, resulting in new e-mail viruses and worms that commandeer personal computers for use by spammers. Viruses such as "Mydoom" can compromise millions of computers in the span of several days. These computers can then start generating high volumes of spam. The situation has been widespread at ESPs and organizations that do not require e-mail authentication. However, ESPs that do employ account authentication have also seen an increase in the hijacking of accounts via other techniques, such as password phishing and Trojans with keystroke loggers. The goal of ESPs is to prevent a compromised account or an account set up by a spammer from sending spam to millions of recipients in a short time-frame [9].

In order to limit the number of e-mails that a user can send, it is also necessary to prevent the automated registration of accounts. This requires a test which verifies a human behind the request and not just a machine running a script (Turing test). CAPTCHA procedures are used for this. However, they represent a weak spot (see Subsect. 4.4.5).

Furthermore it is up to the ESPs, more generally to those organizations providing e-mail access, to implement a limitation of outgoing e-mails. It seems barely possible, if not completely impossible, to deploy and control world-wide implementation.

4.4.8 Address obscuring techniques

Address obscuring techniques aim at the protection of e-mail addresses against misuse by spammers. As conceptual issues vary between different approaches some of the most discussed ones are presented and inspected with regard to their limitations and drawbacks. The sketched approaches are Hall's virtual channels, extended e-mail addresses proposed by Gabber et al. [68], single-purpose addresses introduced by Ioannidis [83] and the similar concept "Tagged Message Delivery Agent".

Hall [77] proposed a virtual channel concept that is applied to selectively sharing e-mail addresses of virtual channels. Essentially, each user's e-mail account is made accessible via a user-controlled set of channels. Each channel has a distinctly structured address which contains within it the account name and a cryptographically secure, i.e. unguessable, pseudorandom security string, known as a channel identifer. Each legitimate correspondent is allowed to know one of these channel addresses. The account owner is provided with simple controls for opening a new channel, closing a channel, and switching a channel by notifying selected correspondents of a new channel that is replacing the current one. A channelized address is an e-mail address of the form *Username-ChannelID-@Host*, e.g. *alice-1xyz6u9uz4-@wonderland.com*. The channel ID contains a channel class indicator (*1*) and a security string (*xyz6u9uz4*). The security string is built by generating pseudorandomly 45 bits and using "base32" encoding to form 9 characters. If, for example, an e-mail user wants to share $2^7 = 128$ channels, an adversary has one chance in 2^{45-7} (about 275 billion) of guessing an open channel with one message. The channel class indicator consists of one digit. This digit allows differentiation between a *send-only* channel, which is useful when one wants to send a message to a public address without receiving e-mails on this address (i.e. permanently closed to everyone), a *private channel*, which is open to e-mails from determined senders (e-mails from other persons may be ignored on such a channel), and *public channel* (permanently open to everyone). Hall proposes an even richer class system. The maintenance of channels, i.e. generating, distributing, deleting etc.) is intended to be handled by a " Personal Channel Agent". The difficulties with this approach are at least twofold:

❑ It makes e-mail communication and the sharing of e-mail addresses complex. For example, it is much easier to tell a friend that your e-mail address is *joe@rwth-aachen.de* than to let him or her know *joe-2xyz6u9uz4-@rwth-aachen.de*.

❑ Keeping channel identifiers secret seems more than challenging in a world where PCs are infected with malware that can read the entries of local address books.

Gabber et al. [68] suggest a similar concept which is based on extended e-mail addresses and aims at hiding them, too. An extended e-mail address of Alice would be *Alice+xV78Yjkpl9@wonderland.com* with *xV78Yjkpl9* being the extension; the address *alice@wonderland.com* is denoted as the "core address". The extension will be calculated as $e(Alice@wonderland.com, Bob@dschungel.com, n_{Bob})$ with e being a function which is not specified but described in terms of requirements and n_{Bob} being a user-specific counter (with the initial value 0). Each time Bob gets a new extended address – maybe because the current address has been incautiously forwarded by Bob to someone else or it has been read by an address harvester – the counter is incremented by 1. In contrast to HALL'S concept, an e-mail address is bound to a specific user. When Alice gets an e-mail from a user claiming to be Bob and to an address with extension e', then Alice checks whether $e' = e(Alice@wonderland.com, Bob@dschungel.com, n_{Bob})$. If $e' \neq e$, the address is not genuine and Alice has different options on how to proceed. One option is to accept this e-mail if the sender belongs to a set of users who may be allowed to use this address, maybe because they are friends of Bob. Another option would be to reject the e-mail and ask the sender to apply for an extended e-mail address. To get such an address, the inquirer is involved in a payment-based procedure which might be CPU-based, for example. While a single user can perform this challenge-response procedure easily, a spammer would be forced to do millions of handshakes. This approach faces the problem of hiding e-mail addresses, too. Furthermore, extended e-mail addresses built this way are far removed from being guessable. To create an e-mail address (circumventing any resource-consuming challenge-response procedure) which can be used by Bob to send e-mails to Alice, an adversary or spammer respectively needs to know the function e, Alice's and Bob's core addresses and Alice's counter n_{Bob}). As a matter of cryptographic principle, the keeping of secrets should not rely on the algorithm used, so that e would be known or easily unguessable. Alice's and Bob's core addresses are public data. In most cases, the counter, although not being public and only being stored on Alice's side, would be easily guessable, as Alice is not believed to create a new extended e-mail address to be used by Bob very often. Thus, the counter should be an "unguessable" value.

The concept of Ioannidis' Single-Purpose Address (SPA) goes even slightly further. It, too, addresses cases in which it is irrelevant if an address is simple and readable (e.g. schryen@winfor.rwth-aachen.de), or completely obscure (e.g. VP72W24KM7IH7FT4O@winfor.rwth-aachen.de) and where it is important to be able to limit the use of an address to just the purposes for which it was given out. The concept is both to prevent a party from sending advertising material in the future (which most online vendors do, despite their assurances to the contrary), and to prevent abuse of the supplied address by third parties that, with or without the cooperation of the merchant, acquire our e-mail address. This is achieved by encoding rules as part of the e-mail addresses in such a way that the potential senders cannot alter these rules without, at the same time, invalidating the alias. These rules are applied when e-mail to the address is received. This way, the user does not have to store any per-address rules locally or keep track of multiple e-mail addresses ruling out the problem that the size of the alias list and the size of filtering rules will grow without bound. The SPA consists of two parts: an indication of the addressee, and an appropriately encoded description of the policy that will be applied when the message is received. The addressee can simply be identified by his or her username, with the policy part given as the extension, as in a "user+extension" convention. Since presumably the "naked" (with no extension) main address of the user would still be valid, it is recommended that users who want to use SPAs get a second address, and set up their systems so that mail to the naked second address is rejected. The creation of the second part of the SPA proceeds as follows (the details parenthesized refer to the author's prototypic implementation):

1. A rule, as part of a user overall e-mail policy, is encoded. For example, a rule could be *"accept this mail between January 30, 2003 and March 20, 2003, and only if the user is sending it from some machine in cs.miskatonic.edu; if accepted, forward the mail to seldon@trantor.gov"* [83, p. 3]. The encoding results in a bit-oriented representation of the rule (112 bit representation), its hash (MD5, 16 bit) or even MAC value is generated and added resulting in a structure called " SPA block (SPAB)" (128 bit representation). Only in the case of a MAC being generated, using a user-specific (symmetric) key, will the SPA block be user-specific.
2. The SPA block is encrypted under a symmetric key (256 bit AES-key in CBC mode) known only to the user creating the SPA.
3. The output of the encryption is a string of randomlooking bits and, as such, it is not suitable for use as an e-mail address. It must, therefore, be encoded (base-32 encoding) using a set of characters that are legal for e-mail addresses. The resulting string forms the second part of the SPA and is called " SPA block encoded and encrypted (SPABEE)".

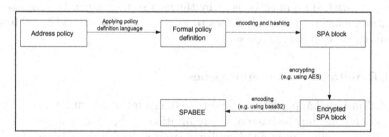

Fig. 4.4: SPABEE generation process

Figure 4.4 summarizes the process of generating a SPABEE. The address of an SPA-e-mail can either be checked by the receiving MTA or by the MDA. The processing has to be done in reverse order, as described. Thus, the processing node needs to have both the symmetric user-specific key for decoding and the e-mail address that the e-mail was sent to. This address is given in the RCPT command that an MTA has access to, but if an MUA is intended to process the SPA, any of the MTAs involved in e-mail delivery must put this information in the header, e.g. in a "Received:" header line. The "user"-part of the SPA address is used for identifying the recipient and the corresponding key for decrypting. The decoded and decrypted SPABEE gives a binary representation which is checked up on being a valid SPAB. This is the case if, and only if, the hash value or MAC corresponds to the binary representation of the rule encoded. If not, the address is not a valid SPA-address and the e-mail will be discarded. Otherwise, the SPAB is decoded, then the e-mail is checked against this policy and, subsequently, the MTA or MUA either delivers it, bounces it, or discards it accordingly. Compromising the system is possible if an attacker gets the symmetric key either from an unprotected key store or due to a successful cryptanalysis. A further attack is to create a SPABEE which represents, after decryption, a valid SPAB. However, this means the generation of a bit sequence that represents, after its decryption, a valid SPAB, i.e., a valid encoded rule and a compliant hash value or MAC. Thus, the deployed algorithms and key lengths have to be chosen appropriately, making these attacks negligible. Like the other obscuring approaches, the protection of users' local address books may become a currently unsolved problem. Furthermore, a legitimate first-contact communication via e-mail is complicated because the sender has no means of easily getting an SPA. Consequently, this approach suffers from the same limitations and drawbacks as Hall's approach.

Tagged Message Delivery Agent (TMDA) (*http://tmda.net*) also uses the concept of using the e-mail address to create SPAs. Aside from formatting and implementation details, the main architectural difference is that policy is not explicitly described in the e-mail address, but rather that the address is used to look up the policy in local tables. This means that, for each special address created, state must be kept by the user so that it can be processed in the future, causing such state tables to grow without bound when addresses without expiration dates are used.

4.4.9 Reputation-based approaches

Reputation-based approaches intend that the recipient (organization) accepts or rejects e-mails on the basis of the reputation of the sender and/or the SO. Kaushik et al. [90] suggest a policy-driven approach with three types of policy. The first type of policy, a Service Level Agreement Policy (SLAP), addresses how a receiving ESP decides to interact with a given sending ESP that has announced that it has e-mail. The second type of policy, a Message Scheduling Policy (MSP), is the output of a SLAP evaluation. The MSP specifies how each message at the sending ESP should be treated. The third type of policy, a Message Resource Allocation Policy (MRAP), encodes the specific requirements of an individual e-mail recipient. The MRAP is used to determine how (and whether) messages should be presented to the actual human recipient. The policy-driven approach allows a fine-graining adjustment of e-mail acceptance/rejection, but it requires effective authentication mechanisms and suffers from misclassification (because it works heuristically).

Email Service Provider Coalition [50] proposes a federated registry model for registering and certifying (legitimate) e-mail senders. The idea is to register bulk mailers, ask them to respond to reports of abuse, and publish the corresponding reputations. By including the registry information in the e-mail header, receiving e-mail nodes are supported in their acceptance/rejection decision. In principle, the LUMOS architecture implements whitelists and supports legitimate e-mail senders, but is far removed from being a solution to spam.

An accreditation and reputation system is presented by ICANN [79]. It is an organizational and technological framework elaborated by Spamhaus, and it introduces a new, sponsored Top Level Domain (sTLD), for example .mail. This sTLD is intended to serve registrants exclusively for e-mail sending processes. A registrant must already have a registered domain key, say *icann.org*, which is a prerequisite for the acquisition of the domain key.sTLD, in this case *icann.org.mail*. There are further requirements which a registrant may have to meet, among them the availability of validated "Whois" information, appropriate technological anti-spam protection, and the domain key having been registered for a period of at least six months. Apart from this, the registrant must inform the central (sponsoring) organization of the IPs and hostnames of the sending e-mail servers. The SO makes an A record entry for the new domain on the DNS, which enables recipient MTAs to use an LMAP or a PKI-based authentication. The sponsoring organization also receives any abuse message concerning key.sTLD and so, at the same time, provides a control mechanism. The framework developed by Spamhaus promises to be effective against a wide range of spamming procedures, yet a fundamental question which remains is this: How can an appropriate technological anti-spam protection be achieved? For example, the framework does not cover cases of spamming "zombie" PCs.

4.4.10 Summary

The technological anti-spam measures discussed and their advantages as well as disadvantages and limitations are summarized in Tables 4.6 and 4.7. Those technological measures which are route-specific are, furthermore, analyzed in terms of their route-specific effectiveness in Sect. 5.3.

Table 4.6: Overview of technological anti-spam measures and their advantages and disadvantages (1)

Technological ASM	Advantages	Disadvantages and limitations
IP blocking	• easy to implement • does not consume many resources	• susceptible to IP spoofing • heuristic procedure possibly leading to misclassification
• blacklisting	• easy blocking of large IP ranges which are known to „host" spammers	• IPs are used by spammers often only for a short time • DNS-based blacklists increase the Internet traffic and make the DNS a more critical resource
• whitelisting	• low or zero false-negative rate	• high false-positive rate
• greylisting	• spammers are forced to implement resource-consuming "resume" functionality	• increase of e-mail traffic due to resending • acceptance/rejection decision cannot be made until envelope data are available • relies on assumption that spammers' MTAs do not implement "resume" functionality
Filtering	• currently most effective anti-spam measure, it keeps the Internet e-mail service alive	• heuristic procedure possibly leading to missclassification • quite resource-consuming • may encourage spammers to send even more e-mails in an attempt to bypass the filters
TCP blocking	• easy to implement	• problematic for ISP customers running their own MTAs
Authentication		
• SMTP extensions	• improve accountability (protection of accounts against exploitation)	• limited effectiveness when username/password stored insecurely on PC
• cryptographic authentication	• provides means to organization- and user-specific authentication, enables accountability through end-to-end authentication	• only spam e-mails with spoofed data are covered • acceptance/rejection decision cannot be made prior ro receiving or downloading the message completely • signatures are invalid when intermediate systems modify the message • reduced accountability when signature is not user-based but organization-based • world-wide standardization or interoperability of data formats, algorithms and infrastructure is necessary • PKI is a complex infrastructure
• path authentication	• covers many cases of address forgery	• only spam e-mails with spoofed data are covered • approaches do not prevent users from fraudulently claiming to be another user within a domain • no protection against spammers who set up valid (DNS) records which are intended to be used for a short time only • DNS becomes a critical resource regarding availability and other insecurities
Verification	• forces spammers to apply appropriate recognition software or to perform social engineering attacks • aims at spam prevention at the earliest stage possible (client)	• e-mail communication becomes more complicated • increased Internet traffic • difficulties in sending legitimate bulk e-mail • CAPTCHA procedures are not secure against social engineering attacks and intelligent recognition software

Table 4.7: *Overview of technological anti-spam measures and their advantages and disadvantages (2)*

Technological ASM	Advantages	Disadvantages and limitations
Payment-based	• aims at spam prevention at the earliest stage possible (client)	• modifications of protocols and client as well as server software are necessary
• CPU-based	• no payment infrastructure required	• hijacked computers suffer from highly increased consumption of CPU time (damage is proportional to the number of infected PCs, thus huge damage occurs when botnets are in use) • if whitelists are included, then sender authentication mechanisms are required • time requirements vary much across the range of CPU speeds
• Memory-based	• see CPU-based	• see CPU-based (with exception of last issue)
• Monetary	• independent of CPU and memory speed	• whitelists are intended, but sender authentication mechanisms are often lacking
• e-cash	• user-specific billing possible	• sender authentication mechanisms are required, usually a PKI is required • digital money infrastructure is necessary • exploitation of 3rd party stamps has financial consequences • free e-mail communication gets lost
• pseudo currency (for providers)	• no digital money infrastructure is required • no user-specific PKI is required	• misuse of ESPs possible • spammers may easily exploit infected computers and send e-mails on behalf of the user and the ESP, respectively • senders of legitimate bulk e-mail may have trouble
Limitation of outgoing e-mails	• easy to implement	• suffers from automatically setting up new e-mail accounts • hijacked computers and accounts are (still) exploitable
Address obscuring	• selective e-mail communication is possible	• users' address books are highly susceptible to harvesting addresses • once aquired, addresses can be usually used for sending arbitrary e-mails • sharing addresses becomes more complicated • illegitimate "first contact" becomes complicated
Reputation-based	• scalable systems • sophisticated systems cover large ranges of spamming	• suffer from misclassification • hijacked computers and accounts are (still) exploitable

5

A model-driven analysis of the effectiveness of technological anti-spam measures

In Chap. 4 a broad range of technological anti-spam measures was presented, some of these already being widely applied while others are still on a conceptual or prototypic level. Up to now, we have been reasonably able to withstand spam e-mails and to use the Internet for regular communication, by deploying complementary anti-spam measures. However, statistics show a percentage of spam constituting more than 50% of all e-mails (see Sect. 2.2), and this rate is simply not acceptable. Even more serious, if we are to avert the danger of losing the Internet e-mail service in its capacity as a valuable, free, and worldwide medium of open communication, anti-spam activities should be performed more systematically than is currently the case with regard to the mainly heuristic anti-spam measures in place. A valuable step in this direction is the assessment of these measures in terms of theoretical and practical effectiveness. Having identified their potentials and limitations, we can better analyze which spamming options are successfully covered and which are still open to spammers. Furthermore, the analysis of the effectiveness of anti-spam measures might help to develop new holistic concepts or to combine existing measures into a bundle of anti-spam procedures which would enable the spam portion to be reduced enormously.

This chapter does not aim at protecting systems from security violations, such as those caused by viruses, Trojan horses, or worms, which are exploited by spammers. It addresses rather the theoretical effectiveness of (route-specific) technological anti-spam approaches and neither empirical nor statistical considerations enter the discussion. Schryen [157] and Schryen [155] provide a description of this chapter's content.

Section 5.1 provides a graph as a formal framework within which the effectiveness of (present and future) technological anti-spam measures can be theoretically analyzed. Section 5.2 uses the graph to derive and categorize all existing delivery routes a spam e-mail may take (spamming options) and which any holistic anti-spam measures would need to cover. Finally, in Sect. 5.3 the effectiveness of (route-specific) anti-spam measures is analyzed, relative to covering the spamming options. Measures which are applied non-route-specifically (or route-invariantly), like spam filters, are assessed generally in Chap. 4.

5.1 A model of the Internet e-mail infrastructure

The Internet e-mail infrastructure is modeled as a directed graph G, to be defined in the first subsection. In the second subsection, the appropriateness of G for modeling the e-mail infrastructure is discussed and it is shown that different types of e-mail delivery are represented by (directed) paths in G. Since any way of making e-mail delivery is obviously also a way of making spam delivery, the set of e-mailing options and the set of spamming options can be regarded as being identical (as can also the corresponding sets of types of delivery) and can hereinafter be understood to be referred to interchangeably.

5.1.1 The definition

Since the Internet e-mail network infrastructure which G is intended to represent is dynamic, it is not useful to model each concrete e-mail node. The different types of Internet e-mail nodes are, on the other hand, static, and it is these which can serve our actual purpose. An e-mail node is here defined as a software unit which is involved in the Internet e-mail delivery process and which works on the TCP/IP application layer. Consideration of software which works exclusively on lower levels, such as routers and bridges, is beyond the scope of this work, as are ways of sending an e-mail without there being any SMTP communication with an e-mail node of the recipient's organization. However, this does not seem to be an important restriction, given that almost all e-mail users receive their e-mails from a server that is SMTP-connected to the Internet (directly or indirectly). The construction of G follows these ideas:

❑ Graph nodes represent types of e-mail nodes as specified above. Directed edges correspond to e-mail connections between two (types of) e-mail nodes, with the edges' direction indicating the orientation "client to server". The edges are assigned a specific value, which is a set of labels representing those protocols which are feasible for the particular edge or connection respectively. Therefore, G can be denoted as a directed, labeled graph.

❑ The set of e-mail nodes to be modeled is mainly gathered from technological documents, such as RFCs, technological reports in the Internet literature, and practical experience (see Subsect. 5.1.2 for details). Hence, completeness can not be guaranteed. Where required, the set has to be extended.

❑ Each e-mail node can be associated with protocols for incoming connections and protocols for outgoing connections. They are gathered from the same documents and sources as are mentioned above (see Subsect. 5.1.2 for details), so again, completeness cannot be guaranteed. Communication between the e-mail nodes (EN) EN_A and EN_B is possible if, and only if, there is at least one protocol which can be used by EN_A for an outgoing connection and by EN_B for an incoming connection, i.e. if the intersection of the protocol sets is not empty. Hence, an edge (A, B) is modeled if, and only if, EN_A as client can communicate with EN_B as server, where EN_A corresponds to A and EN_B corresponds to B. The assigned labels correspond to the intersection of the protocol sets.

Now we can formally describe G: Let $G = \{V, E, c\}$ be a directed, labeled graph with vertex set V and edge set E, and let $c : E \rightarrow L$ be a total function on E where L denotes a set of (protocol) labels. First the structure of the graph is presented graphically (see Fig. 5.1) and formally. Its semantics are then explained in more detail.

The set of vertices can be depicted as the disjoint union of five vertex sets $V_1, \ldots, V_5$. Each of these sets is attached to one of the organizational units participating in e-mail delivery: *sender, Sending Organization (SO)* or *ESP, Internet, Receiving Organization (RO)*, and *recipient*. Where recipients do not use an ESP for the reception of e-mails but run their own e-mail receiving and processing environment, the organizational units *RO* and *recipient* merge. This, however, does not affect the structure of the graph, which retains its general validity.

Let the set of vertices be $V = V_1 \cup \ldots \cup V_5$ with

$V_1 = \{\text{MTA}_{\text{send}}, \text{MUA}_{\text{send}}, \text{OtherAgent}_{\text{send}}\}$,
    set of vertices attached to *sender*

$V_2 = \{\text{MTA}^{inc}_{\text{sendOrg}}, \text{MTA}_{\text{sendOrg}}, \text{WebServ}_{\text{sendOrg}}\}$,
    set of vertices attached to the *SO,*

$V_3 = \{\text{SMTP-Relay}, \text{GW}_{\text{SMTP,B}}, \text{GW}_{\text{A,SMTP}}, \text{GW}_{\text{A,B}}\}$,
    set of vertices attached to *Internet*

$V_4 = \{\text{MTA}^{inc}_{\text{recOrg}}, \text{MTA}_{\text{recOrg}}, \text{MDA}_{\text{recOrg}}, \text{MailServ}_{\text{recOrg}}, \text{WebServ}_{\text{recOrg}}\}$,
    set of vertices attached to the *RO,*

$V_5 = \{\text{MUA}_{\text{rec}}\}$,
    set of vertices attached to *recipient*

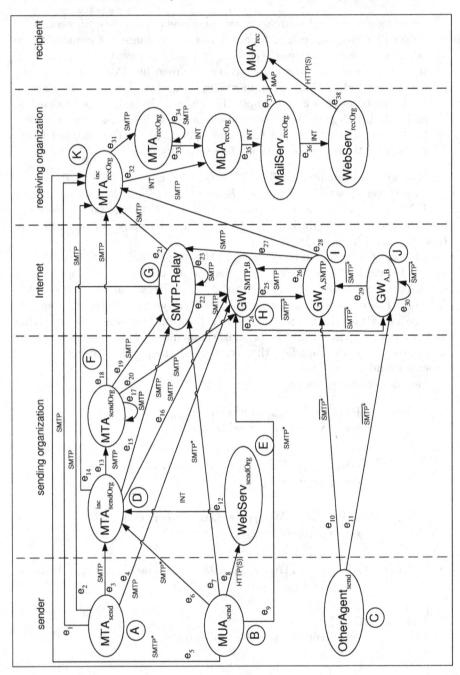

Fig. 5.1: Internet e-mail infrastructure as a directed graph

Let the set of (protocol) labels be $L =$ $\{\text{SMTP}, \text{SMTP}^*, \overline{\text{SMTP}^*}, \text{HTTP(S)}, \text{INT}, \text{MAP}\}$, and let $E = \{e_1, \ldots, e_{39}\}$ and c be defined as follows:

$$e_1 = (\text{MTA}_{\text{send}}, \text{MTA}^{(1)}_{\text{recOrg}}) \qquad\qquad c(e_1) = \text{SMTP}$$

$$e_2 = (\text{MTA}_{\text{send}}, \text{SMTP-Relay}) \qquad\qquad c(e_2) = \text{SMTP}$$

$$e_3 = (\text{MTA}_{\text{send}}, \text{MTA}^{inc}_{\text{sendOrg}}) \qquad\qquad c(e_3) = \text{SMTP}$$

$$e_4 = (\text{MTA}_{\text{send}}, \text{GW}_{\text{SMTP},B}) \qquad\qquad c(e_4) = \text{SMTP}$$

$$e_5 = (\text{MUA}_{\text{send}}, \text{MTA}^{inc}_{\text{recOrg}}) \qquad\qquad c(e_5) = \text{SMTP}^*$$

$$e_6 = (\text{MUA}_{\text{send}}, \text{MTA}^{inc}_{\text{sendOrg}}) \qquad\qquad c(e_6) = \text{SMTP}^*$$

$$e_7 = (\text{MUA}_{\text{send}}, \text{SMTP-Relay}) \qquad\qquad c(e_7) = \text{SMTP}^*$$

$$e_8 = (\text{MUA}_{\text{send}}, \text{WebServ}_{\text{sendOrg}}) \qquad\qquad c(e_8) = \text{HTTP(S)}$$

$$e_9 = (\text{MUA}_{\text{send}}, \text{GW}_{\text{SMTP},B}) \qquad\qquad c(e_9) = \text{SMTP}^*$$

$$e_{10} = (\text{OtherAgent}_{\text{send}}, \text{GW}_{A,\text{SMTP}}) \qquad\qquad c(e_{10}) = \overline{\text{SMTP}^*}$$

$$e_{11} = (\text{OtherAgent}_{\text{send}}, \text{GW}_{A,B}) \qquad\qquad c(e_{11}) = \overline{\text{SMTP}^*}$$

$$e_{12} = (\text{WebServ}_{\text{sendOrg}}, \text{MTA}^{inc}_{\text{sendOrg}}) \qquad\qquad c(e_{12}) = \text{INT}$$

$$e_{13} = (\text{MTA}^{inc}_{\text{sendOrg}}, \text{MTA}_{\text{sendOrg}}) \qquad\qquad c(e_{13}) = \text{SMTP}$$

$$e_{14} = (\text{MTA}^{inc}_{\text{sendOrg}}, \text{MTA}^{inc}_{\text{recOrg}}) \qquad\qquad c(e_{14}) = \text{SMTP}$$

$$e_{15} = (\text{MTA}^{inc}_{\text{sendOrg}}, \text{SMTP-Relay}) \qquad\qquad c(e_{15}) = \text{SMTP}$$

$$e_{16} = (\text{MTA}^{inc}_{\text{sendOrg}}, \text{GW}_{\text{SMTP},B}) \qquad\qquad c(e_{16}) = \text{SMTP}$$

$$e_{17} = (\text{MTA}_{\text{sendOrg}}, \text{MTA}_{\text{sendOrg}}) \qquad\qquad c(e_{17}) = \text{SMTP}$$

$$e_{18} = (\text{MTA}_{\text{sendOrg}}, \text{MTA}^{inc}_{\text{recOrg}}) \qquad\qquad c(e_{18}) = \text{SMTP}$$

$$e_{19} = (\text{MTA}_{\text{sendOrg}}, \text{SMTP-Relay}) \qquad\qquad c(e_{19}) = \text{SMTP}$$

$$e_{20} = (\text{MTA}_{\text{sendOrg}}, \text{GW}_{\text{SMTP},B}) \qquad\qquad c(e_{20}) = \text{SMTP}$$

$$e_{21} = (\text{SMTP-Relay}, \text{MTA}^{inc}_{\text{recOrg}}) \qquad\qquad c(e_{21}) = \text{SMTP}$$

$$e_{22} = (\text{SMTP-Relay}, \text{GW}_{\text{SMTP},B}) \qquad\qquad c(e_{22}) = \text{SMTP}$$

$$e_{23} = (\text{SMTP-Relay}, \text{SMTP-Relay}) \qquad\qquad c(e_{23}) = \text{SMTP}$$

$$e_{24} = (\text{GW}_{\text{SMTP},B}, \text{GW}_{A,B}) \qquad\qquad c(e_{24}) = \overline{\text{SMTP}^*}$$

$$e_{25} = (\text{GW}_{\text{SMTP},B}, \text{GW}_{A,\text{SMTP}}) \qquad\qquad c(e_{25}) = \overline{\text{SMTP}^*}$$

$$e_{26} = (\text{GW}_{A,\text{SMTP}}, \text{GW}_{\text{SMTP},B}) \qquad\qquad c(e_{26}) = \text{SMTP}$$

$$e_{27} = (\text{GW}_{A,\text{SMTP}}, \text{SMTP-Relay}) \qquad\qquad c(e_{27}) = \text{SMTP}$$

$$e_{28} = (\text{GW}_{A,\text{SMTP}}, \text{MTA}^{inc}_{\text{recOrg}}) \qquad\qquad c(e_{28}) = \text{SMTP}$$

$$e_{29} = (\text{GW}_{A,B}, \text{GW}_{A,\text{SMTP}}) \qquad\qquad c(e_{29}) = \overline{\text{SMTP}^*}$$

$$e_{30} = (\text{GW}_{A,B}, \text{GW}_{A,B}) \qquad\qquad c(e_{30}) = \overline{\text{SMTP}^*}$$

$$e_{31} = (\text{MTA}^{inc}_{\text{recOrg}}, \text{MTA}_{\text{recOrg}}) \qquad\qquad c(e_{31}) = \text{SMTP}$$

$$e_{32} = (\text{MTA}^{inc}_{\text{recOrg}}, \text{MDA}_{\text{recOrg}}) \qquad\qquad c(e_{32}) = \text{INT}$$

$$e_{33} = (\text{MTA}_{\text{recOrg}}, \text{MDA}_{\text{recOrg}}) \qquad\qquad c(e_{33}) = \text{INT}$$

$$e_{34} = (\text{MTA}_{\text{recOrg}}, \text{MTA}_{\text{recOrg}}) \qquad\qquad c(e_{34}) = \text{SMTP}$$

$$e_{35} = (\text{MDA}_{\text{recOrg}}, \text{MailServ}_{\text{recOrg}}) \qquad c(e_{35}) = \text{INT}$$
$$e_{36} = (\text{MailServ}_{\text{recOrg}}, \text{WebServ}_{\text{recOrg}}) \qquad c(e_{36}) = \text{INT}$$
$$e_{37} = (\text{MailServ}_{\text{recOrg}}, \text{MUA}_{\text{rec}}) \qquad c(e_{37}) = \text{MAP}$$
$$e_{38} = (\text{WebServ}_{\text{recOrg}}, \text{MUA}_{\text{rec}}) \qquad c(e_{38}) = \text{HTTP(S)}$$

Each vertex corresponds to a type of e-mail node. An edge $e = (v_1, v_2)$, with a label $c(e) \in L$ attached, exists if, and only if, the Internet e-mail infrastructure allows e-mail flow between the corresponding node types; $c(e)$ denotes the set of feasible protocols. The set SMTP contains SMTP (as a protocol) extended by all IANA-registered SMTP service extensions, also referred to as ESMTP, such as SMTP Service Extension for Authentication [114], Deliver By SMTP Service Extension [117], SMTP Service Extension for Returning Enhanced Error [58], and SMTP Service Extension for Secure SMTP over Transport Layer Security [78]; see *www.iana.org/assignments/mail-parameters* for a list of SMTP service extensions. The set SMTP* contains the set SMTP and all SMTP extensions specified for e-mail submission from an MUA to an e-mail node which has an SMTP incoming interface. This e-mail node can be an MTA, as specified in RFC 2821, or a Message Submission Agent (MSA), as specified in RFC 2476 [72]. With reference to the latter, $\text{MTA}_{\text{sendOrg}}^{inc}$ can alternatively be denoted as $\text{MSA}_{\text{sendOrg}}$ and $\text{MTA}_{\text{recOrg}}^{inc}$ as $\text{MSA}_{\text{recOrg}}$, respectively. Port 587 is reserved for e-mail message submission. Most e-mail clients and servers can be configured to use port 587 instead of port 25; however, this is not always possible or convenient, and in such cases, port 25 can serve for message submission as well. Using an MSA, numerous methods can be applied to ensure that only authorized users can submit messages. These methods include authenticated SMTP, IP address restrictions, secure IP, and prior POP authentication, where clients are required to authenticate their identity prior to an SMTP submission session ("SMTP after POP"). $\overline{\text{SMTP*}}$ is the union of three sets of protocols. The first contains all Internet application protocols excepting SMTP*, and the second, all proprietary application protocols used on the Internet: this inclusion takes tunneling procedures into account. The third set – since use of application protocols is not mandatory for the exchange of data in a network – consists of all Internet protocols on the transport and network layer of the Department of Defense (DoD) model, such as TCP and IP. MAP is the set of all e-mail access protocols used to transfer e-mails from the recipient's e-mail server to his or her MUA. IMAP version 4 [32] and POP version 3 [115] are among the most deployed protocols here. The set HTTP(S) contains the protocols HTTP [73] as well as its secure versions "HTTP over SSL" [64] and "HTTP over TLS" [141]. Finally, the set INT denotes protocols for and procedures in internal e-mail delivery, that is, it is concerned with processes inside the RO, such as getting e-mails from an internal MTA and storing them into the users' e-mail boxes.

5.1.2 The appropriateness

The appropriateness of graph G in the context of modeling the Internet e-mail infrastructure is given by the fact that different types of e-mail delivery can be described by a set of specific (directed) paths in G. This issue is addressed in three steps:

1. The e-mail nodes modeled are motivated.
2. For the e-mail nodes, possible protocols for incoming connections and protocols for outgoing connections are identified. The edges in G were defined on the basis of these protocols (see Subsect. 5.1.1).
3. A set of (directed) paths in G is identified. This models different types of e-mail delivery.

Technical e-mail nodes can be assigned to the organizational unit that acts as the sender of an e-mail, to the sender's organization (sender's ESP), to the recipient, to the recipient's organization (recipient's ESP), and to the Internet subsuming all other organizational units. On the application layer, the sender can use an MTA, an MUA as defined in RFC 2821 [93], or any other agent. These nodes correspond to the nodes in G denoted as $\mathrm{MTA_{send}}$, $\mathrm{MUA_{send}}$, and $\mathrm{OtherAgent_{send}}$, respectively. If an SO participates in e-mail delivery, it accepts incoming e-mails with an SMTP-based MTA, denoted as $\mathrm{MTA}^{inc}_{sendOrg}$ in G. Alternatively, e-mails may be sent to an SO by way of the web environment, meaning that all e-mails are passed to an internal MTA by a receiving web e-mail server, denoted as $\mathrm{WebServ_{sendOrg}}$. An SO may make internal SMTP-based delivery using two or more consecutive MTAs, denoted as $\mathrm{MTA_{sendOrg}}$. No other e-mail nodes are generally used by ESPs, exceptions being proprietary e-mail nodes. However, since any internal non-standard processing of an (outgoing) ESP is required by interorganizational e-mail delivery agreements to be completed with an MTA, such e-mail nodes are of no relevance in the overall e-mail delivery chain and can be ignored. ROs take, as a rule, only SMTP-based e-mail deliveries and, although exceptions do exist, they are so uncommon as to be likewise negligible. As in the case of the SO, the MTA responsible for incoming SMTP connections, denoted as $\mathrm{MTA}^{inc}_{recOrg}$, may be followed by two or more consecutive MTAs, denoted as $\mathrm{MTA_{recOrg}}$, before the MDA, denoted as $\mathrm{MDA_{recOrg}}$, deposits the message in a "message store" (mail spool), which a mail server, denoted as $\mathrm{MailServ_{recOrg}}$, accesses in order to deliver it to the recipient's MUA either directly, denoted as $\mathrm{MUA_{rec}}$, or via a web-based e-mail server, denoted as $\mathrm{WebServ_{recOrg}}$. E-mails terminating in a systems other than SMTP require the existence of an e-mail gateway, but, like the analogous situation at the SO's site, this issue is beyond the scope of this model. When the Local Mail Transfer Protocol (LMTP) [112] is used to relay messages to the MDA, the MDA is termed Local Delivery Agent (LDA). Before an e-mail passes the first MTA of the RO it may be relayed by an intermediate SMTP relay which accepts an e-mail sent by a node residing on sender' site or on the SO's site and transfers it to another e-mail node (when this node pretends to be the original client it is referred to as SMTP proxy). This includes the scenario where an e-mail is forwarded to another e-mail node because of a mailbox-specific forwarding rule. The SMTP relay represents an intermediate Internet e-mail node using SMTP both at the incoming and the outgoing interface. When other interfaces are used, three further intermediate types are possible. These are used, for example, for SMTP tunneling and are known as gateways: $GW_{SMTP,B}$ nodes accept SMTP e-mails and transfer e-mails with a protocol other than SMTP; $GW_{A,SMTP}$ performs the inverse process at incoming and outgoing interfaces, nodes of type $GW_{A,B}$ use SMTP neither for incoming nor for outgoing messages, where A and B can be the same protocol (when $A = B$, we usually talk about a proxy but, for simplicity, we subsume this under gateway).

Because the term "proxy" is used in different contexts, some remarks on it seem appropriate here. The notion "proxy" generally denotes a service that allows clients to make indirect network connections to other network services. Proxies pretend to act as the original client and do not disclose the actual client; only the access on proxies' log files enables the identification of the actual client. The notion "proxy" does not give any information about the dissimilarity of the protocols used for incoming and outgoing connection. Some MTAs or relays are configured as proxies meaning that they do not insert a *Received* entry in the e-mail header. When an MTA or other client on a third party computer is remotely controlled by a spammer, this client acts as a proxy, too. Then it is called a "zombie PC". Even gateways can implement a proxy function.

Figure 5.2 provides an overview of existing e-mail nodes, using a class diagram. It should be noted that the e-mail nodes are logical nodes representing pieces of software, several of which might be executed in one physical node in a particular instance of e-mail delivery (for example MTA^{inc}_{recOrg} and MDA_{recOrg}).

Having motivated the nodes and vertices respectively, we now have a look at the protocols and connections by applying the design criteria for edges in G (see above): an edge $e = (v_1, v_2)$ exists if, and only if, the Internet e-mail infrastructure allows e-mail flow between the corresponding node types. To this end, each node v of G is explored with reference to the edges incident upon v:

MTA_{send} With a local MTA on the user's side only SMTP connections are possible. SMTP connections can be established to an ESP's incoming MTA (e_3), to Internet nodes accepting SMTP connections, viz. an SMTP relay (e_2) and a gateway (e_4), or to an MTA of the RO or recipient(e_1). Other connections are not possible.

MUA_{send} An e-mail sender who operates an MUA can basically connect either to all nodes with an SMTP interface for incoming connections, or to a web server of the SO. HTTP(S)-based connections to other nodes are

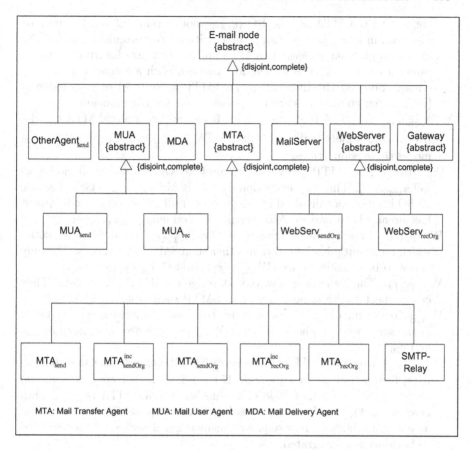

Fig. 5.2: Internet e-mail nodes

covered by the node OtherAgent$_\text{send}$. In the former case, the MUA can connect to the same nodes as the MTA$_\text{send}$ (e_5, e_6, e_7, e_9). However, given the involvement of an MUA the set of protocols has to be extended to SMTP*. If a connection is made to a web server, then either HTTP or the secure version HTTPS may be used. Other connections are not possible and are not modeled.

OtherAgent$_\text{send}$ Other agents are defined as agents that use connections other than SMTP-based ones ($\overline{\text{SMTP*}}$). ESPs and organizations today generally accept only SMTP-based e-mail connections, such that they can only connect to gateways in the Internet (e_{10}, e_{11}) as modeled.

WebServ$_\text{sendOrg}$ A web server of an ESP sends its e-mails to an internal MTA (e_{12}). Connections to other nodes generally do not exist.

MTA$^{inc}_\text{sendOrg}$ The MTA that is responsible for incoming messages most commonly SMTP-connects to another internal MTA (e_{13}). It may also SMTP-connect to (an MTA of) the RO (e_{18}) – notice that SO and RO may be identical, in which case we can assume, without compromising the validity of the graph, that at least two MTAs of the ESP are involved. A third, rarely used possibility is for the MTA to establish a connection to other e-mail nodes on the Internet, to an SMTP relay (e_{15}) or to a gateway (e_{16}). Other connections are not possible and are not modeled.

$\text{MTA}_{\text{sendOrg}}$ An MTA receiving e-mails from another internal MTA can deliver to the same e-mail nodes that $\text{MTA}_{\text{sendOrg}}^{inc}$ can. Edges $e_{17}, \ldots, e_{20}$ model these connections.

SMTP-Relay An SMTP relay can connect to the same e-mail nodes as $\text{MTA}_{\text{sendOrg}}$. The only exception to this is $\text{MTA}_{\text{sendOrg}}$ itself, because an SO is either not involved in the process at all or its e-mail environment has already been passed. Accordingly, we find edges $e_{21}, \ldots, e_{23}$.

$\text{GW}_{\text{SMTP,B}}$ E-mail nodes, denoted as $\text{GW}_{\text{SMTP,B}}$, are defined as nodes which make outgoing connections other than SMTP-based ones. The only nodes to be considered are $\text{GW}_{\text{A,B}}$ (e_{24}) and $\text{GW}_{\text{A,SMTP}}$ (e_{25}).

$\text{GW}_{\text{A,SMTP}}$ This denotes gateways with outgoing SMTP connections. They can connect to the same nodes as an SMTP relay ($e_{26}, \ldots, e_{28}$).

$\text{GW}_{\text{A,B}}$ Regarding outgoing connections, this kind of gateway can be treated in the same way as a node of type $\text{GW}_{\text{SMTP,B}}$. Hence, we find edges e_{29} and e_{30}.

$\text{MTA}_{\text{recOrg}}^{inc}$ A recipient MTA that accepts SMTP connections can either deliver, forward, or reject an e-mail. If the e-mail is delivered, it is passed either to the local MDA (e_{30}) or to another internal MTA (e_{31}); in both cases we find internal e-mail processing. Because forwarding or rejection of an e-mail initializes a new sequence, as mentioned earlier, edges dedicated to both are not integrated.

$\text{MTA}_{\text{recOrg}}$ An internal MTA, receiving e-mails from $\text{MTA}_{\text{recOrg}}^{inc}$, either passes an e-mail to another internal MTA (e_{34}) using SMTP or to the local MDA (e_{33}). This process is denoted as internal delivery.

$\text{MDA}_{\text{recOrg}}$ The MDA is responsible for storing an e-mail in the recipient's local e-mail box residing on the mail server $\text{MailServ}_{\text{recOrg}}$ (e_{37}). This is the second step of the internal e-mail delivery.

$\text{MailServ}_{\text{recOrg}}$ Most mail servers provide an interface for recipients' MUAs which access the user's e-mails with a mail access protocol such as IMAP or POP. These protocols are pull protocols, the MUA initiating the dialogue with the mail server. However, when a connection of this type is established, e-mails are directed to the MUA. Alternatively, a mail server can provide an internal interface for a web server (e_{36}).

$\text{WebServ}_{\text{recOrg}}$ The web server is an intermediate node between the mail server and the MUA and allows HTTP-based access on e-mails (e_{38}). This kind of platform-independent e-mail access is widely available and convenient: web browsers are usually installed on users' devices.

MUA$_{rec}$ The destination of an e-mail is the recipient's MUA. MUA$_{rec}$ does not have any outgoing edges, because any outgoing connection relates to the forwarding of an e-mail and is thus treated as a new sequence.

According to the construction of G, e-mail delivery routes are represented by paths in G. As it is essential for today's e-mail delivery process that the way in which an e-mail node received an e-mail does not restrict the way it passes the e-mail forward, each path p corresponds to a feasible e-mail delivery route. It should be noted that completeness is intended but not guaranteed as is not the completeness of e-mail nodes nor their communication connections. We are only interested in complete e-mail deliveries, which means that the e-mail has reached the recipient's e-mail box on his or her e-mail server or the MTA of the RO, which applies a forwarding rule or rejects the message. That is, forwarding an e-mail and sending a bounce e-mail starts a new sequence. Furthermore, only those e-mail deliveries are regarded which are either initiated by a sender's client or, for example, in case of bouncing or forwarding e-mails, by an ESP's MTA.

Each option for sending one e-mail allows, in principle, the sending of many, e.g. millions of e-mails, as spammers do. Thus, the set of options for sending one e-mail has to be taken into account when identifying options for sending spam e-mails. Obviously, the set of all paths $p = (v_{start}, \ldots, \text{MailServ}_{recOrg})$ with $v_{start} \in V_{start} := V_1 \cup V_2$ gives us all options for sending (spam) e-mails, thus providing a formal approach to spamming options. In the following section, these paths are formally derived and categorized.

5.2 Deriving and categorizing the spam delivery routes

(Spam) e-mail delivery routes are derived in Subsect. 5.2.1 by means of automata theory. In a second step (in Subsect. 5.2.2), the routes are clustered in a way that each cluster contains routes that correspond to e-mail options which can be treated similar in the context of spam.

5.2.1 Deriving the spam delivery routes

The goal of this subsection is to derive the set P of all paths $p = (v_{start}, \ldots, \text{MailServ}_{recOrg})$ with $v_{start} \in V_1 \cup V_2$. P is arrived at by applying some basic ideas from automata theory: the graph G is transformed into a Deterministic Finite Automaton (DFA) $A = (S, \Sigma, \delta, Start, F)$ where S is a finite set of states, Σ is an alphabet, "$Start$" is the initial state, $F \subseteq S$ is the set of final states, and δ is a function from $S \times \Sigma$ to S. This automaton recognizes a language that (bijectively) corresponds to P, such that $w = (w_1 \ldots w_n) \in L(A) \Leftrightarrow (w_1, \ldots, w_n) \in P$, where $L(A)$ is the language recognized by A. The construction is self-evident and can be described informally as follows: The set of states S corresponds to the nodes of G extended by an artificial state "Start" which serves as the initial state. Σ corresponds to the nodes of G, as well. An edge (v_1, v_2) means that the transition function δ includes $\delta(s_1, s_2) = s_2$, that is, state s_2 is reached if, and only if, the symbol s_2 is "read" by A. In order to account for the starting node, δ also needs to include $\delta(\text{Start}, s_2) = s_2$ with s_2 being a state corresponding to any node of the set of starting nodes V_{start}. F only contains the state corresponding to the node $\text{MTA}_{\text{recOrg}}^{inc}$.

Given the equivalence between DFAs and regular expressions, the language recognized by the DFA A – and thus P – can be described with a regular expression. For simplicity, the states are labeled with capital letters which are assigned to the corresponding nodes (see Fig. 5.1). Elements of Σ are set in lowercase letters. Given two regular expressions r_1 and r_2, $\sim$ denotes the relationship between r_1 and r_2 with $r_1 \sim r_2 :\Leftrightarrow L(r_1) = L(r_2)$; let Λ be the regular expression with $L(\Lambda) = \varepsilon$. Using the edges of G, we get $L(A) = L(\text{Start})$ with

$$\text{Start} \sim aA \vee bB \vee cC \vee dD \vee fF \tag{5.1}$$

$$A \sim kK \vee gG \vee dD \vee hH \tag{5.2}$$

$$B \sim dD \vee gG \vee eE \vee hH \tag{5.3}$$

$$C \sim iI \vee jJ \tag{5.4}$$

$$D \sim kK \vee fF \vee gG \vee hH \tag{5.5}$$

$$E \sim dD \tag{5.6}$$

$$F \sim kK \vee gG \vee fF \vee hH \tag{5.7}$$

$$G \sim kK \vee gG \vee hH \tag{5.8}$$

$$H \sim jJ \vee iI \tag{5.9}$$

$$I \sim hH \vee gG \vee kK \tag{5.10}$$

$$J \sim iI \vee jJ \tag{5.11}$$

$$K \sim \Lambda \tag{5.12}$$

Let α, β, γ be regular expressions, then recursive relationships can be dissolved, using the rule

$$\frac{\alpha \sim \beta\alpha \vee \gamma, \ \varepsilon \notin L(\beta)}{\alpha \sim \beta^*\gamma} \tag{5.13}$$

Using (5.6), (5.12), and (5.13) we get

$$\text{Start} \sim aA \vee bB \vee cC \vee dD \vee fF \tag{5.14}$$

$$A \sim k \vee gG \vee dD \vee hH \tag{5.15}$$

$$B \sim dD \vee gG \vee edD \vee hH \tag{5.16}$$

$$C \sim iI \vee jJ \tag{5.17}$$

$$D \sim k \vee fF \vee gG \vee hH \tag{5.18}$$

$$F \sim k \vee gG \vee fF \vee hH \sim f^*(k \vee gG \vee hH) \tag{5.19}$$
$$G \sim k \vee gG \vee hH \sim g^*(k \vee hH) \tag{5.20}$$
$$H \sim jJ \vee iI \tag{5.21}$$
$$I \sim hH \vee gG \vee k \tag{5.22}$$
$$J \sim j^*iI \tag{5.23}$$

Applying (5.23) on (5.17) and (5.21) yields

$$C \sim iI \vee jj^*iI \tag{5.24}$$
$$H \sim jj^*iI \vee iI \tag{5.25}$$

(5.1) can now be simplified to

$$\text{Start} \overset{(5.24)}{\sim} aA \vee bB \vee c(iI \vee jj^*iI) \vee dD \vee fF$$
$$\sim aA \vee bB \vee ciI \vee cjj^*iI \vee dD \vee fF$$
$$\overset{(5.19)}{\sim} aA \vee bB \vee ciI \vee cjj^*iI \vee dD \vee ff^*(k \vee gG \vee hH)$$
$$\overset{(5.20)}{\sim} aA \vee bB \vee ciI \vee cjj^*iI \vee dD \vee ff^*(k \vee gg^*(k \vee hH) \vee hH) \tag{5.26}$$

Now, still the symbols A, B, D, H, and I have to be dissolved where only H and I feature a recursive structure. First, I is simplified to

$$I \overset{(5.20)}{\sim} hH \vee gg^*(k \vee hH) \vee k \sim hH \vee gg^*k \vee gg^*hH \vee k$$
$$\sim (h \vee gg^*h)H \vee gg^*k \vee k \tag{5.27}$$

With (5.27) we get

$$H \overset{(5.27)}{\sim} jj^*i((h \vee gg^*h)H \vee gg^*k \vee k) \vee$$
$$i((h \vee gg^*h)H \vee gg^*k \vee k)$$
$$\sim jj^*i(h \vee gg^*h)H \vee jj^*igg^*k \vee jj^*ik \vee$$
$$i(h \vee gg^*h)H \vee igg^*k \vee ik$$
$$\sim (jj^*i(h \vee gg^*h) \vee i(h \vee gg^*h))H \vee$$
$$jj^*igg^*k \vee jj^*ik \vee igg^*k \vee ik$$
$$\overset{(5.13)}{\sim} (jj^*i(h \vee gg^*h) \vee i(h \vee gg^*h))^*$$
$$(jj^*igg^*k \vee jj^*ik \vee igg^*k \vee ik) \tag{5.28}$$

As no recursions are present, (5.26) can now be dissolved by simple substitutions. For straightforwardness, H is not substituted although this is possible with (5.28).

Start $\overset{(5.15,5.16)}{\sim}$ $a(k \vee gG \vee dD \vee hH) \vee (dD \vee gG \vee edD \vee hH) \vee ciI \vee$

(5.18) $cjj^*iI \vee d(k \vee fF \vee gG \vee hH) \vee ff^*(k \vee gg^*(k \vee hH) \vee hH)$

$\overset{(5.18,5.20)}{\sim}$ $a(k \vee gg^*(k \vee hH) \vee d(k \vee fF \vee gG \vee hH) \vee hH) \vee$
  $b((d \vee ed)D \vee gg^*(k \vee hH) \vee hH) \vee (ci \vee cjj^*i)((h \vee gg^*h)H$
  $\vee gg^*k \vee k) \vee$
  $d(k \vee fF \vee gg^*(k \vee hH) \vee hH) \vee ff^*(k \vee gg^*(k \vee hH) \vee hH)$

$\overset{(5.19,5.20)}{\sim}$ $a(k \vee gg^*(k \vee hH) \vee d(k \vee ff^*(k \vee gG \vee hH) \vee gg^*(k \vee hH) \vee$
  $\vee hH) \vee hH) \vee$
  $b((d \vee ed)(k \vee fF \vee gG \vee hH) \vee gg^*(k \vee hH) \vee hH) \vee$
  $(ci \vee cjj^*i)((h \vee gg^*h)H \vee gg^*k \vee k) \vee$
  $d(k \vee ff^*(k \vee gG \vee hH) \vee gg^*(k \vee hH) \vee hH) \vee$
  $ff^*(k \vee gg^*(k \vee hH) \vee hH)$

$\sim$ $a(k \vee gg^*k \vee gg^*hH \vee d(k \vee ff^*(k \vee gg^*(k \vee hH) \vee hH) \vee gg^*k \vee$
  $gg^*hH \vee hH) \vee hH) \vee$
  $b((d \vee ed)(k \vee ff^*(k \vee gG \vee hH) \vee gg^*(k \vee hH) \vee hH) \vee$
  $gg^*(k \vee hH) \vee hH) \vee (ci \vee cjj^*i)((hH \vee gg^*H \vee gg^*k \vee k) \vee$
  $d(k \vee ff^*(k \vee gg^*(k \vee hH) \vee hH) \vee gg^*k \vee gg^*hH \vee hH) \vee$
  $ff^*(k \vee gg^*k \vee gg^*hH \vee hH)$

$\sim$ $a(k \vee gg^*k \vee gg^*hH \vee d(k \vee ff^*(k \vee gg^*k \vee gg^*hH \vee hH) \vee gg^*k \vee$
  $gg^*hH \vee hH) \vee hH) \vee$
  $b((d \vee ed)(k \vee ff^*(k \vee gg^*(k \vee hH) \vee hH) \vee gg^*k \vee gg^*hH \vee hH) \vee$
  $gg^*k \vee gg^*hH \vee hH) \vee cihH \vee cigg^*H \vee$
  $cigg^*k \vee cik \vee cjj^*ihH \vee cjj^*igg^*H \vee cjj^*igg^*k \vee cjj^*ik \vee$
  $d(k \vee ff^*(k \vee gg^*k \vee gg^*hH \vee hH) \vee gg^*k \vee gg^*hH \vee hH) \vee$
  $ff^*k \vee ff^*gg^*k \vee ff^*gg^*hH \vee ff^*hH$

$\sim$ $ak \vee agg^*k \vee agg^*hH \vee ad(k \vee ff^*k \vee ff^*gg^*k \vee ff^*gg^*hH \vee$
  $ff^*hH \vee gg^*k \vee gg^*hH \vee hH) \vee ahH \vee$
  $(bd \vee bed)(k \vee ff^*k \vee ff^*gg^*k \vee ff^*gg^*hH \vee ff^*hH \vee gg^*k \vee$
  $gg^*hH \vee hH) \vee bgg^*k \vee bgg^*hH \vee bhH \vee cihH \vee cigg^*H \vee$
  $cigg^*k \vee cik \vee cjj^*ihH \vee cjj^*igg^*H \vee cjj^*igg^*k \vee cjj^*ik \vee$
  $d(k \vee ff^*k \vee ff^*gg^*k \vee ff^*gg^*hH \vee ff^*hH \vee gg^*k \vee gg^*hH \vee hH$
  $ff^*k \vee ff^*gg^*k \vee ff^*gg^*hH \vee ff^*hH$ (5

As (5.29) shows, (spam) e-mail delivery routes are numerous and call for a categorization of a manageable format.

5.2.2 Categorizing the spam delivery routes

A useful way of proceeding is to place in one category delivery routes which are defined by the same types of organizational unit; the types are "sender", "Sending Organization (SO)" or "ESP", "Internet", "Receiving Organization (RO)", and "recipient" (see Fig. 5.1). Because complete e-mail delivery invariably presupposes a RO and the recipient has no influence on the process, these units can be ignored. Categories arise, then, from the respective participation or non-participation of a local sender, an ESP (as the SO) and the Internet (application level infrastructure), giving eight possible combinations. The categories are shown in Table 5.1.

Table 5.1: Spamming categories

No.	Scenario	Sender	Sending organization	Internet
-	-			
-	-			X
I	Provider itself spams or its MTAs were corrupted; direct connection to MTA_{recOrg}		X	
II	Provider itself spams or its MTAs were corrupted; use of intermediate Internet nodes like relays		X	X
III	Spammer uses local client; direct connection to MTA_{recOrg} (via dial-in or LAN connection)	X		
IV	Spammer uses local client; use of intermediate Internet nodes like relays (via dial-in or LAN connection)	X		X
V	Spammer uses local client; use of e-mail provider (via dial-in or LAN connection)	X	X	
VI	Spammer uses local client; use of e-mail provider (via dial-in or LAN connection) which uses intermediate Internet nodes like relays	X	X	X

In the e-mail communication network, as modeled above, an Internet node can never be the first participant in a delivery process: an e-mail goes out from a node in either a sender's or a SO's environment, including instances of computers infected or controlled remotely. The types in the first two rows of Table 5.1 are, therefore, merely theoretical possibilities. Scenarios I and II occur when e-mail providers or their MTAs are corrupt. Given that ESPs and the corresponding MTAs are limited in number in comparison with users, it should be possible to effectively deal with these ways to send spam e-mails. In all other scenarios spam e-mails issue from a local client, the obvious starting point, and this is probably what happens most of the time. Scenario III is one in which the spammer does not use an ESP, although of course, he or she uses an ISP operating on layers no higher than the transport layer, that is the ISP generally does simple forwarding of TCP packets or IP packets. The spammer connects to an MTA of the RO directly and so is restricted to the e-mail ports implemented there. This, however, will usually be port 25 or 587, making it easy for ISPs to stop most spam e-mails sent in this way by simply blocking TCP packets to these ports. Scenario III also contains a specific case of zombie PCs (see below). Spamming in the manner of scenario IV is much harder to tackle because, this time, the spammer may use all Internet nodes, including gateways. In scenario V, to circulate spam, the spammer simply takes advantage of the e-mail service offered by an ESP. Even if a limit is imposed upon the number of e-mails permitted per day and account, there remains the task of preventing the spammer from setting up new accounts automatically. Scenario V also includes the case of zombie PCs – those PCs which are exploited and controlled remotely by spammers, often via Trojan horses –, which connect to a user's SO and ESP respectively. Zombie PCs are also called bots when they belong to a botnet which is controlled by botnet masters. Aided by a botnet and thousands of bots, an attacker is able to send massive amounts of spam e-mail [175]. More than half of all spam e-mails are assumed to be sent via botnets [80, 145, 144], either via a user's SO or by the usage of a direct connection to the recipient's MTA (scenario III). Scenario VI seems quite unlikely. The spammer uses an ESP which forwards e-mails, sending them to intermediate nodes on the Internet. This might occur if an ESP supported spamming activities of customers.

If we now assign to these six categories the spam delivery routes in (5.29), we obtain

$$Start \quad \sim$$

$$I: \quad d(k \vee ff^*k) \vee ff^*k \vee$$

$$II: \quad d(ff^*gg^*k \vee ff^*gg^*hH \vee ff^*hH \vee gg^*k \vee gg^*hH \vee hH) \vee$$
$$ff^*(gg^*k \vee gg^*hH \vee hH) \vee$$

$$III: \quad ak \vee$$

$$IV: \quad agg^*k \vee agg^*hH \vee hH \vee ahH \vee bgg^*k \vee bgg^*hH \vee bhH \vee cihH \vee cigg^*$$
$$cigg^*k \vee cik \vee cjj^*ihH \vee cjj^*igg^*H \vee cjj^*igg^*k \vee cjj^*ik \vee$$

$$V: \quad ad(k \vee ff^*k) \vee (bd \vee bed)(k \vee ff^*k) \vee$$

$$VI: \quad ad(ff^*gg^*k \vee ff^*gg^*hH \vee ff^*hH \vee gg^*k \vee gg^*hH \vee hH) \vee$$

$$(bd \vee bed)(ff^*gg^*k \vee ff^*gg^*hH \vee ff^*hH \vee gg^*k \vee gg^*hH \vee hH) \qquad (5.30)$$

(5.30) can be simplified to

Start $\sim$

$\quad I : \ d(k \vee ff^*k) \vee ff^*k \vee$

$\quad II : \ (d \vee \Lambda)(ff^*gg^*k \vee ff^*gg^*hH \vee ff^*hH) \vee d(gg^*k \vee gg^*hH \vee hH) \vee$

$\quad III : ak \vee$

$\quad IV : \ (a \vee b)(gg^*k \vee gg^*hH \vee hH) \vee cj^*i(hH \vee gg^*H \vee gg^*k \vee k) \vee$

$\quad V : \ (ad \vee bd \vee bed)(k \vee ff^*k) \vee$

$\quad VI : \ (ad \vee bd \vee bed)(ff^*gg^*k \vee ff^*gg^*hH \vee ff^*hH \vee gg^*k \vee gg^*hH \vee hH)$

$$(5.31)$$

with (see (5.28))

$$H \sim (jj^*i(h \vee gg^*h) \vee i(h \vee gg^*h))^*$$
$$(jj^*igg^*k \vee jj^*ik \vee igg^*k \vee ik)$$

The regular expression in (5.31) is constructed and represented in a form which permits us to match up each individual line with a corresponding set of delivery routes, defined by the same types of e-mail node. Having formally identified spam delivery routes, we can assess the effectiveness of the most frequently discussed and applied anti-spam measures in Sect. 5.3.

5.2.3 Some example delivery routes and their formal representations

To illustrate how (common) options of sending (spam) e-mails are covered by the formal representation in (5.31), some of the former ones are exemplified:

❏ A user being in the office or at home uses an MUA, e.g. Outlook (Express), and sends an e-mail to the MTA of his or her ESP. The message is then relayed by some consecutive MTAs of this ESP before the message is delivered to an MTA of the recipient's ESP. This route is covered by the regular expression bdf^*k (scenario V). It also covers the case in which a MUA is remotely controlled by a botnet master and messages follow the path which is described above.

❏ An e-mail user can also use a web interface for sending e-mails. This is particularly useful when he or she is abroad and PCs are available in an Internet cafe or in a conference's e-mail room. Then, a message is sent consecutively to the ESP's web server, to at least two MTAs, and, finally, to an MTA of the recipient's ESP. This route corresponds to $bedf^*k$ (scenario V).

❏ Senders of bulk e-mails often use a mass e-mail program residing on their host. When spammers use such a local MTA they often camouflage the spam source by sending the messages to an open proxy which subsequently sends messages to an MTA of the RO (agk, scenario IV).

❏ Trying to obfuscate the spam e-mail's source, mass e-mail tools can be used that are designed to connect with (a chain of) SOCKS 4 or SOCKS 5 proxies. The chain's last proxy SMTP-connects with an MTA of the RO. This delivery route is covered by the expression cj^*ik (scenario IV).

❏ A script, e.g. a Common Gateway Interface (CGI) script, running on the spammer's or a 3rd party's host can HTTP-connect to a (misconfigured) web server which provides e-mail services to the public. For example, the entering of "adding new user inurl:addnewuser" into a search engine leads to many web servers which allow anyone to set up a new user account and send an arbitrary number of e-mails on behalf of this account. The web server itself connects to a (usually local) MTA which, subsequently, sends the message to an MTA of the RO. In our model, the bundle consisting of the web server and the (local) MTA is referred to as gateway ($GW_{A,SMTP}$). cik is the regular expression covering this part of scenario IV.

5.3 The effectiveness of route-specific anti-spam measures

Anti-spam measures can be distinguished according to whether they control only particular delivery routes of the set derived in Subsect. 5.2.2, or whether they operate irrespectively of the delivery routes spam may take (see Fig. 5.3). Both types require distinct discussions. Non-route-specifical (or route-invariant) measures are assessed in Sect. 4.4. Route-specific anti-spam measures are analyzed relative to covering the spamming options in the following.

Route-specific anti-spam measures include

❏ blocking mechanisms accepting or rejecting e-mails on the basis of the IP address of the delivering MTA,

❏ blocking TCP port 25 which is used to send e-mails,

❏ limiting the number of outgoing e-mails per account and unit of time, for example per day,

❏ authentication mechanisms that base on SMTP extensions, (general) cryptographic authentication, and path authentication.

They can be mapped onto the e-mail infrastructure with the help of the individual lines of the regular expression in (5.31), each representing delivery routes that are defined by the same type of e-mail node involved. By providing the lines in rows and the anti-spam methods in columns, Table 5.2 reveals

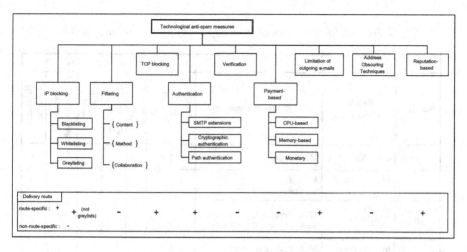

Fig. 5.3: Technological anti-spam measures

which spam delivery routes are combated by which method. An "x" indicates effective coverage, a blank space indicates the impossibility thereof. The table is explained in the following paragraphs, which are dedicated to the individual anti-spam methods.

5.3.1 IP blocking

The blocking of e-mails is a widely used mechanism by which e-mails are accepted or weeded out on the basis of the IP address of the sending node (see Subsect. 4.4.1). IP addresses of notorious nodes are listed on local and/or public blacklists. There are limits to what can be achieved by all of these. Blacklists are weapons against repeatedly used nodes, but spammers tend to change their IP addresses continually, either by switching to other ISPs or by taking advantage of exploits on unsuspected third party nodes. For example, spammers can use relays and gateways running on computers with unsuspected IP addresses. The more permanent IP addresses on blacklists tend to be those of corrupt ESPs, so it is mostly spam issued from these which is blocked (scenario I). A sure way to broaden the target is to block a full range of IPs (scenario V), for example of ISPs or even of a country known to harbor spammers. However, this can easily lead to a digital divide, and any measure running this risk hardly seems feasible in the long run, which is why the corresponding "x" in Table 5.2 is bracketed.

5.3.2 TCP blocking

Blocking all (outgoing) TCP traffic on port 25 (see Subsect. 4.4.3) is a simple option for ISPs for banishing spam sent from spammers' and exploited computers when port 25 is used (scenario III and the first two versions of scenario

Table 5.2: Effectiveness of (route-specific) anti-spam measures

Scenario	Regular expression	Nodes involved	IP blocking	TCP blocking	SMTP extensions	Cryptographic authentication	Path authentication	Limitation of outgoing e-mails	Reputation-based
I	d (k ∨ ff*k) ∨ ff*k	MTAs of provider	x						x
II	(d ∨ Λ)(ff*gg*k) ∨ dgg*k	MTA of provider, then relay(s)							
II	(d ∨ Λ)(ff*gg*hH) ∨ dgg*hH	MTA of provider, then relay(s) and gateway(s)							x
II	(d ∨ Λ) (ff*hH) ∨ dhH	MTA of provider, then at least gateway(s)							
III	ak	Local MTA	x				x		x
IV	(a ∨ b) gg*k	Local MTA or MUA, then relay(s)							
IV	(a ∨ b)(gg*hH ∨ hH)	Local MTA or MUA, then relay(s) and gateway(s)	x			x	x		x
IV	cj*i (hH ∨ gg*H ∨ gg*k ∨ k)	Local agent other than MTA or MUA, then at least gateway(s)							
V	(ad ∨ bd ∨ bed)(k ∨ ff*k)	Local MTA or MUA, then MTA(s) of provider	(x)		(x)			(x)	(x)
VI	(ad ∨ bd ∨ bed)(ff*gg*k ∨ gg*k)	Local MTA or MUA, then MTA(s) of provider, then relay(s)							
VI	(ad ∨ bd ∨ bed)(ff*hH ∨ hH)	Local MTA or MUA, then MTA(s) of provider, then at least gateway(s)			(x)		x	(x)	(x)
VI	(ad ∨ bd ∨ bed)(ff*gg*hH ∨ gg*hH)	Local MTA or MUA, then MTA(s) of provider, then relay(s) and gateway(s)							

IV). It should be noted that this, at the same time, hits deliveries from MTAs running on users' or companies' computers. Spam deliveries involving other ports or gateways, on the other hand, are not covered (the third version of scenario IV is not covered).

For many consumer-oriented ISPs, the simplest solution to stop e-mail worms and spam from their network is to block outbound port 25 traffic. However, blocking port 25 can be problematic for customers who need to run their own mail server or communicate with a mail server on a remote network to submit e-mail (such as a web hosting company or a hosted domains mail server) [9].

5.3.3 SMTP extensions

Protocol extensions such as SMTP-AUTH [114], "SMTP after POP" and "SMTP after IMAP" have been provided to support authentication of users or SMTP clients (see Subsect. 4.4.4). Like the limitation of outgoing e-mails, this measure requires a local e-mail agent to use an ESP. SMTP extensions can address spoofing of sender names and/or host names and are intended to improve accountability. However, user names and passwords are generally not kept protected on user's PCs and are available to malicious code on zombie PCs. The corresponding entries are thus bracketed, too.

5.3.4 Cryptographic authentication

A powerful and promising way to secure e-mail communication are environments which enable the recipient to authenticate the sender or, at least, the SO. Public Key Cryptography supplies the mathematical and algorithmic basis for digitally signing documents, and Public Key Infrastructures (PKIs) provide the organizational framework. At present, implementations serve for the authentication of organizations and (second level) domains: most users do not (as yet) possess a pair of keys. The SO signs an e-mail with its private key, and the recipient uses the public key to verify the organization's domain and, to rule out forgery, matches it with the domain in the sender's address shown in the "From:" field. Cryptographic authentication presumes that the SO is not corrupt and that its MTAs do not suffer from exploits (scenarios I and II are not covered). It is effective where spammers use MTAs of their own or where exploits on unsuspected computers are concerned, for example, spamming machines remotely controllable via a Trojan horse: an e-mail sent by such a spamming machine, which circumvents the MTAs and the signing software of the SO, will fail to be authenticated by the recipient (scenarios III and IV are covered). Misuse of the user's private account information - and of the password in particular - to issue spam, on the other hand, poses quite a serious challenge, since the SOs cannot distinguish between genuine and forged e-mails (scenarios V and VI are not covered). A shortcoming of cryptographic authentication and PKI respectively may also show up on a different plane in that spammers can readily obtain keys for a domain intended, and then used, solely for the temporary purpose of spamming.

5.3.5 Path authentication

Another method of authentication is path authentication which the LMAP proposals belong to (see Subsect. 4.4.4). These operate by checking whether a message that gives, say, *buffy@sunnydale.com* as its origin was actually sent from an MTA of the corresponding *sunnydale.com* organization. A negative result indicates forgery or that the sender has used an external e-mail relay. The LMAP family is effective in controlling direct e-mail deliveries – a local MTA is used (scenario III) – and those indirect deliveries that make use of relays and gateways (scenarios IV and VI). The weaknesses that the LMAP family exhibits are similar to those of the measures that base on cryptographic authentication.

5.3.6 Limitation of outgoing e-mails

A fairly simple method is to limit the maximum number of e-mails which can be sent per account and within a given period (see Subsect. 4.4.7). This is only available where an ESP is made use of and, even then, the automatic set-up of infinitely many e-mail accounts presents a wide loophole. Some ESPs apply CAPTCHA (Completely Automated Public Turing Test to Tell Computers and Humans Apart) procedures which require a number or a word appearing in a picture to be retyped before an account can be set up. However, Mori and Malik show how it is possible to automatically recognize the content of 92% of all pictures created by the Yahoo CAPTCHA process [110]. A different attack on visual CAPTCHA processes is as follows: the spammer places the ESP's picture on his or her own web site and tricks users into believing that reading the text and entering it in a text field will give them access to adult information. The spammer then transfers the retyped text into the corresponding text field on the ESP's form. All this can be done automatically. In short, current implementations to ensure a manual set-up of e-mail accounts - and by this means to keep the number of accounts per user low - are liable to be evaded and of doubtful value. This renders the quantitative restriction of e-mails a less than effective measure against spam; the corresponding entries are thus bracketed.

5.3.7 Reputation-based

Reputation-based approaches (see Paragraph 4.4.9) intend the recipient (organization) to accept or reject e-mails on basis of the reputation of the sender and/or the SO. Sophisticated systems should be able to differ between reliable and non-reliable organizations and senders. However, these approaches suffer from hijacked hosts which send spam e-mails on behalf of unsuspicious e-mail users. Therefore the entries related to scenario V and VI are bracketed.

5.3.8 Conclusion

When summing up the effectiveness of the anti-spam measures indicated in Table 5.2, it must be stressed that no anti-spam measure is currently capable of effectively stopping those spam deliveries which take advantage of ESP infrastructures (scenario V). The main problems are third party exploits and that it is all too easy for spammers to set up e-mail accounts automatically. The former is a plague, which is becoming more acute as botnets, networks of compromised and remotely controlled machines flourish among spammers [175]. However, model driven analysis of the effectiveness of (route-specific) anti-spam measures gives valuable hints on how to integrate them in a modified e-mail infrastructure that covers all options to send spam e-mails. Such an infrastructure is proposed in Chap. 6.

6

An infrastructure framework for addressing spam

Although many anti-spam measures have already been proposed and implemented, they all suffer from theoretical limitations and drawbacks (see Chap. 4 and Sect. 5.3), and we still face in practice a high volume and a high portion of spam e-mails. This makes it necessary to continue with research regarding both the development and deployment of effective anti-spam countermeasures. This far, no single measure has proved to be the silver bullet against spam, and it is doubtful whether any single, simple solution will ever be able to reduce or stop spam. Rather it seems appropriate to look for solutions that provide a complementary application of several anti-spam measures.

The infrastructure framework presented in this chapter features such a complementary application – a brief description of the framework is provided by Schryen [153], an extended version including quantitative resource analysis provides Schryen [156]. It is intended to have the following characteristics, which we assume to be preconditions for effectiveness in the long run and a widespread adoption by the Internet e-mail community, that includes ESPs, other sending/receiving organizations, e-mail users, and Internet authorities:

☐ Both technological and organizational modifications must be minor. The OECD [124, 14.] sums it up: *"A solution to spam should not make the Internet so cumbersome to use that people stop using it. The cure should not be worse than the disease."*

☐ An openness must be present, insofar as the framework provides for principles, and not for concrete algorithms or data formats.

☐ Spam should be stopped as close to its true source as possible. The prevention of spam has a higher priority than does its detection.

☐ Means to support the sending of solicited bulk e-mails have to be provided.

☐ The deployment of the key elements can be done smoothly and flexibly, i.e. the adoption of the infrastructure can occur evolutionarily.

☐ The infrastructure must not undertake an "arms' race" with spammers (for example, filters do undertake such a race).

This chapter aims at the conceptual development and analysis of an infrastructural e-mail framework and is structured as follows: Sect. 6.1 provides an overview of the framework and of the interaction of its key components. The framework includes both organizational and technological elements, which are discussed in detail in Sects. 6.2 and 6.3 respectively. The theoretical effectiveness of the framework is then assessed in Sect. 6.4. Deployment issues are covered in Sect. 6.5, before this chapter closes with a consideration of the limitations and drawbacks in Sect. 6.6. Although an analysis of the economic impact of our framework is desirable, we omit such an analysis for the following reasons: As already mentioned in Sect. 2.4, spam-related costs (and thus any possible savings) have not been quantified reliably, as is the case with economic benefits. Besides the quantification of cost savings we would also have to consider upcoming costs, which occur due to the introduction of the infrastructure framework. These costs comprise in particular those that are related to the operation of Counter Managing & Abuse Authorities. However, such costs depend heavily on the business model which the Counter Managing & Abuse Authorities underlie, and in order to keep our framework flexible, we do not make any assumptions about the business model. Summing up, a quantitative analysis of the economic impact would rely on many vague assumptions, and probably lead to low reliable results.

6.1 Overview of the framework

The core ideas of the framework are (1) to limit the number of e-mails that can be sent during a specific time-window and per account, (2) to restrict the automatic set-up of e-mail accounts and (3) to provide means for controlling this limitation of e-mail traffic by introducing an element of centralism [147, 150].[1] In order to support these ideas, a new organizational role is introduced: the Counter Managing & Abuse Authority (CMAA). The framework is intended to include several organizations, each of them taking on the full CMAA role. These organizations are either new and designated ones or established ones, such as trustworthy ESPs. In our framework, in principle, an SO, for example an ESP, either directly transmits an e-mail to the RO or sends the e-mails to a CMAA organization, which then relays the message to the SO. The former option is today's default option for sending e-mails, but is intended to be used in our framework only if the RO trusts the SO with regard to the implementation of effective anti-spam measures. Otherwise, the latter option applies, which means that the CMAA first checks whether the sender would exceed the number of e-mails he or she is allowed to send on one day. Depending on

---

[1] In principle, the framework follows the idea that a credit of, for example, 100 messages per day is a very large number for an individual, but an inconsequential number for a spammer. It also aims to prevent a compromised account or infected host from sending spam to millions of recipients in a short time frame.

the result, the CMAA would then either bounce the e-mail or relay it to the RO, whereby any CMAA organization offers a relaying service.

This replacement of the direct SMTP connection between the SO and the RO by a relaying procedure represents an element of centralism, which allows for controlling and accounting the (volume of) e-mail traffic. This control is intended to enormously reduce the sending of unsolicited bulk e-mail. Solicited bulk e-mail may still be sent if a person or organization accepts (legal) responsibility for a proper usage. The (anti-spam) control is also intended to make additional anti-spam measures undertaken by ROs obsolete. As the control mechanism is unlikely to prevent all spamming, it seems reasonable to complementarily provide a forum for e-mail users' complaints about unsolicited e-mails. Therefore, every CMAA organization is intended to also operate a central anti-spam abuse system. The abuse system and the relaying system are connected to each other in that numerous complaints about the spamming activities on behalf of a specific sender may lead to the blocking of that sender's CMAA account and, thus, to the bouncing of further e-mails from this sender. For the rest of this chapter, we use the shorter term CMAA for "CMAA organization", unless we explicitly provide the term CMAA to designate the organizational role.

An important feature of the framework is the option of the SO to send an e-mail directly to the RO in order to reduce a CMAA's workload. However, whether an e-mail that has not been relayed and counted by a CMAA is accepted by an RO depends on the RO's policy, which could include a dynamic white list of trustworthy SOs. This alternative procedure, which is today's standard in e-mail delivery, makes the framework flexible and scalable in both its operation and deployment.

In order to implement the accountability, on which the framework is based, the SO sets up a record for each sender's e-mail account prior to the first relaying. The records are stored in a database, herein denoted as Counter Database (CDB). As a CMAA is also responsible for the locking of accounts due to abuse complaints, these complaints are stored in another database, herein denoted as Abuse Database (ADB). A third database, the Organization Database (ODB), serves for the storage of information about those SOs that are registered on the CMAA for the usage of its services. Figure 6.1 illustrates the infrastructure framework. For the purpose of simplification, those infrastructure elements that are responsible for the administration of the databases are omitted. They are presented in Sect. 6.3.

In order to successfully tackle spammers' needs to send a huge number of e-mails, possibly millions of them, some obvious requirements have to be fulfilled, which are addressed in the following two sections in detail:

❑ The records have to be protected from (illegal) manipulation. This imposes stringent requirements on the database and system security.

❑ The set-up and removal of records is restricted to trustworthy parties only, such as trustworthy ISPs and SOs. Furthermore, due to the expected high

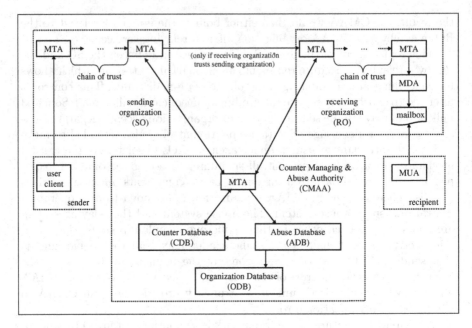

Fig. 6.1: Overview of the infrastructure framework

number of "adding" or "deleting" transactions, these operations must be supported by automatization.

❑ The third parties that are allowed to use the services of an CMAA, including the adding and the removal of specific records, have to fulfill a bundle of requirements:

◊ They must ensure that the accounts they are responsible for cannot be set-up automatically, thus preventing spammers from using an arbitrary number of accounts.

◊ They have to take care that their systems are secured against misuse, i.e. an attacker must not be able to manipulate the CDB on behalf of the respective organization.

◊ They have to ensure that their e-mail users need to use mechanisms that protect their accounts from being misused as well as possible, e.g. by using a password for sending an e-mail.

❑ The account-specific credits must be low enough to prevent unsolicited bulk e-mail, but high enough to not disturb solicited e-mail communication. This requirement includes the provision of means for regular bulk e-mailers.

The introduction of additional (logical or physical) organizational units (CMAAs) that are responsible for the implementation or the control of the described tasks requires organizational, technological, and financial support and, therefore, seems to be unnecessary and even counterproductive. However, some reasons support its appropriateness:

1. The operation of CMAA (role) services is critical for the success of the framework and requires both the willingness and the technological ability to operate a CMAA properly. Organizations that reside in developing countries or in countries with a non-restrictive anti-spam environment may only improperly fulfill these requirements; organizations that are notorious for addressing spam only lackadaisically are likewise unqualified. A CMAA that is operated and controlled by a trustworthy organization seems to be much more appropriate for providing the required services.

2. The list of trustworthy organizations is CMAA-specific and is maintained by each CMAA. The administration of decentralized white lists and black-lists by ROs would become obsolete. Each organization receiving an e-mail that has been relayed (and counted) by a CMAA can assume that the SO is a trustworthy one. Therefore, ROs would only be required to maintain data for all CMAAs, such as IP lists of trustworthy MTAs.

3. The infrastructure will not eradicate spam, but should support an abuse system. Currently decentralized abuse systems could be consolidated by integrating this service into the portfolio of the CMAAs.

Although the framework makes demands on SOs and, therefore, seems to resemble reputation-based approaches, such as LUMOS or the sTDL approach of Spamhaus (see Subsect. 4.4.9), it differs from them in two main issues:

☐ The presented reputation-based approaches keep the e-mail communication direct, i.e. the SO directly SMTP-connects with the RO. It is the RO that has to prove the reputation or accreditation of a particular SO. In contrast, our framework provides an additional organizational unit, which relays e-mails, and, thus, makes the communication indirect. Therefore, with our approach, it is not up to each RO to prove the reputation of a particular SO; this is a CMAA's task.

☐ With our approach, the SO's fulfillment of requirements is not sufficient for the successful delivering of a message. In addition, a restriction on the remaining account-specific credit applies.

However, as with reputation-based approaches, it remains an important task to formulate a set of requirements for SOs, which are effective regarding the misuse of a CMAA's services and the fulfillment of which can be verified. Because of this importance, these issues are addresses in Subsect. 6.2.4 in detail.

6.2 Organizational solution

The framework involves technological as well as organizational modifications to the Internet e-mail infrastructure and the e-mail processes. The organizational modifications, which are addressed in this section, result from the introduction of a new organizational role: the CMAA. As mentioned above, the framework is intended to involve several organizations each of them taking on the full CMAA role. However, a few outstanding key questions must be addressed prior to implementation and deployment:

1. Who will operate a CMAA?
2. How is a CMAA certified and by whom?
3. Which CMAA is responsible for which organization?
4. How does an organization register for the usage of CMAA services?

These issues are addressed in the following subsections. However, the organizational structure of the framework is simple and illustrated in Fig. 6.2.

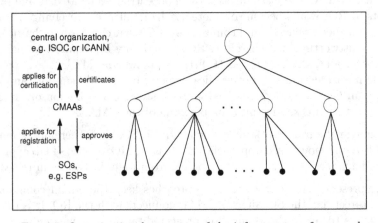

Fig. 6.2: *Organizational structure of the infrastructure framework*

6.2.1 Integrating CMAAs into the Internet

The introduction and the maintenance of a new organizational role that is as important and central as the CMAA demands a control and a policy that is independent of technological, economic, social, political, and cultural players. Therefore, we propose to entrust an established and well-accepted Internet organization, such as the Internet Society (ISOC) or the Internet Corporation for Assigned Names and Numbers (ICANN), with the ruling of CMAA issues. The ISOC is the organizational home of the groups responsible for Internet infrastructure standards, including the Internet Engineering Task Force (IETF) and the Internet Architecture Board (IAB), and includes the Internet Engineering Steering Group (IESG). ICANN is an internationally organized, non-profit corporation and is dedicated to preserving the operational stability of the Internet. In the following, we denote the trustworthy organization as " Central Organization (CO)".

It is the task of the CO to specify precise requirements for a CMAA, receive submissions, inspect the applications, officially certify applying organizations as CMAAs, and, if necessary, withdraw CMAA certificates. It is also desirable that the CO provides standardized software for CMAAs and their customer organizations. More information about the intended software is given in Subsects. 6.2.2 and 6.2.4.

In principle, designated CMAA organizations may be set up. However, it seems reasonable to assume that, at least in the beginning, mainly already established network organizations, such as trustworthy ESPs, anti-spam organizations, and universities, will serve as CMAAs, because they already dispose of the technological experience, tools, and staff, all of which is helpful, if not crucial, to running a CMAA. The motivation to gain certification and serve as a CMAA can result from two goals: (1) If the CMAA services offered have to be paid for by the organizations that make use of them, then there may be an economic incentive. Furthermore, it saves the costs of registering for an external CMAA. (2) It may increase the organization's reputation.

6.2.2 Certificating an organization as a CMAA

The effectiveness of the framework regarding the reduction of spam e-mails heavily relies on the trustworthiness of the CMAA organizations. Therefore, the requirements on organizations that apply for certification as a CMAA should be stringent. We propose that the CO considers the following evaluation criteria for CMAA applicants:

❏ An applying organization should have either a good reputation in the Internet community or at least references from such organizations. The reputation could include a high integrity in network-based services, an active involvement in anti-spam activities, and a good reputation with regard to anti-spam blacklists maintained by well-accepted organizations.

❏ The applicant should be under legislation that allows for prosecution in the case of any tolerating or supporting of spam activities. Any spam-promotive behavior, be it intentional or negligent, must be triable. Additionally, an applicant may be obliged to pay a deposit, that is forfeited in the case of a strong violation of the requirements on a CMAA. These requirements and any case of strong violation would have to be precisely specified in the contract signed by the CO and a particular CMAA.

❏ The organization's data in the "whois" database must have been successfully validated.

❏ The implementation of technological requirements that are mandatory for the operation of a CMAA must be accomplished. These include

 ◇ the protection of services and databases against security vulnerabilities,

 ◇ a system redundancy in order to guarantee the operational availability of CMAA services in the case of system crashes and heavy traffic, and

◇ an appropriate load balancing system for a time-efficient use of the redundant systems in order to guarantee an appropriate throughput.

The last issue addresses a performance requirement which is necessary to keep the Internet e-mail service a "real-time" system. We propose that the CO supports applicants with standardized and certified software for the operation of tasks that each CMAA has to perform. The usage of such software could even be regulated by the CO.

The certification process is intended to involve personal contacts between the applying organization and the CO, and the agreement is formally defined by a contract. The list of certified organizations, their contact information, the CMAA policy that has to be signed by each certified organization, and organization-specific information, such as service fees, should be provided by the CO. Complaints about a violation against the CMAA policy should be directed to the CO, which can withdraw CMAA certificates if this is deemed necessary.

6.2.3 Mapping organizations onto CMAAs

It is the decision of each organization that sends e-mails on behalf of its users whether it should use the services of one or more CMAAs, so that we have an $(m : n)$ relationship between SOs and CMAAs. Usually, an SO would use only one CMAA. However, there is no limitation to one CMAA intended, as an SO may choose to use more than one for the reason of increased reliability of its own e-mailing service. The framework is scalable in that it allows SOs to bypass any CMAA and to omit the registration on any CMAA. The pressure on these organizations to register is determined by the extent to which the Internet e-mail community accepts the importance of CMAAs, i.e. to which extent the community of ROs makes the decision of whether an e-mail is accepted or rejected dependent on the participation of a CMAA (or trustworthy SO). If the CMAAs' role is widely adopted by the Internet e-mail community, an SO's omission of a registration at a CMAA results in the rejection of messages sent to users of many or even most organizations.

If an organization has decided to register for CMAA services, then, the question arises as to which CMAA to choose. The mapping of organizations onto CMAAs can follow the market or the regulation paradigm:

Market paradigm One option would be to leave the decision to the particular SO. Then, a market emerges with CMAAs as sellers and SOs as buyers. However, in order to support the wide diffusion and adoption of the CMAAs' integration, the CO should regulate some issues that may otherwise hamper the diffusion of the usage of CMAAs, such as an unlimited fee range.

Regulation paradigm Another option would be to regulate the mapping and to assign a CMAA to an SO. Examples of regulatory approaches can be found at ICANN, which is responsible for IP address space allocation, protocol identifier assignment, TLD name system management, and root server system management functions.

6.2.4 Registering for the usage of CMAA services

One of the most critical requirements of the proposed infrastructure is the integrity of registered organizations. Although it seems impossible to exclude all those organizations that tolerate or even support spamming in advance, a set of requirements that applicants have to fulfill may be helpful for the (increasing) reduction of fraudulent or careless organizations. The fulfillment of these requirements has to be controlled by the CMAAs. Similar requirements can be found in [79].

❑ The organization's data in the "whois" database must have been successfully validated. This includes that the administrative contact has signed the application form and proved his/her identity by attaching a copy of a valid identity card. In the case of a repeated misuse of CMAA services and of the toleration or even support of spammers, this contact can be prosecuted.

❑ Each organization being registered has to sign the anti-spam policy to which it must adhere. In the case of a violation, the organization or its administrative contact can be prosecuted.

❑ The following technological requirements apply:

◇ The administration client (see Fig. 6.3) has to be installed. Like the administration server, this software should be provided by the CO.

◇ A private/public key pair must be generated, and the public key must be added to the DNS. The private key has to be stored securely, i.e. it either has to be stored encryptedly on a server or, even better, on a secure external device, such as a smart card.

◇ For the purpose of authentication and authorization (when sending an e-mail to a CMAA), LMAP records have to be added to the DNS.

◇ The component – be it a software or a hardware unit – that signs messages on behalf of the organization must be protected against attacks and any misuse. The CO should provide such software and specify the requirements on the hardware to be used.

◇ It has to be ensured that a reverse DNS query, with any name server of the applying organization as an argument, results in a FQDN whose "SLD.TLD" part is the name under which the organization is registered at its CMAA (see (6.1) on p. 134).

◇ One of the most important requirements on applying organizations is the demand for a manual set-up of accounts. The automatic set-up must be prohibited because, otherwise, the limitation of the number of e-mails per account and day would be pointless. One option would be to initiate an offline registration procedure, which demands a letter-based application, that includes both user identification by signature and the provision of a valid mail address. Another option would be to implement a CAPTCHA procedure (see Subsect. 4.4.5). However, CAPTCHA procedures suffer from several drawbacks. We propose that the underlying algorithm has been evaluated by the CO and that the CO provides CAPTCHA software, which can be used.

⋄   In order to protect e-mail accounts from easy misuse, an authentication mechanism, for example a password-based one, has to be applied. If SMTP-based connection is used, then SMTP-AUTH [114] can be used. Web-based e-mailing services are usually implemented with password-based protection.

In contrast to the CMAA certification process, the registration process is not intended to involve a personal contact. The reason for this is that it would be too cumbersome, as the number of registering organizations is much higher than the number of CMAA applicants.

6.3 Technological solution

This section describes the technological specification of the framework. This specification consists of the description of the three central data stores, the CDB, the ADB, and the ODB, and of the processes that are related to database administration, to e-mail relaying and bouncing, and to the usage of the abuse system. Regarding the following process descriptions, it is not relevant whether the SO is identical with the CMAA or not. In the former case, the roles "SO" and "CMAA" are both realized by the same organization, and although some process simplifications may then be possible, in principle, the processes are even then intended to run as described.

Further, it should be noted here that all of the technologies required to implement this proposal currently exist. The framework leverages existing technologies and services to reduce spam. The overall infrastructure framework and its key components are illustrated in Fig. 6.3.

6.3.1 Databases

Most services offered by a CMAA need to access its CDB. For example, the decision of whether an e-mail is relayed or bounced relies on the data of the particular CDB. We propose any CDB to maintain for every single CMAA-registered e-mail account the following data:

☐   *account* is the e-mail address of the user. E-mails can be sent on its behalf. An example would be any e-mail address, e.g. *guido@schryen.net*

☐   *credit* contains the current number of e-mails that can be sent on the current day. Its initial value is set to *max*.

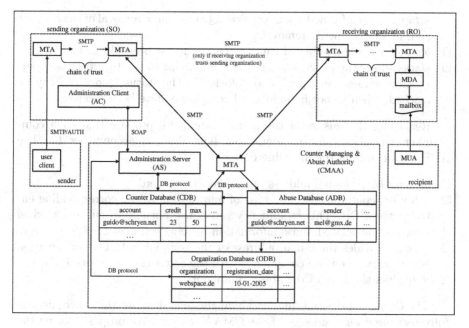

Fig. 6.3: Infrastructure framework

- ❏ *max* is the number of e-mails that can be sent per day on behalf of the particular account.
- ❏ *bounce_status* indicates whether a bounce e-mail has already been sent to the *account*. This would happen when the e-mail limit is first exceeded. Then, *bounce_status* would have to be changed to indicate that no further bounce e-mail is necessary.
- ❏ *setup_org* contains the SLD and the TLD, for example *freenet.de*, of the organization that set up the record and which offers the e-mail account to the particular user. Only the organization that set up a record is authorized to relay e-mails on behalf of the e-mail address stored in that particular record.
- ❏ *setup_date* gives the date of the set-up procedure and allows for statistical evaluations.
- ❏ *holder* provides the name and the mail address of the holder of the account. This information is mandatory, if the credit of the account exceeds the default credit, thus offering the option of sending solicited bulk e-mail on behalf of that particular account. If this account is misused for the sending of unsolicited bulk e-mail, then the holder information may be used for prosecution.
- ❏ *idle_days* is the number of days the account has not been used. When certain thresholds are exceeded, the responsible organization – stored in

setup_org – is informed about the possibly upcoming removal of the account and, finally, about its removal.
- *blocks* gives the number of times the account has been blocked so far.
- *status* allows the provision of information about the status of the account. Possible values are "open" and "blocked". The status "blocked" may be reached, when a specific number of complaints have been received.

Regarding the misuse of the abuse system, we propose that each complainant can only submit one abuse complaint about an account per day. The ADB would contain the following data:

- *account* is the e-mail address of the database record.
- *setup_org* contains the same type of information as the corresponding entry in the CDB. This redundancy serves the purpose of efficiency, when organization-related abuse information is being composed.
- *sender* provides the e-mail address of the complainant. This information is necessary to ensure compliance with the restriction mentioned above.
- *date* gives the date of the abuse complaint.

The ODB contains information about the organizations that have successfully registered for the usage of the CMAA services. We propose storing the following information:

- *organization* contains the same type of information as the corresponding entry in the CDB.
- *registration_date* gives the date of the registration process.
- *complaints1, ..., complaints30* provide the number of abuse complaints for the last 30 days, whereby 30 is an arbitrary number.
- *admonishments1, ... admonishments6* allows the storage of the number of admonishments for the last six months. Again, six is an arbitrary number.
- *status* provides information about whether the organization has been excluded or whether it may still use the CMAA services.

It should be noted that the protection of e-mail addresses that are stored in the databases is very important, because the databases would otherwise provide valuable resources for spammers. The proposed extension of the infrastructure would then be even counterproductive. Although the usage of hash values or encrypted addresses would seem to be solutions to this problem, they suffer from the following drawbacks: If only hash values of e-mail addresses are stored, then the e-mail addresses cannot be recovered efficiently. However, the e-mail addresses are needed for some CMAA messages, for example for messages that aim at the removal of a user account. If the addresses are stored encryptedly, they can be recovered by applying the decrypt function. However, most CDB administration processes and the e-mail delivery process include the sending of an e-mail address that would have to be encrypted or decrypted. Because of the high number of expected queries, the use of cryptographic functions would probably consume too much time. There-fore, the usage of other mechanisms, such as authorization-based ones, should be explored. This discussion reflects the challenge to many infrastructures and systems in finding an appropriate balance between security, functionality, and (time-related) efficiency.

6.3.2 Database administration processes

Access to the CDB is granted to SOs that have been approved for the usage of the CMAA-specific CDB and to the CMAA itself. SOs are allowed to set up, modify, and remove records, herein denoted as processes P1, P2, and P3. The CMAA is responsible for the periodical maintenance of the CDB records in many regards. It has

- ❑ to reset values of each record, for example, the credit, by a fixed time of the day (P4),
- ❑ to trace accounts that have not been used for a specific time in order to remove those particular accounts or to inform the responsible SO about the possible upcoming removal (P5), and
- ❑ to block accounts due to spam complaints (P6).

The administration of ADB and ODB is reserved for the CMAA. It is responsible for both the detection of accounts, for which many abuse com-plaints have arrived, and the detection of SOs that are responsible for such "suspicious" accounts. As a consequence, accounts have to be blocked and SOs have to be admonished or even excluded from all CMAA services (P7). All complaint and admonishment information stored in the ODB has to be updated periodically, because complaints only refer to the last 30 days and admonishments only to the last six months (P8).

As the data that are exchanged between an SO and an CMAA are com-pletely structured, the usage of e-mails seems to be improper. Rather, the Simple Object Access Protocol (SOAP), which is an XML based W3C stan-dard for a platform-independent communication between applications [188], provides means for this communication.

Process P1: setting up a CMAA record

P1 is illustrated in Fig. 6.4, which models the process with an UML 2.0 activity diagram.

The process, by which a CMAA record is set up, is initiated by a user when he or she wants to set up an e-mail account at an SO, for example an ESP. The user usually applies online by using a web form, and he or she is intended to have two options regarding credit: if the user needs more than the default credit, for example 1000 e-mails per day instead of the default value 50, then he or she has to authenticate. This authentication

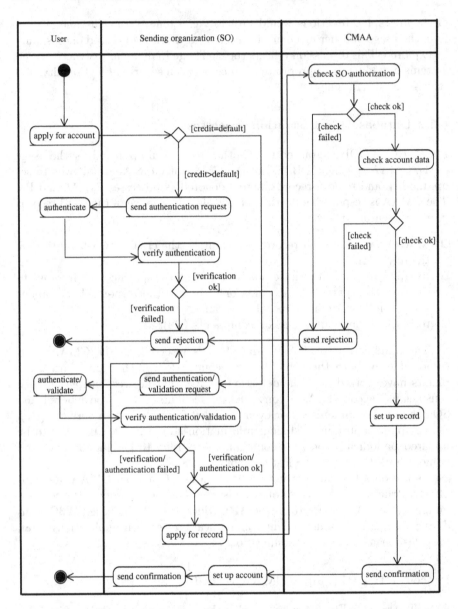

Fig. 6.4: Activity diagram modeling the set-up of a CDB record

□ is intended to be submitted offline by mail or fax,
□ must disclose the user's identity and address,
□ must specify the desired credit,
□ includes the user's explicit agreement that he/she accepts to take (even legal) responsibility for any misuse of the account, and
□ is intended to be valid for an unlimited period.

The lacking limitation is motivated by the need of many senders of solicited bulk e-mail to continuously exceed the default number of e-mails. For example, senders of newsletters would otherwise have to regularly undergo the authentication procedure. On the other hand, the benefit for the senders of unsolicited bulk e-mail, who authenticated themselves or compromised an account, should be limited due to the abuse system, which helps to identify and block such accounts. Users who want to only casually exceed the default number of e-mails are likely apt to apply for a much higher credit, too. The acceptance of such applications are unlikely to lead to an increased number of e-mails sent by the users. However, by their applications for an increased credit, users are accountable. The accountability and the users' agreement to take responsibility for any misuse of their accounts support prosecution of users, even if their accounts have been compromised by a third party. This issue represents a hazard to the users', which might, therefore, be deterred to apply for an increased credit.

For a possible prosecution due to spamming, we propose ensuring that the user underlies an opt-in legislation. If the user applies for an account with default credit, then, either the same authentication procedure applies or an effective CAPTCHA procedure has to validate that a human user is applying. If the authentication/validation succeeds, then the SO applies for a CDB record at its CMAA. The CMAA first checks the authenticity. We propose applying a (cryptographic) signature-based procedure for this, because this approach makes it rather difficult, if not practically impossible, to spoof sender data, which would easily lead to the setting up of an arbitrary number of accounts. The SOs' public keys must be stored in the DNS. If the authentication fails for any reason, a rejection message is sent to the SO. Otherwise, the CMAA has to proceed with the authorization of the SO to set up a record for the particular e-mail account. The SO is granted this permission if it is responsible for the e-mail account. This responsibility is defined as follows: either the *SLD.TLD* domain of the e-mail address is a domain of the SO, for example *schryen@winfor.rwth-aachen.de*, where *rwth-aachen.de* is a domain of RWTH Aachen University, or the domain is hosted by the SO, for example, the domain of the e-mail address *guido@schryen.de*, *schryen.de* is hosted by the SO. In both cases, each authoritative name server for the given domain belongs to the SO. This verification can be undertaken by using the DNS: let *DNSNS(domain)* be the operation that requests the DNS for a name server of *domain*, let *RDNS(IP)* be the operation that requests the DNS for the host that matches *IP*, let *SLDTLD(address)* be the operation that returns the

SLD. TLD part of a host or an e-mail address, let *setup_org* be the SLD.TLD part of the organization that requests the record set-up, and let *address* be the e-mail address for which a record is requested. Then, the requirement can be verified by using two, possibly cascading, accesses to the DNS:

$$SLDTLD(RDNS(DNSNS(SLDTLD(address)))) = setup\_org^2 \quad (6.1)$$

If the verification of responsibility succeeds, the CMAA sets up the record and sends a confirmation to the SO, which then sets up the particular e-mail account and sends a confirmation message to the user. If the verification fails, the CMAA sends a rejection to the SO, which then sends a rejection message to the user.

The CMAA SOAP server application has to consider that holder data must be provided if the value of *max* is higher than the default value, which still has to be defined.

Process P2: modifying a CMAA record

SO is allowed to modify the *max* value and/or the *holder* value only. If the *max* value is reset to the default value, holder data need not to be provided. Otherwise the provision of holder data is mandatory. When an SO sends a modification request to the CMAA, the CMAA proceeds analogously to its operations in P1 (see Fig. 6.4).

Process P3: removing a CMAA record

The deletion of a CMAA record only requires that the SO provide the account name. Regarding the SO's SOAP message, the notes on P2 apply.

Processes P4 and P5: resetting the credits of CMAA records and tracing idle CMAA accounts

By a fixed time of the day, the CMAA would have to reset the values of each record. The tracing idle CMAA accounts can be shared with this procedure.

Process P6 and P7: blocking CMAA accounts or/and SOs

The CMAA should daily consolidate abuse complaints. This consolidation may lead to the blocking or removal of user accounts. Furthermore, if too many complaints refer to different accounts of one specific SO, then, the SO has to be admonished or even excluded from all CMAA services. The following issues of processes P6 and P7 are worth a mention:

---

[2] Note that for a successful authorization, each requesting organization is responsible for the provision of adequate DNS entries (see Subsect. 6.2.4).

❑ When the number of abuse complaints on a specific account exceeds the daily limit, the account is blocked for one day. Each account may be blocked a number of times, which are still to be specified. If the total number of blocking exceeds this value, then the account is removed and the responsible SO is informed about this deletion.

If the user of an account that has to be blocked is accountable, for example, because he/she has applied for a non-default credit, then, it is up to the CMAA to initiate legal prosecution, to inform all other CMAAs, and/or to refuse any further setup of an e-mail account for this user.

❑ It may happen that SOs ignore, tolerate or even support the abuse of e-mail accounts. Therefore, for each organization, all complaints about those accounts that the organization is responsible for are counted and stored in the ODB, which contains for each SO the number of abuse complaints for each of the last six months. We differentiate between three abuse states that an organization can be assigned: low, medium, and strong. The status results from the application of the CMAA's policy on the SO's six-month complaint history and the SO's number of past admonishments. The following actions have to be taken by the CMAA, depending on the SO's status:

◇ If the history is assessed as "low", nothing has to be done.
◇ If the value is "medium", then the CMAA sends an admonishment to the SO and records this.
◇ In the case of a "strong" violation, that particular SO would have to be excluded from all CMAA services. The status would be set to "excluded", all accounts that had been set up by the SO would be removed, and the SO and all other CMAAs would be informed about this exclusion.

Process P8: removing complaint and admonishment information

Complaints older than 30 days and admonishments older than 6 months are intended to be removed from the ODB. The removal of complaints has to be executed once a day; the deletion of admonishment information once a month.

6.3.3 E-mail delivery process

The process of sending an e-mail has to be extended by the integration of a CMAA. Although a CMAA's involvement makes the delivery process more complicated, the modifications are intended to be hidden from the user, who may continue using his/her e-mail client software without any changes. Figure 6.5 shows the process by using an activity diagram. Figure 6.3 (see p. 129) provides an infrastructure view of this process. The process can be divided into the following components:

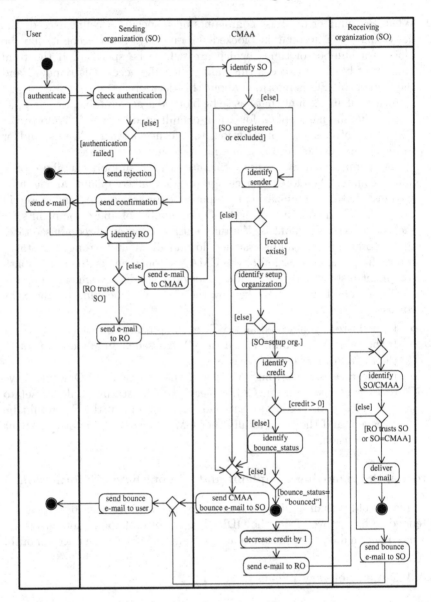

Fig. 6.5: Activity diagram modeling the e-mailing process

1. User authentication
   First, the user has to authenticate, so that his/her account is protected
   from misuse by an unauthorized person. We propose using the IETF standard SMTP-AUTH [114] with a (user, password) SASL authentication
   mechanism [113]. However, for effective protection from misuse, the password must be strong, i.e. not guessable and not too short, and protected
   from being read by malicious software. If the authentication fails, the
   process is terminated, otherwise the user can send the e-mail to his/her
   SO.

2. SO's relaying decision
   For each recipient of the e-mail, the SO looks for the RO in the internal
   database that stores the names of those organizations that accept direct
   e-mail communication with the own organization. If the RO is listed, then
   the e-mail is sent directly to the RO, otherwise it is sent to the SO's
   CMAA. The case where the SO is identical to the RO is covered implicitly.
   In such a case, the involvement of an CMAA is not intended. However, it
   should still be an option for a SO to let a CMAA count those e-mails that
   are not directed to another SO, in order to protect their users' accounts
   from being spammed. For the sake of simplicity, this option is omitted in
   Fig. 6.5.

3. CMAA's relaying decision
   The CMAA checks whether the SO is registered and not excluded – the SO
   data can be obtained from the e-mail's FQDN, which has to be successfully
   validated against the IP of the sending host by using an LMAP-based procedure (see Subsect. 4.4.4, Path Authentication)[3] –, if the CMAA main-
   tains a record for the sender and if the SO is allowed to send e-mails on
   behalf of the sender account. If one of these conditions is not fulfilled, the
   CMAA refuses the relaying and sends a bounce e-mail to the SO, which,
   then sends a bounce e-mail to the sender. If all tests succeed, the CMAA
   checks the sender's credit. If no credit is available, the relaying is refused
   and, provided that no bounce e-mail due to the unavailable credit has
   been sent, a bounce e-mail is sent to the SO. It is important to send, at
   most, one bounce e-mail per day and account due to credit unavailability,
   because it would be otherwise possible to maliciously initiate the sending of an arbitrary number of bounce e-mails to a compromised account:
   once a password is read or guessed, an attacker could easily send e-mails
   on behalf of this account thereby causing the CMAA to send a bounce
   e-mail for each e-mail that exceeds the account's e-mail limit. If the credit
   is larger than 0, then the credit is decreased by 1 and the e-mail is relayed
   to the SO.

---

[3] If the validation fails, the process terminates. In order to keep the activity diagram
in Fig. 6.5 as simple as possible, this issue is not modeled in it.

4. RO's acceptance decision

   When an organization receives an e-mail, it first operates an LMAP-based validation as described above. If the validation fails, the process terminates. Otherwise, the RO checks whether the SO is whitelisted regarding a direct e-mail communication or if the delivering host belongs to a CMAA. If this check is successful, the e-mail is accepted and delivered to the e-mail's recipient. Otherwise, the e-mail acceptance is refused and a bounce e-mail is sent to the SO.

If a CMAA participates in e-mail delivery, its MTAs add *Received* entries to the header as described in RFC 2821. No further modification is necessary.

6.3.4 Abuse complaint process

The success of the abuse system depends on the user participation in the sending of abuse e-mails to the CMAAs. In order to make a user send a spam complaint to a CMAA, he/she has to know to which CMAA the complaint has to be directed. We envisage at least two options for providing this information: either the CMAA that relays a message adds a new header entry to the e-mail, for example: *X-Compliant: <abuse-e-mail-address>*, or adds this information to the e-mail's body as part of a CMAA signature. The first option would be preferable for keeping an e-mail text free from any CMAA (meta) information and for easing the implementation. The reason is that the header entry could be added at the beginning of the message without seeking the appropriate position in the body, which could contain several MIME parts thereby complicating the e-mail's structure. The second option allows the recipient to easily identify the abuse address without having to make the header entries visible. Furthermore, many users are likely to know little or nothing about the (existence of an e-mail) header.

When a user wants to complain about a received e-mail, then the user would have to send an abuse e-mail to the responsible CMAA via his or her organization. The CMAA that receives the complaint e-mail would have to perform three checks: (1) Is the e-mail a complaint message? (2) Does the CMAA maintain a record for the account being complained about? (3) Does the ADB already contain a complaint tuple (account,sender,date)? The purpose of the third check is to prevent the abuse system from being misused by users sending multiple complaints about the same account in order to discredit it. Only if all checks are positive, is a new complaint record added to the ADB. The *setup_org* data can be obtained by requesting the CDB.

The content and format of a complaint e-mail is not specified here, in order to avoid an overstandardization; however, an abuse e-mail must contain the account and the date of the e-mail being complained about. Furthermore, each complaint message has to labeled as such a message because the CMAAs have to handle it different from a "regular" message. The content and format may vary between different CMAAs, although for the purpose of consistency, it is useful to standardize these issues.

6.4 Theoretical effectiveness

In Sect. 5.1 we proposed a model of the current Internet e-mail infrastructure, and we used this model for deriving spam delivery routes and assessing the effectiveness of anti-spam measures. Figure 6.6 shows the model again.

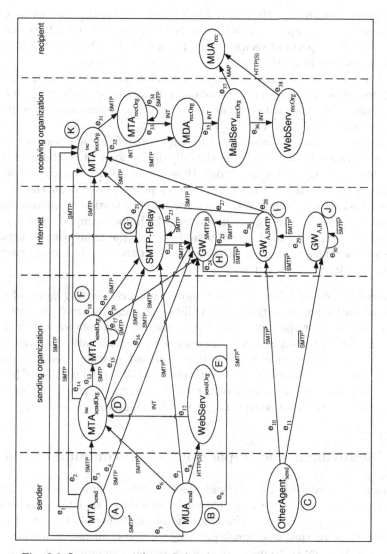

Fig. 6.6: Internet e-mail network infrastructure as a directed graph

Regarding the modeled section of the Internet e-mail infrastructure, our framework does not add a new element. From a technological point of view, the CMAA simply represents an SMTP relay. Therefore, we can still use this model and the derived spam delivery routes. Analogously to Fig. 5.2 (see p. 114), Table 6.1 shows the routes and explains to which extent our framework addresses them. The framework addresses all scenarios completely by adhering to three principles:

1. Some delivery routes, that are difficult to control, are classified as insecure. These routes comprise those that do not include a CMAA relay (scenario III and large parts of scenarios II , IV, and VI). ROs are recommended for refusing e-mails that have taken such delivery routes.
2. Each RO can maintain a whitelist and decide which organizations it trusts. If one of these organizations sends or relays spam e-mails, each RO can exclude that organization from any direct e-mail communication at any time (scenarios I and V).
3. In most cases, an SO would send an e-mail to an RO that does not include that SO on its whitelist. Then, the only option for a successful delivery is to use a CMAA's relaying service. However, in order to be allowed to use such a service, the SO must have successfully registered for the CMAA services. This registration requires the implementation of organizational and technological anti-spam measures, which, for example, avoid the automatic setup of e-mail accounts and prevent the hampering of existing e-mail accounts. The relaying scenarios cover the complementary parts of the scenarios II, IV, and VI.

As mentioned in Subsect. 5.3.8, today's's most challenging issues of technological anti-spam activities include third party exploits and the fact that it is all too easy for spammers to set up e-mail accounts automatically. Both problems are addressed in our framework with a combination of prevention and limitation of the possible harm: the framework provides means to ensure that (1) only a manual set-up of accounts is allowed, (2) the number of (spam) e-mails per account and day is restricted, (3) users are informed about the misuse of their accounts so that they can take countermeasures.

6.5 Deployment and impact on e-mail communication

An essential precondition for the wide deployment of a new e-mail infrastructure seems to be that its key elements can be introduced smoothly and flexibly, i.e. that the adoption of the infrastructure (additions) can occur evolutionarily. Our infrastructure framework provides for this challenge as follows: The framework is designed to use both a direct e-mail communication and an indirect one by integrating CMAAs. This flexibility means a scalability of the framework that allows the avoidance of a "big bang" at its introduction, but leaves the (time) schedule for using CMAAs to each organization. An ESP, for example, can decide not to use CMAAs at all, to use CMAAs for incoming

Table 6.1: Effectiveness of the proposed framework

Scenario	Regular expression	Nodes involved	Effect of the proposed framework
I	d (k ∨ ff*k) ∨ ff*k	MTAs of provider	❏ Organizations can control e-mails via local white lists, that contain trustworthy sending organizations.
II	(d ∨ Λ)(ff*gg*k) ∨ dgg*k	MTA of provider, then relay(s)	❏ Organizations accept incoming SMTP connections only from relaying hosts that belong to a (trustworthy) CMAA.
	(d ∨ Λ) (ff*gg*hH) ∨ dgg*hH	MTA of provider, then relay(s) and gateway(s)	❏ The relaying service is only offered to (registered) organizations that have implemented both technological and organizational measures against the misuse of e-mail accounts.
	(d ∨ Λ) (ff*hH) ∨ dhH	MTA of provider, then at least gateway(s)	❏ Misused accounts can be identified and blocked by a CMAA.
III	ak	Local MTA	❏ These e-mails are sent from a host which neither belongs to a CMAA nor to a whitelisted organization. ❏ These e-mails **do not have to be accepted** by a receiving organization.
IV	(a ∨ b) gg*k	Local MTA or MUA, then relay(s)	❏ These e-mails come from hosts that are not whitelisted and do not belong to a CMAA (no CMAA would accept e-mails from hosts of unregistered parties).
	(a ∨ b) (gg*hH ∨ hH)	Local MTA or MUA, then relay(s) and gateway(s)	❏ These e-mails **do not have to be accepted** by a receiving organization.
	cj*i (hH ∨ gg*H ∨ gg*k ∨ k)	Local agent other than MTA or MUA, then at least gateway(s)	
V	(ad ∨ bd ∨ bed) (k ∨ ff*k)	Local MTA or MUA, then MTA(s) of provider	(see remarks on scenario I)
VI	(ad ∨ bd ∨ bed) (ff*gg*k ∨ gg*k)	Local MTA or MUA, then MTA(s) of provider, then relay(s)	(see remarks on scenario II)
	(ad ∨ bd ∨ bed) (ff*hH ∨ hH)	Local MTA or MUA, then MTA(s) of provider, then at least gateway(s)	
	(ad ∨ bd ∨ bed) (ff*gg*hH ∨ gg*hH)	Local MTA or MUA, then MTA(s) of provider, then relay(s) and gateway(s)	

e-mails, to register for a CMAA's services, or even to apply for a CMAA certificate. Although no organization is forced to participate in the centralized services, market pressure – assuming that the infrastructure has been widely adopted – will push them to do so, as they are otherwise in danger of being excluded from large parts of the world-wide e-mail communication. This consequence would make the ESP probably unattractive or even unacceptable from the users' view.

If we categorize communication scenarios according to the SO and RO types, we get those categories illustrated in Fig. 6.7. Organizations that are certified or registered are not limited in their e-mail communication. Other organizations would not be allowed to send e-mails to certified or registered organizations, which would usually insist on the registration or certification of the SO. This means that the overall e-mail communication becomes limited. The area of limitation is indicated by the "X" in Fig. 6.7. The grade of limitation will depend on the extent to which the CMAAs will be accepted and used. If the proposed infrastructure is either widely accepted or hardly accepted, then, the limitation is low, because most e-mail communication belongs to one of the categories, which are displayed as ellipses. A high limitation, i.e. "X" indicates a large subset of e-mail communication, would result from a balanced distribution.

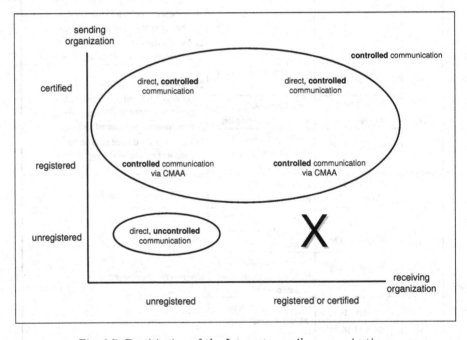

Fig. 6.7: Partitioning of the Internet e-mail communication

A successful deployment of the proposed framework also requires its adoption by the ISOC, ICANN, and/or large ESPs. This adoption includes both the maintenance of a CO, that has to fulfill the role described in Subsect. 6.2.1, and the propagation of the framework in the Internet e-mail community. However, at this early stage no reliable information about the acceptance of the framework can be provided.

6.6 Drawbacks and limitations

The implementation of the framework requires both organizational and technological modifications of today's Internet e-mail infrastructure. These modifications have to be propagated by Internet organizations and providers in order to become widely accepted. However, even then, the framework has its drawbacks and limitations:

☐ Spam e-mails are unlikely to be eliminated, because some options for spamming still remain, even if they consume more resources than today:

◇ E-mail accounts can be set up manually at registered organizations and then used for spamming. If the accounts have a default credit, for example 50 e-mails per day, a spammer would have to set up 20,000 accounts to send 1 million e-mails per day. This takes time and human resources, which would decrease the spammer's profit.

◇ If a spammer sets up an account with an increased credit, then, he or she has to provide personal information that has to be validated. In the case of the misuse of such an account, the spammer could be prosecuted. However, in practice, we have to take into account that personal data have been misused and that prosecution is difficult, because some national authorities do not cooperate appropriately.

◇ Accounts of legitimate users can be compromised by malicious software, such as keylogging programs, which spy out passwords, or software that looks for passwords in the file system. Although a bounce e-mail would be sent to the user's account, it would take some time to fix the user's host.

◇ Organizations that have successfully registered for CMAA services may be corrupt or may tolerate spammers. They would be excluded from CMAA services, and the administrative contact could be prosecuted. However, the same limitations as described above apply.

◇ An SO that is stored on an RO's whitelist can bypass any CMAA and send an unlimited number of (spam) e-mails. It is up to the RO to cope with this problem by informing or admonishing the SO and/or by even removing it from the whitelist.

☐ The approach requires a critical mass of organizations to drive the framework's adoption.

☐ The DNS becomes an even more critical and important resource than it is today for the following reasons:

◇ The DNS has to provide entries for public keys of registering organizations. Ideally, the public keys are signed by a trustful organization.

◇ LMAP records of SOs and CMAAs have to be added to the DNS. Currently, no single approach has been adopted as a world-wide standard.

◇ DNS spoofing would have an impact on the sending of spam e-mails: a CMAA's decision to relay an e-mail depends on the LMAP record. If LMAP data are spoofed, then a third party could send e-mails on behalf of another registered organization.

◇ The availability of DNS servers is closely related to the availability and functionality of the Internet e-mail infrastructure. This attracts attacks on the availability of these servers, such as Distributed Denial of Service (DDoS) attacks.

❑ The CMAAs' systems represent a critical resource, too:

◇ The availability of the relays and administration servers is critical with regard to the operational maintenance of large parts of Internet e-mail traffic. Therefore, the consequences of a successful DDoS attack are tremendous.

◇ The servers have to handle a huge amount of traffic and requests. This requires a careful implementation of load balancing systems, if e-mail communication is not to become (timely) inefficient.

◇ The CMAAs' CDBs contain large numbers of valid e-mail addresses and have to be protected from unauthorized accesses. Address harvesters will make ambitious efforts to get access to CDBs. Options for protecting CDB e-mail addresses from being read unauthorizedly are discussed in Subsect. 6.3.1.

❑ We have to take privacy concerns into account when e-mail relaying is done by only several central organizations.

The empirical analysis of the abuse of e-mail addresses placed on the Internet

This chapter is dedicated to the (empirical analysis of the) resource "e-mail addresses", which is vital for any potential bulk mailer and spammer. Its availability is part of spammers' demands on technological capability, as illustrated in Fig. 4.1 (see p. 44). The assumption that the Internet is an attractive source of addresses for spammers, motivates the empirical analysis of the abuse of Internet e-mail addresses. The key issues of this chapter's content can be also found in [151] and in [152].

In Sect. 7.1, the relevance of inspecting e-mail address harvesting is discussed. Section 7.2 illustrates prior studies and findings. Both a methodology and a honeypot conceptualization for the implementation of an empirical analysis of the abuse of e-mail addresses is presented in Sect. 7.3. Finally, in Sect. 7.4, the prototypic implementation of such an empirical study and its findings are described.

7.1 The relevance of inspecting e-mail address harvesting

Valid e-mail addresses are among the most valuable resources for spammers, and the identification of address sources and spammers' exploiting procedures is crucial to preventing spammers from procuring addresses and subsequently misusing them. It is widely known that, besides generating addresses with brute force mechanisms and dictionary attacks, spammers procure valid e-mail addresses by harvesting the Internet or, illegally, by purchasing or stealing them from various organizations. However, only little is known about the quantitative properties of e-mail address abuse on the Internet and how to measure these. Gaining insight into this field can comprise

❑ the assessing of the extent of the current harassment and its development over time,
❑ the measuring of the effectiveness of AOTs, such as the embedding of addresses into images or the "masking" of addresses textually, e.g. by using an address such as *aliceREMOVETHISTEXT@wonderland.tv*,

❑ the empirical assessment of such obfuscating techniques which restrict addresses' usability, e.g. by using single-purpose addresses [83] or e-mail aliases [71], and

❑ the discovery of specific marketing and addressing activities.

The investigation of spammers' topic oriented marketing and addressing activities (see above) is closely related to the quality of e-mail addresses. Spammers are known to collect as many valid e-mail addresses as possible but little is known about spammers' capabilities and interest in carefully directed, consumer- or topic-oriented marketing. A taxonomy (of the quality) of e-mail addresses is shown in Fig. 7.1.

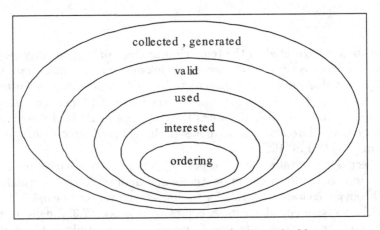

Fig. 7.1: Taxonomy (of the quality) of e-mail addresses

The inner ellipses are more valuable for spammers than the outer ones, due to the latter's losses caused by non-selective advertising. Only a portion of collected or generated e-mail addresses are valid ones, i.e. e-mails addressed to non-valid ones are refused by the addressee's host, as these mailboxes do not exist. The valid ones can be divided into used addresses and those that are no longer accessed and are, thus, useless for spammers. A way of distinguishing between the two is provided by an opt-out option included in some spam e-mails, which, when used incautiously by the spam recipient, indicates that the address is in use. Spammers can even go a step further when adopting physical marketing strategies using knowledge about consumer-specific interests and behavior: for example, an Internet user participating actively in a German discussion group that focuses on medical products is presumably interested in medical products offered in the German language. The innermost ellipse contains the e-mail addresses belonging to users who buy the products and, thus, from whom the spammer profits.

7.2 Prior studies and findings

The author is aware of five empirical studies that focus on the extent of spam harm that is caused by placing e-mail addresses on Internet services:

1. In 1999, the Australian Coalition Against Unsolicited Bulk Email (CAUBE.AU) seeded e-mail addresses to the Usenet, to the web and to Internet contact databases. The study [23], which took almost one year, focused on spam sources and contents. Regarding the attractiveness of particular services, the study found that "[...] *the effectiveness of an e-mail address exposure [...] is almost identical for posting a single message to USENET as it is for posting the address to a single web page.*"

2. In 2002, the US Federal Trade Commission (FTC) seeded 175 different locations on the Internet (including web pages, newsgroups, chat rooms, message boards, and online directories for web pages, instant message users, domain names, resumes, and dating services) with 250 new, undercover e-mail addresses [65]. During the six weeks after the postings, the key findings were:

   ⋄ "*86 percent of the addresses posted to web pages received spam. It didn't matter where the addresses were posted on the page.*"
   ⋄ "*86 percent of the addresses posted to newsgroups received spam.*"
   ⋄ "*Chat rooms are virtual magnets for harvesting software. One address posted in a chat room received spam nine minutes after it first was used.*"
   ⋄ "*Addresses posted in other areas on the Internet received less spam, the investigators found. Half the addresses posted on free personal web page services received spam, as did 27 percent of addresses posted to message boards and nine percent of addresses listed in e-mail service directories. Addresses posted in instant message service user profiles, 'Whois' domain name registries, online resume services, and online dating services did not receive any spam during the six weeks of the investigation.*"
   ⋄ "*In almost all instances, the investigators found, the spam received was not related to the address used. As a result, consumers who use e-mail are exposed to a variety of spam – including objectionable messages – no matter the source of the address.*"

3. In 2002, the Center for Democracy & Technology embarked on a project
   [24] to attempt to determine the source of spam. Hundreds of different
   e-mail addresses were set up, which led to the major findings that

   ◇ *"[...] e-mail addresses posted on Web sites or in newsgroups attract
   the most spam"*,
   ◇ *"for the most part, companies that offered users a choice about receiving commercial e-mails respected that choice"*,
   ◇ *"some spam is generated through attacks on mail servers, methods that
   don't rely on the collection of e-mail addresses at all."*

4. The "Project Honey Pot" (*www.projecthoneypot.org*) is a distributed
   honeypot network to track e-mail harvesters and the spammers who send
   to harvested addresses. It was opened to public volunteers in October 2004
   and, as of June 20 2005, the project is monitoring more than 250,000 active spamtrap e-mail honeypots. The core idea is to provide a honeypot
   software to be installed on web servers by administrators, and to collect
   data about address harvesters (from these servers) and about spam e-
   mails received on harvested addresses (from assigned e-mail servers). The
   collected data are stored and processed on a central honeypot server. The
   technological background as well as an analysis of the data collected during the first six month are provided by Prince et al. [136]. The empirical
   results comprise the following findings:

   ◇ *"Approximately 6.5 percent of the traffic visiting our honey pots subsequently turns out to be spam harvesters."*
   ◇ *"The average time from a spamtrap address being harvested to when
   it receives its first message is currently 11 days, 7 hours, 43 minutes,
   and 10 seconds."*
   ◇ *"[...] we have characterized two distinct classes of harvesters. [...] The
   first class – the hucksters – are characterized by a slow turnaround from
   harvest to first message (typically at least 1 month), a large number
   of messages being sent to each harvested spamtrap address, and typical product-based spam [...]. The second class – the fraudsters – are
   characterized by an almost immediate turnaround from harvest to first
   message (typically less than 12 hours), only a small number of messages sent to each harvested spamtrap address, and fraud-based spam
   [...]."*

5. The FTC conducted a study [67] in 2005 that explored the current state
   of e-mail address harvesting, the effectiveness of anti-spam filters and the
   effectiveness of using masked e-mail addresses. In the course of three days,
   150 e-mail addresses were posted to 50 Internet locations in total, consisting, in each case, of 12 in the category "FTC web page", "message
   boards", "blogs", and "chat rooms" respectively, and 2 in Usenet groups.
   One key finding of the study – which lasted five weeks – regarding the
   attractiveness of categories for harvesters, is that *"[...] 99.6 percent of the
   total amount of spam received were received by Unfiltered Addresses that*

had been posted on 11 of the 12 web pages, [...]" [67, p. 4]. This study indicates that spammers continue to harvest addresses posted on Internet locations.

The studies differ in their goals as well as in their (methodological) framework and implementation, e.g. there are differences in the analysis periods, the number of seeded addresses, the number and kind of locations used, and the categories considered. This must be taken into account when comparing results. All studies share the result that the extent to which e-mail addresses are harvested and misused for spamming is considerable. This significance stresses the necessity of preventing or reducing the harvesting of e-mail addresses placed on the Internet and motivates both the development of address-obfuscating techniques and (the deployment of a framework which supports) empirical studies which serve as a "controlling instrument".

7.3 A methodology and honeypot conceptualization

An empirical analysis of the usage of e-mail addresses that are seeded on the Internet, such as those described in Sect. 7.2, is usually realized by using a honeypot. In this case, the conceptualization of the honeypot belongs to the methodology which aims at the systematical guiding of the implementation of such an empirical analysis. Regarding the planning of the analysis, the author assumes the following methodological issues to be the most important ones:

1. the determination of the analysis' goals including the questions to be addressed,
2. the selection of appropriate Internet locations as well as e-mail addresses to be seeded,
3. the development of proper data and database models,
4. the conceptualization of the honeypot's IT infrastructure, and
5. the selection and application of evaluation procedures that address the analysis' goals.

It is especially items 2 and 3, for which some kinds of generic "frameworks" seem to be appropriate. Therefore, these items are worked out in the following two subsections. The other items are exemplified in Sect. 7.4, where the prototypic implementation of an empirical study is described.

7.3.1 A framework for seeding e-mail addresses

Internet locations can be categorized by the use of the dimensions "service", "language", and "topic", as illustrated in Fig. 7.2.

There is a broad range of services, which include e-mail addresses and which are open to harvesters in principle (see Subsect. 4.3.1), such as web pages, chats, and newsgroups. Regarding the placement of e-mail addresses,

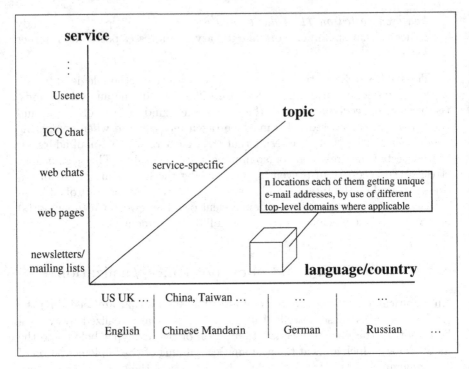

Fig. 7.2: Categories of Internet locations

the services differ in many ways. For example, web pages permissively allow the seeding of textual e-mail addresses as well as addresses which are embedded in a graphic (here referred to as the "representation form" of an e-mail address), whereas newsletters and mailing lists are limited to textual addresses, and administrators of some newsgroups do not permit the placement of e-mail addresses in the body of an article at all. A further dimension is spanned by the languages and countries involved in the empirical study. The Internet locations can also be categorized according to the topic they are dedicated to. The classification of web pages and newsletter/mailing lists, for example, can follow any e-business classification (for example, possible topics are "education", "auctions", "logistics" etc.). Newsgroups can be classified according to the topics they are dedicated to and which are reflected in the newsgroup's name. Depending on the study's objectives, it might be desirable to define the topics service-specifically. After defining the categories for address placement, one or several locations per category can be selected. Finally, the type of addresses to be seeded has to be defined. This relates to the e-mail addresses' top-level domain as well as to the representation form of the address. In order to trace back spam e-mails, it is necessary to use unique e-mail addresses which are, ideally, invisible to users and thus transparent to harvesters only.

7.3.2 Data(base) models for storing e-mails

E-mails can be stored in flat files, such as used on e-mail servers, or, more structured, in databases, the latter option facilitating data analysis. Because data analysis is the primary goal of the empirical analysis of the abuse of e-mail addresses, a database model is proposed in this subsection. According to database theory, first, a semantic data model ought to be designed before the database model is created. The rest of this subsection follows this procedure by presenting an object-oriented data model, an equivalent relational data model, and a relational database model. The development of these two equivalent data models is driven by the goal to support the use of databases that follow one of the two currently most important modeling paradigms: structural modeling and object-oriented modeling. The representation of a relational database model is due to the fact that such a model was chosen for storing e-mails in the prototypic implementation of an empirical study.

The object-oriented data model

Modeling the structure and the content of Internet e-mails is not a straight-forward procedure, as different modeling issues which are partially opposed to each other have to be addressed: simplicity, completeness, correctness, and practice-orientation. As the class model below is intended to address spam issues, all compromises as well as the level of abstraction were made in favor of adequately covering spam issues. The modeling language used for the representation of the object-oriented data model is UML 2.0.

The basic structure and content of an Internet message (e-mail) is specified with the Internet standard Request for Comments (RFC) [142]. An e-mail consists of header fields (collectively called "the header of the message") followed, optionally, by a body. Many other Internet standards have emerged, which extend RFC 2822 and, except for one exemption, are obviously relevant to spam (see below). These are not regarded in detail, or not at all in this model. If necessary, they have to be integrated into this model later. RFC 2076 [130] and its updated, but not yet standardized version [131] compile information from other e-mail-related RFCs and also integrate a few commonly occurring e-mail parts which are not defined in RFCs.

In particular, no security aspects are regarded in the basic model, as no spam e-mail observed by the author featured any security item, e.g. not included are: Secure MIME (S/MIME) [139], Open Pretty Good Privacy (PGP) [19], and Privacy Enhancement for Internet Electronic Mail (PEM) [100, 91, 11, 89].

As RFC 2822 was designed to send only plain text e-mails with ASCII symbols, thus excluding any binary documents, e.g. executable files, pictures, videos, and compressed files, from being attached, the Internet community has accepted the Multipurpose Internet Mail Extensions (MIME) standard, as specified in RFCs 2045-2049 [61, 62, 109, 63, 60] as extension; these RFCs have been updated – but not obsoleted – by several RFCs, only some of which are relevant in this context and are mentioned below. The MIME e-mail extension is the exemption mentioned above. Since malfunctioning codes, like viruses, worms and Trojan horses are often attached to (spam) e-mails using MIME, it is important to consider this in the modeling process. RFC 2045 specifies the various headers used to describe the structure of MIME messages. The second document, RFC 2046, defines the general structure of the MIME media typing system and defines an initial set of media types. The third document, RFC 2047, describes extensions to RFC 2822 to allow non-US-ASCII text data in Internet mail header fields. For completeness, but beyond the scope of our modeling purposes, the remaining documents are mentioned: The fourth document, RFC 2048, specifies various IANA registration procedures for MIME-related facilities. The fifth and final document, RFC 2049, describes MIME conformance criteria and provides some illustrative examples of MIME message formats, acknowledgements, and the bibliography.

Figure 7.3 gives a comprehensive view of the static model of e-mail data flowing through the Internet. It is described with a top-down approach.

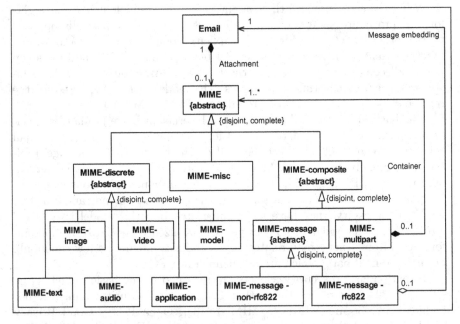

Fig. 7.3: Class diagram of e-mail (related) data

The class *E-mail* models an e-mail as we can see it, with an e-mail client excluding all MIME attachments. As sketched above, the MIME standard extends the Internet Message Format by redefining the format of messages to allow for

1. textual message bodies in character sets other than US-ASCII,
2. an extensible set of different formats for non-textual message bodies,
3. multi-part message bodies, and
4. textual header information in character sets other than US-ASCII.

An e-mail can contain a MIME attachment modeled with the abstract class *MIME*, thus the cardinality is a $(0 \dots 1)$ one. In the spam context each MIME attachment is strongly linked to its associated e-mail (environment). Thus, in this class model, the co-existence of an e-mail object is mandatory. RFC 2045 and RFC 2047 specify general, MIME type-independent details.

The MIME standard specifies eight top-level media types (RFC 2046 and RFC 2077 [116]) each of them featuring several subtypes. A current list of subtypes is provided by the IANA web page [82]. The six discrete top-level media types provide a standardized mechanism for tagging entities as *audio*, *image*, or several other kinds of data and are modeled as subclasses of the abstract class *MIME-discrete*. The composite *multipart* and *message* media types allow mixing and hierarchical structuring of entities of different types in a single message and are modeled as subclasses of the abstract class *MIME-composite*. The top-level media type *multipart* consists of one or more entities of independent data types and includes several other, nested MIME attachments thus involving a recursive structure. A MIME-multipart object is a container for one or more independent MIME objects. If a MIME object is part of a MIME-multipart object, then, in the present modeling context, this relationship is regarded as fix, in that the deletion of the MIME-multipart object results in the deletion of the nested MIME object; this kind of relationship is the same as that between the class *E-mail* and *MIME* (see above). The top-level media type *message* subsumes many possible message subtypes, including an e-mail message modeled with the class *MIME-message-rfc822*. All other subtypes are subsumed with the class *MIME-message-non-rfc822*. The subtype *rfc822* realizes the embedding of exactly one e-mail message and thus there is an aggregation relationship with the class *Email*; as an embedded e-mail can exist even if its embedding e-mail does not exist any more, no composition is used. Although RFC 2046 strongly discourages the use of non-standardized top level types, their occurrence cannot be excluded. As a precaution, these types are subsumed with the artificial top-level media type *MIME-misc*.

These MIME issues suggest a modeling with a class hierarchy. No further modeling of subtypes is included, as, in practice, subtypes are added quite dynamically and the model would, thus, soon become obsolete.

The classes shown in Fig. 7.3 are now described in more detail, whereas the modeling is based on the following understanding:

☐ It is pragmatic to renounce modeling get()- and set()-methods, as all attributes are practically accessible and writable for every e-mail node participating in the e-mail delivery process. Generally, no complex methods going beyond this type of access are used.

❑ The names of attributes are adopted from the RFCs mentioned above, where they are called *field name*.

❑ The types of attributes are adopted from the RFCs, too, where they are denoted as *field body*. In contrast to the RFC specification, where the types are described on a syntactic level in Augmented Backus-Naur Form (ABNF) [34], here, only the semantics are relevant and, thus, these are regarded as complex data types. It should be explicitly noted that the names of the complex data types are adopted from RFC 2822 but are meant to also include non-ASCII data (in encoded form), as specified in RFC 2047.

❑ Many attributes are conceptually read-only like "message-Id", but practically they are all writable by non-cooperating e-mail nodes. Thus, they are modeled as writable.

❑ RFC 2822 is in accordance with the *Internet Best Current Practice* for using specific key words in IETF documents [16]. One key word standardized in its meaning is "SHOULD BE". Each occurrence of this key word is realized as an attribute with optional content or as (0,1)-cardinality. RFCs 2045-2049 are interpreted in the same way.

❑ As all e-mail nodes have full access to all e-mail parts, all attributes are public. Pragmatically, any access symbol for access, like "+", is omitted.

Figure 7.4 illustrates how an e-mail is modeled (without any MIME attachments). The attributes and their semantics are not explained here, as they are commented on in detail in RFC 2822 [142]. Only some noteworthy issues are taken up here:

❑ According to RFC 2822 the attribute *from* is of the type *Mailbox-list*, thus containing one or more mailboxes, each of them looking like buffy@sunnydale.com. However, in practice, many e-mails and also spam e-mails do not only contain the mailboxes, but also the names of the attached holders, e.g. Buffy Summers <buffy@sunnydale.com>. Since, in RFC 2822, this structure is referred to as *address*, the type is changed into *Address-list*. For the same reason, this adaption is applied to the *sender* field.

❑ The fields *from* and *orig-date* and also *resent-from* and *resent-date* are mandatory in RFC 2822; the field *sender* is mandatory if *from* contains more than one entry. However, as spam e-mails have been observed to be non-compliant in this regard, these requirements are omitted.

❑ Some attributes with array types are labeled as *bag*. According to UML 2.0, this means that no order is intended. In contrast, the label *ordered* means the opposite.

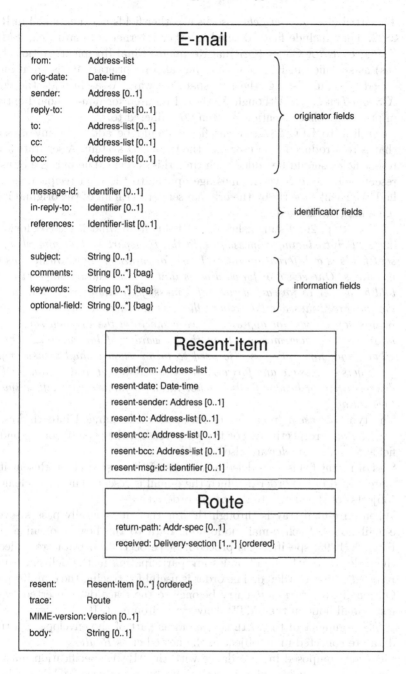

Fig. 7.4: Class diagram of an e-mail

❑ The attribute *optional-field* absorbs all other fields not mentioned in RFC 2822. They include fields defined in other Internet standards, e.g. SMTP Enhanced Error Codes (Original-Recipient, Final-Recipient, Action, Status) as specified in RFC2034 [58], but also proprietary fields often introduced with an *X-*, e.g. the anti-spam software Assassin adds the entry *X-Spam-Level: . . . .* Although *X-* should be used for non-standard entries, in practice, this convention is often not adhered to.

❑ According to RFC 2822, resent fields should be added to any message that is reintroduced by a user into the transport system. A separate set of resent fields should be added each time this is done. The purpose of using resent fields is to have the message appear to the final recipient as if it had been sent directly by the original sender, with all of the original fields remaining unchanged.

RFC 2822, p. 26, distinguishes resent fields from what is called "forwarding": *"Reintroducing a message into the transport system and using resent fields is a different operation from 'forwarding'. 'Forwarding' has two meanings: One sense of forwarding is that a mail reading program can be told by a user to forward a copy of a message to another person, making the forwarded message the body of the new message. A forwarded message in this sense does not appear to have come from the original sender, but is an entirely new message from the forwarder of the message. On the other hand, forwarding is also used to mean when a mail transport program gets a message and forwards it on to a different destination for final delivery. Resent header fields are not intended for use with either type of forwarding."*

The type of *resent-from* and *resent-sender* are changed into *Addresslist* and *Address*, respectively. For the same reason, the type of corresponding fields *from* and *sender* are also altered.

Sets of resent fields – modeled as objects of the nested class Resent-item – are added in the order in which the e-mail is resent. Thus, the elements (objects) of the attribute *resent* are ordered.

❑ When an e-mail travels through the Internet, it generally passes several e-mail nodes. Each e-mail node adds data to the header of an e-mail; RFC 2821 [93] specifies this procedure (see Sect. 3.1). Data are added in the order in which e-mail nodes are participating in the delivery, so the *received* data are ordered. The order is useful for tracing the e-mail's path. Optionally, a *return-path* entry belongs to the trace data inserted by the last e-mail node in the SMTP delivery environment. It gets the <*reverse-path*> argument of the MAIL command as part of the envelope. All trace data are collected in an object of the nested class *Route*.

❑ Messages composed in accordance with the MIME specification must include a header field giving information about the used MIME-version if any: currently the actual version number is 1.0. Due to the modeling of MIME-objects with a recursive structure, the attribute MIME-version is

part of the class *E-mail* although it is specified in the MIME specification
and not in RFC 2822.

☐ The (optional) body of an e-mail contains its actual content. If no mime-
extension is used, then the body can be used to contain US-ASCII characters modeled with an attribute *body* of type *String* here. If the content
is included in an attached MIME document, then the attribute must not
be used.

An example of an *E-mail* object is given by the object diagram in Fig. 7.5,
which represents a real world spam e-mail with an attached MIME document,
which the author received. For simplicity, a middle part of the delivery path
stored in the attribute *received* was cut out.

The MIME classes are modeled in accordance with the RFCs mentioned above including RFC 2183 [180] which adds the header field *content-
disposition* (see Fig. 7.6). Regarding the procedures for the coding and decoding of attached media documents from their natural format into 7bit US-
ASCII format and vice versa respectively, the reader is referred to RFC 2045.

Again, attributes and their semantics are not explained in detail here.
The interested reader is referred to the MIME RFCs. However, some issues
are worth being mentioned:

☐ In order to also cover those spam e-mails featuring non-standardized subtypes, the attribute *content-subtype* should also be able to catch up unknown subtypes.

☐ Due to the heterogeneity of a media document included as a MIME attachment, the type *MediaDocument* can be interpreted and stored flexibly
as a Binary Large Object (BLOB).

☐ The absence of a content-type header usually indicates that the corresponding body has a content-type of *text/plain; charset=US-ASCII*. This
default rule is modeled with default values for the attribute *content-type*
in class *MIME* and the attributes *content-subtype* and *parameters* in class
MIME-text.

☐ As class *MIME-composite* has no attributes – it was integrated only for di-
dactic reasons, as RFC 2045 distinguishes between discrete and composite
top-level media types – this class is skipped over here.

☐ The top-level media type *message* subsumes many quite different forms
of messages, including e-mail messages and *News* articles. Dependent on
the subtype, there are different fields and, thus, different attributes in the
corresponding classes. From this point of view it makes sense to model all
the message subtypes defined by IANA with their own classes. However, as
spam e-mails are unlikely to use the top-level media type *message* heavily, modeling renounces on this in favor of simplicity. Consequently, the
modeling abstracts from the fact that subtypes of *message* often impose
restrictions on what encodings are allowed.

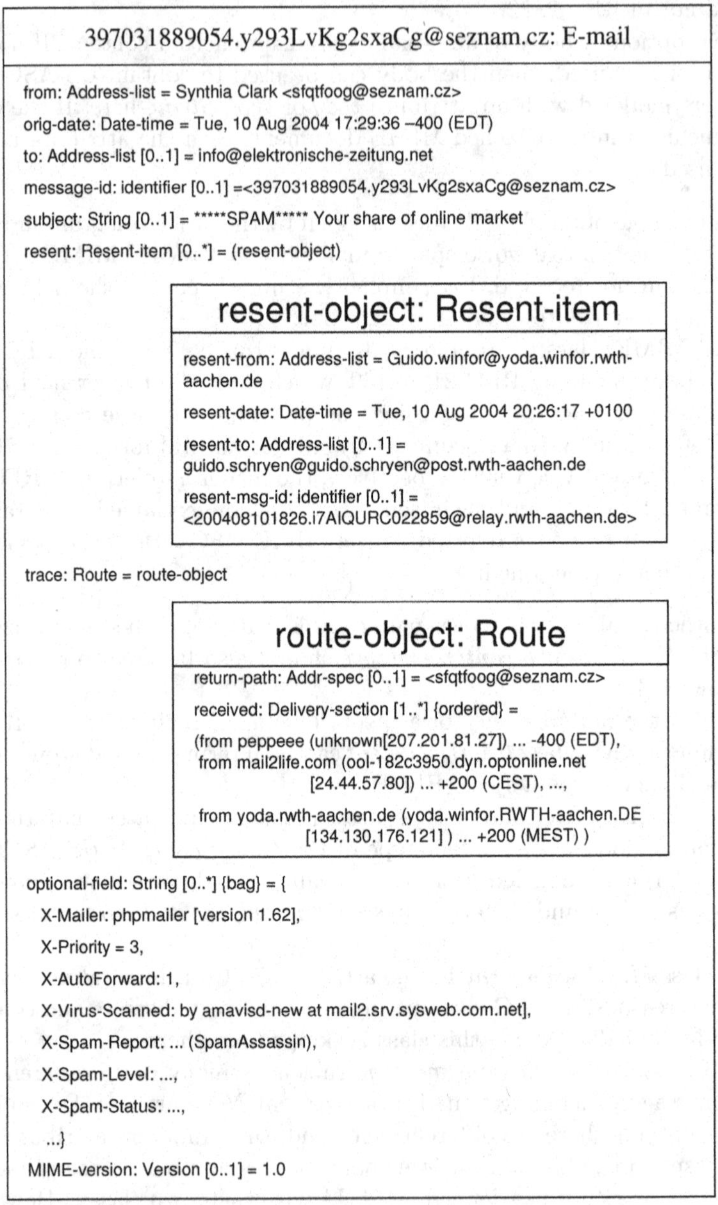

397031889054.y293LvKg2sxaCg@seznam.cz: E-mail

from: Address-list = Synthia Clark <sfqtfoog@seznam.cz>

orig-date: Date-time = Tue, 10 Aug 2004 17:29:36 –400 (EDT)

to: Address-list [0..1] = info@elektronische-zeitung.net

message-id: identifier [0..1] =<397031889054.y293LvKg2sxaCg@seznam.cz>

subject: String [0..1] = *****SPAM***** Your share of online market

resent: Resent-item [0..*] = (resent-object)

resent-object: Resent-item

resent-from: Address-list = Guido.winfor@yoda.winfor.rwth-aachen.de

resent-date: Date-time = Tue, 10 Aug 2004 20:26:17 +0100

resent-to: Address-list [0..1] = guido.schryen@guido.schryen@post.rwth-aachen.de

resent-msg-id: identifier [0..1] = <200408101826.i7AlQURC022859@relay.rwth-aachen.de>

trace: Route = route-object

route-object: Route

return-path: Addr-spec [0..1] = <sfqtfoog@seznam.cz>

received: Delivery-section [1..*] {ordered} =

(from peppeee (unknown[207.201.81.27]) ... -400 (EDT),
from mail2life.com (ool-182c3950.dyn.optonline.net
      [24.44.57.80]) ... +200 (CEST), ...,

from yoda.rwth-aachen.de (yoda.winfor.RWTH-aachen.DE
      [134.130.176.121]) ... +200 (MEST))

optional-field: String [0..*] {bag} = {

X-Mailer: phpmailer [version 1.62],

X-Priority = 3,

X-AutoForward: 1,

X-Virus-Scanned: by amavisd-new at mail2.srv.sysweb.com.net],

X-Spam-Report: ... (SpamAssassin),

X-Spam-Level: ...,

X-Spam-Status: ...,

...}

MIME-version: Version [0..1] = 1.0

Fig. 7.5: Object diagram of an (spam) e-mail

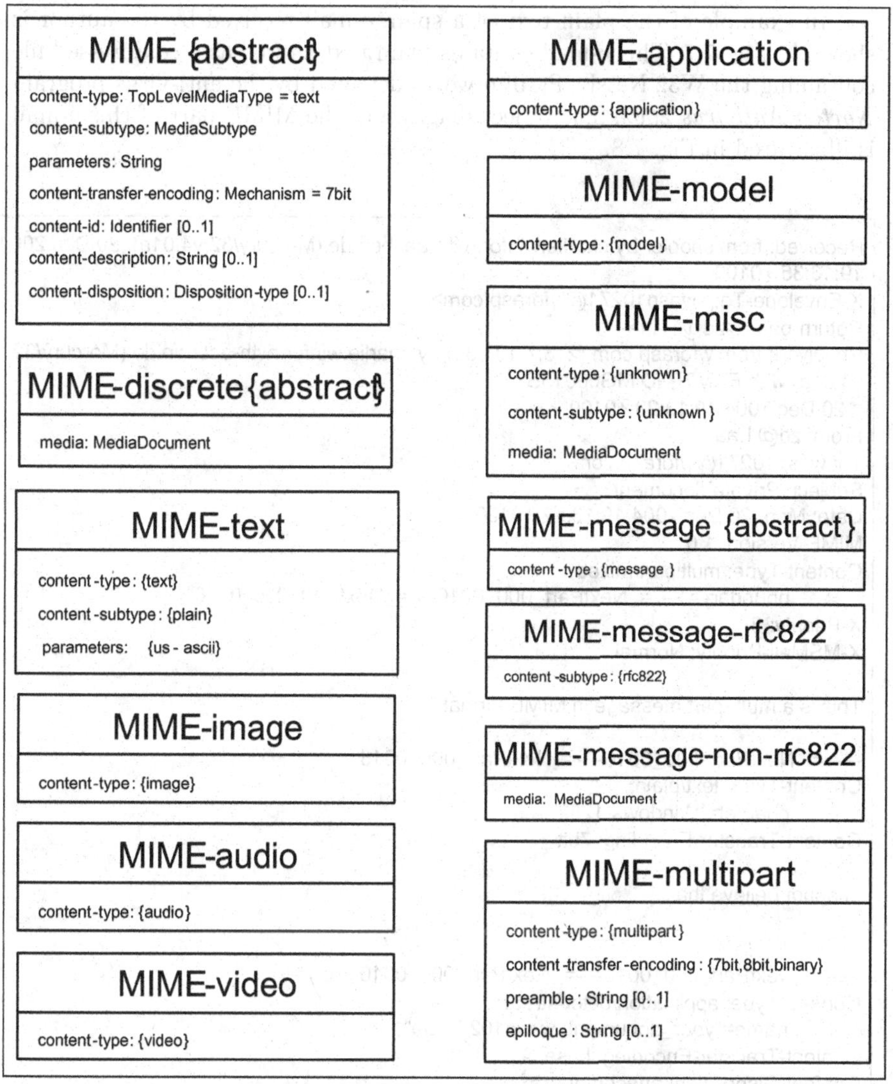

Fig. 7.6: Class diagrams of MIME attachments

An example of the plain text of a spam e-mail received by the author is shown in Fig. 7.7. This e-mail contains plain text as well as a compressed file containing the W32.Netsky.P@mm worm detected by the anti-virus program *Norton Antivirus 2004*. The object diagram of the MIME-part of this e-mail is illustrated in Fig. 7.8.

```
Received: from spooler by charlie.winfor.rwth-aachen.de (Mercury/32 v4.01a); 20 Dec 2004
19:13:35 +0100
X-Envelope-To: <wasp10271@wforasp.com>
Return-path: <zd@1.aa>
Received: from wforasp.com (213.7.193.30) by charlie.winfor.rwth-aachen.de (Mercury/32
v4.01a) with ESMTP ID MG00013B;
    20 Dec 2004 19:13:23 +0100
From: zd@1.aa
To: wasp10271@wforasp.com
Subject: Private document
Date: Mon, 20 Dec 2004 19:13:12 +0100
MIME-Version: 1.0
Content-Type: multipart/mixed;
        boundary="----=_NextPart_000_0016----=_NextPart_000_0016"
X-Priority: 3
X-MSMail-Priority: Normal

This is a multi-part message in MIME format.

------=_NextPart_000_0016----=_NextPart_000_0016
Content-Type: text/plain;
        charset="Windows-1252"
Content-Transfer-Encoding: 7bit

I cannot believe that.


------=_NextPart_000_0016----=_NextPart_000_0016
Content-Type: application/octet-stream;
        name="your_document_wasp10271.zip"
Content-Transfer-Encoding: base64
Content-Disposition: attachment;
        filename="your_document_wasp10271.zip"

UEsDBAoAAAAAAePlDGjiB3egHMAAIBzAABUAAAAZGV0YWIscy50eHQgICAgICAgICAgIC
Ag
...
LnBpZIBLBQYAAAAAQABAIIAAADycwAAAAA=

------=_NextPart_000_0016----=_NextPart_000_0016--
```

Fig. 7.7: *Plain text of a spam e-mail with a MIME-multipart attachment containing a worm*

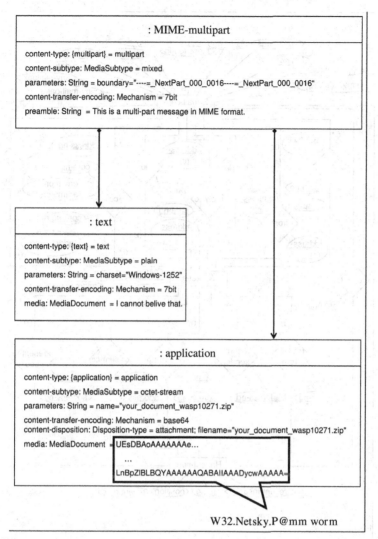

Fig. 7.8: *Object diagram of a spam e-mail with a MIME-multipart attachment containing a worm*

The relational data model

The relational data model is presented by using Entity Relationship Diagrams (ERDs). The ERDs in the Figs. 7.9 and 7.10 correspond to the class diagrams of e-mails and MIME attachments (see Figs. 7.4 and 7.6).

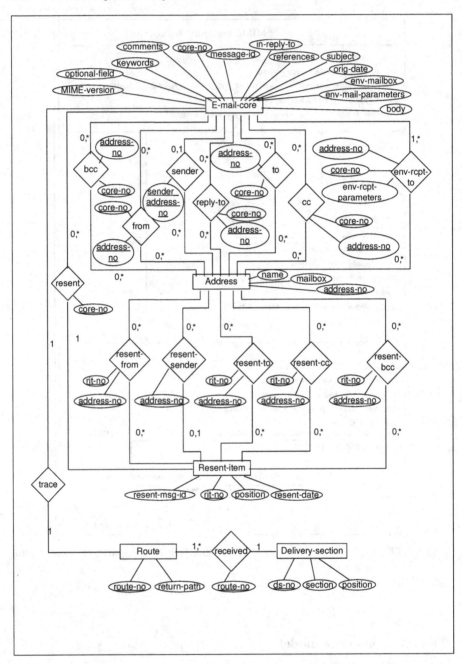

Fig. 7.9: Entity-relationship diagram corresponding to class E-mail

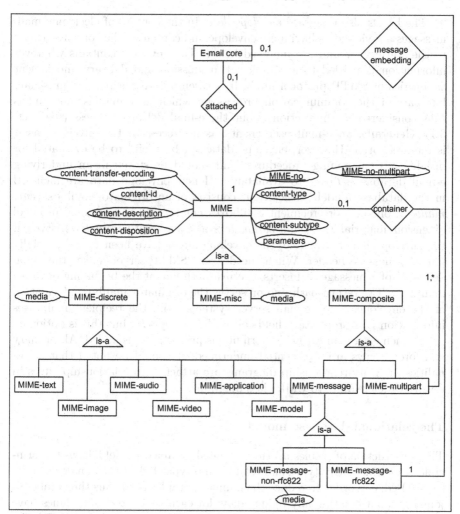

Fig. 7.10: Entity-relationship diagram corresponding to MIME classes

The ERDs also integrate *envelope data*. In the context of electronic mail, messages are viewed as having an envelope and contents. The contents belong to the static view and are modeled below. The envelope contains whatever information is needed to accomplish transmission and delivery and is sent as a series of SMTP protocol units. It is essentially not a part of an e-mail, but part of the communication process by which an e-mail is sent and is thus considered in the section about the e-mail delivery process (see Sect. 3.1). Generally, an e-mail user client has no access to the envelope, as it is removed prior. However, envelope data can be useful to be evaluated for insights into spamming procedures, and should be stored in an underlying e-mail database subject to availability. Hence, envelope data are included in the database model. Basically, it consists of an originator mailbox (*env-mailbox*), one or more recipient mailboxes *env-rcpt-to*, and optional protocol extension material (*env-mail-parameters* and *env-rcpt-parameters*). Even if the envelope is not available, the envelope might have been folded partially into the message header: When the delivery SMTP server makes the "final delivery" of a message, it inserts a return-path line at the beginning of the e-mail data. The return-path line preserves the originator mailbox information of the envelope. Some e-mail server systems store the recipient mailboxes information in a proprietary field called *X-Envelope-To*, but this is optional.

To each entity, an artificial attribute as primary key is added. All primary and foreign keys are represented underlined. It should be noted that cardinalities in entity-relationship diagrams are attached to relationship edges in reverse order relative to UML class diagrams.

The relational database model

The construction of (tables in) the relational database model follows the principle of melting entity types and relationship types linked with an edge $(0, 1)$- or $(1, 1)$-edge in order to reduce the number of tables (and thus the number of joins) without creating any redundancy; for each $(0, 1)$-edge null values have to be regarded. This can be done by explicitly allowing the value "NULL". For the same reason, transforming all MIME entity types and MIME relationship types results in one table. Consequently, a MIME-multipart entry must not contain a value in the *media* column, i.e. the column entry must be *NULL*. The table *Mime* also contains an attribute *mime-nr-multipart* which stores the MIME number of the parent (multipart) MIME entry, if available. The attribute *core-nr* realizes the *message embedding* relationship, i.e. it stores the *core-nr* of the embedded message, if the MIME *content-type* is *message/rfc822*. Table 7.1 shows the relational database model that can be used for storing (spam) e-mails.

Table 7.1: Relational database model for storing e-mails

Tables	Attributes
E-mail-core	core-no, orig-date, message-id, in-reply-to, references, subject, comments , keywords, optional-field, mime-version, body, return-path, sender_address-no, mime-no, env-mailbox, env-mail-parameters
Address	address-no, mailbox, name
Resent-item	rit-no, resent-msg-id, resent-date, position, core-no, address-no
Delivery-section	ds-no, section, position, core-no
Env-rcpt-to	core-no, address-no, env-rcpt-parameters
From	core-no, address-no
Reply-to	core-no, address-no
To	core-no, address-no
Cc	core-no, address-no
Bcc	core-no, address-no
Resent-from	rit-no, address-no
Resent-to	rit-no, address-no
Resent-cc	rit-no, address-no
Resent-bcc	rit-no, address-no
Mime	mime-no, content-type, content-subtype, parameters, content-transfer-encoding, content-id, content-description, content-disposition, media, mime-no-multipart, core-no

7.4 The prototypic implementation of an empirical study

This section describes the prototypic implementation of an empirical study of the abuse of e-mail addresses. The implementation follows the methodology and the honeypot conceptualization, as described in the previous section. The study's main objective is to assess, on a quantitative basis, the extent of the current harassment and its development over time. The presented "framework" is intended to be extensible to measuring the effectiveness of address-obfuscating techniques. First, the study's specific goals and the seeding of e-mail addresses are described in Subsect. 7.4.1. Then, in Subsect. 7.4.2, an adaptation of the database model is presented. The honeypot's IT infrastructure is shown in Subsect. 7.4.3. Finally, in Subsect. 7.4.4, the findings of the empirical study are illustrated.

7.4.1 The goals and the conceptualization of the seeding

The specific goals of the empirical study that was conducted comprise the determination of

- ❑ the relative and absolute attractiveness of particular Internet services,
- ❑ the development of e-mail addresses' attractiveness over time,
- ❑ the relevance of an e-mail address' top level domain,
- ❑ differences in the seeding of addresses at language-specific locations, and
- ❑ the relationship between the content of e-mails and the locations on which the recipients' addresses were placed.

The last issue addresses the question of to which extent spammers have already shifted from simply employing used e-mail addresses towards acquiring addresses of users likely to be interested (specific marketing). It should be mentioned explicitly that the implementation of address obfuscating techniques is beyond the scope of the empirical study.

The main idea for getting spam e-mails is to place e-mail addresses on Internet locations, ensuring that each e-mail address is placed on, at most, one spot. This procedure allows the association of each spam e-mail with that particular Internet location on which the spam e-mail's recipient address was placed. According to the framework for seeding e-mail addresses (see Subsect. 7.3.1), (types of) Internet locations have to be defined by considering the dimensions "service", "topic", and "language/country". Services included are US and German "web pages" and "newsletters", and German-speaking as well as English-speaking "Usenet groups". The topics of the first two services are listed in Table 7.2, and they follow the classification of e-business models according to Wirtz [189]. The topics and the names of the Usenet groups are listed in Table 7.3.

As illustrated in Fig. 7.2 (see p. 150), each location category is represented by a cube. In our study, each cube contains three locations, i.e. a location is a specific web side, newsletter, or newsgroup. Each location gets four addresses (one de- , one com-, one net-, and one org-address). Therefore, for each cube, 12 e-mail addresses had to be created and placed. Of course, each e-mail address must be unique, and must not be seeded more than once.

As thousands of e-mail addresses had to be created, these were generated automatically by using a random generator for the user part of the addresses. In order to prevent e-mail addresses from being guessed or generated with brute force attacks, it was necessary to define them randomly as well as to give them an appropriate number of characters. An example of an e-mail address that was created in this way is *wasp10208@wforasp.com*.

The specific Internet locations serving as lures were chosen manually, just as the placement of the e-mail addresses had to be implemented manually. As

Table 7.2: Topics specific to the services "web pages" and "newsletters"

Class	Topic	Class	Topic
	personal web page	context	search engines, web catalogues
administration	departments, authorities, offices		meta search engines
	federations, unions	commerce	auctions
	social welfare organizations		payment
	churches, sects		logistics and transport
	associations, clubs		web portals
	educational institutions		shops, malls
content	information		finance, insurances
	entertainment		tourism
	education		jobs
	infotainment		motor vehicles
connection	discussion board		property
	peer-to-peer (not the service itself)		social contacts
	chats (not the service itself)		health
	greeting cards		gambling, lottery
	Internet providers		adult material
	community providers		(computer) hardware
	(content) mobile providers		software

soon as an e-mail address had been spread, its location and activation date
were stored.

7.4.2 The adaptation of the database model

For the sake of an extensive and efficient evaluation, in the prototypic implementation, the database model (see Subsect. 7.3.2) was modified as follows:

❑ The table "E-mail-core", which contains the core e-mail data, is extended
by columns for

  ◇ the IP address of the delivering host – the address can be extracted
     from the "received" entries –,
  ◇ the Top Level Domain (TLD) and the Second Level Domain (SLD) –
     these domains can be determined with reverse DNS lookups –,
  ◇ the name of the e-mail program that was used for sending the e-mail
     – the name of the e-mail program is extracted from the (optional)
     "x-mailer" field, but it can be spoofed, of course –,
  ◇ the number of MIME attachments broken down by the follow-
     ing types: "application/octet", "application/zip", "application/ps",

Table 7.3: Topics specific to the service "Usenet groups"

German-speaking	English-speaking
de.comp	alt.*
de.admin	comp .*
de.alt	free .*
de.comm	novell .*
de.etc	microsoft .*
de.markt	rec .*
de.rec	sci .*
de.sci	soc .*
de.soc	uk .*
de.talk	
de.org	
de.test	

*:several newsgroups in the corresponding category were selected

"application/pdf", "application/msword", other "application" subtypes, "audio", "image/jpeg", "image/gif", other "image" subtypes,
"message/rfc822", other "message" subtypes, "model", "text/plain",
"text/html", other "text" subtypes, and "video", and

◇ further data, such as data on embedded viruses and data on the blacklisting status of the delivering MTA.

❑ In order to simplify programming, the entity type "MIME-message-rfc822"
is linked to the entity type "Mime" and not, as the ERD in Fig. 7.10
indicates, to the entity type "E-mail core. Therefore, in the table "MIME",
the column "core-no" was replaced by the column "mime-no-multipart".

7.4.3 The IT infrastructure of the honeypot

An e-mail server was set up, namely *charlie.winfor.rwth-aachen.de*, and three
domains were reserved – *wforasp.com, wforasp.net*, and *wforasp.org* – for covering the e-mail addresses of four top level domains. All e-mails addressed to
these domains are directed to this e-mail server.

Each incoming e-mail was classified either as a regular e-mail (ham e-
mail), e.g. regular newsletters or such containing comments from users of
discussion forums, or as a spam e-mail. This procedure was mainly executed
by humans but supported by an e-mail parser (written in the script language
"PHP"), which used increasing whitelists and blacklists. A second task of the
e-mail parser was to decompose each incoming e-mail: all entries of the header

and the content were analyzed, as was the (MIME) structure of the body. Next, the e-mails' elements were stored in a (MySQL) database; spam and ham e-mails were stored into separate databases. As many spam e-mails are not RFC-compliant, the parser's robustness against RFC violations was one of the implementation goals. Simple data analysis was undertaken by using SQL queries, whereas more complex procedures were conducted by the use of Microsoft Excel. Figure 7.11 provides an overview of the IT infrastructure of the honeypot.

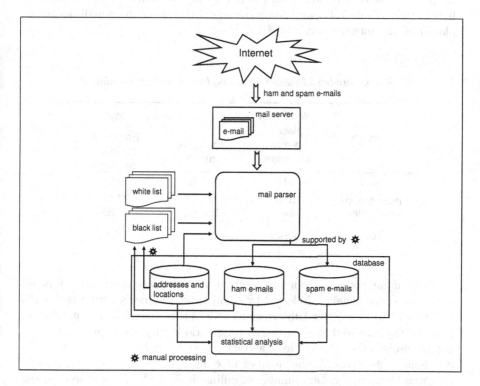

Fig. 7.11: The infrastructure of the e-mail honeypot

A detailed description of the pre-evaluation process that parses, classifies, and stores e-mails into the databases is given by the Figs. A.1 and A.2 in Appendix A.

7.4.4 Empirical results and conclusions

The total number of e-mails received on the honeypot is 57,273, 47% (26,882) of which is spam. Of all spam e-mails received on the e-mail server, 69.9% (18,792) result from placements on the Internet (denoted as honeypot spam e-mails), whereas the others – directed to addresses which have never been generated and which have been placed nowhere, such as *admin@wforasp.com* – are due to spammers' guessing attempts, e.g. by the use of brute force or dictionary attacks. The number of placed e-mail addresses and their respective residence periods underlying this evaluation differ between the Internet services; only e-mails received before January 31 2006, 12pm MET have been considered. The average time period for e-mail addresses placed on the web is almost a year, as is the time period for addresses used for newsletter subscriptions. The time period related to newsgroup placements is approximately half of that. Table 7.4 shows some statistical details of the e-mail addresses placed on the Internet services.

Table 7.4: Number of placed e-mail addresses and their online days

Service	Number of placed e-mail addresses	Numer of online days	
		Empirical mean	Empirical standard deviation
web	917	318.99	75.66
newsgroups	390	186.38	37.17
newsletters	848	361.62	67.39
Total	2,155	--	--

Most honeypot spam e-mails result from web placements (62.3% of all honeypot spam e-mails), followed by spam caused by newsgroup placements (6.3%) and to newsletter subscriptions (1.27%). However, as the number of placed e-mails as well as their online time periods vary, these proportions do not precisely reflect the services' attractiveness for harvesters. To take these two issues into account, the number of e-mails received on each service is weighted by using the total number of online days of all e-mails placed on the corresponding service. Let $sp_i, i \in \{w, ng, nl\} =: S$ be the number of spam e-mails received on placements on the service **web**, **newsgroups**, and **newsletters** (see below), and let $od_i, i \in S$ be the total number of online days of all e-mail addresses placed on service i. Then, the weighted number of received spam e-mails is calculated by

$$sp_i' := sp_i \times \frac{\sum_{j \in S} od_j}{od_i} \qquad (7.1)$$

The computation in (7.1) is time-invariant in that all online days are equally weighted. Table 7.5 shows the results which indicate that web placements attract more than two-thirds (70%) of all honeypot spam e-mails, followed by newsgroup placements (28.6%) and newsletter subscriptions (1.4%) – the latter hardly leading to the receiving of spam e-mails. Language-specific proportions do not considerably differ from the proportions in total.

Table 7.5: Empirical statistics for the service- and language-specific abuse of e-mail address placements

Service i	Language	sp_i	od_i	$od_i / \sum_{j \in S} od_j$ [a]	sp'_i [a]	$sp'_i / \sum_{j \in S} sp'_j$ [a]
web	German	5,478	156,212	42.77%	12,807	63.81%
	English	11,270	136,302	45.45%	25,356	69.73%
	Total	16,748	292,514	43.54%	38,468	70.01%
newsgroups	German	965	51,520	14.11%	6,840	34.09%
	English	737	21,170	6.90%	10,676	29.36%
	Total	1,702	72,690	10.82%	15,731	28.63%
newsletters	German	182	157,468	43.12%	422	2.10%
	English	160	149,188	48.65%	329	0.91%
	Total	342	306,656	45.64%	749	1.36%
Total overall		18,792	671,860	--	--	--

Language-specific numbers refer to different (language-specific) main units.

[a] Due to different main units the number in a "total" row does not represent the sum or (weighted) average of the corresponding language-specific numbers.

The honeypot also allows the analyzing of the relevance of the e-mail address' top-level domain (TLD) to receiving spam. Table 7.6 shows the empirical data. Proportions do not have to be weighted according to online days, because, at each Internet location, one address of each TLD was placed at the same time. Trying to reject the null hypothesis that the empirical proportion

Table 7.6: Spam e-mails by top level domain of abused e-mail address

Top-level domain	Spam resulting from e-mail addresses placed		Spam resulting from e-mail addresses not placed	
	Quantity q_i	Proportion (%)	Quantity	Proportion (%)
de	3,833	20.45	155	1.92
com	6,147	32.80	507	6.27
net	5,117	27.30	609	7.53
org	3,645	19.45	6,815	84.28
total	18,742	--	8,086	--

of spam sent to e-mail addresses which were placed on the Internet follows a discrete uniform distribution we use the chi-square test. We compute

$$\chi^2 = \sum_{j=1}^{4} \frac{(q_i - 4688.5)^2}{4688.5} \approx 880.13 \qquad (7.2)$$

and compare this value with the 0.01 critical value from the chi square distribution with 3 degrees of freedom

$$\chi^2_{p=0.01,df=3} \approx 12.84. \qquad (7.3)$$

Because $\chi^2 > \chi^2_{p=0.01,df=3}$, the null hypothesis has to be rejected on significance level 0.01. Therefore we cannot assume the proportions to be uniformly distributed.

Interestingly, the empirical data regarding spam on e-mail addresses which were not placed on the Internet differ from the data considered above, in that spam e-mails directed to "org" addresses amount to almost 85%. Brute force and dictionary attacks seem to focus on e-mail addresses with the TLD "org". When we look at the extent to which e-mail addresses placed on the web have been flooded with spam, we find that more than 43% of addresses on the web have been abused, whereas about 27% was the case for addresses on newsgroups and only about 4% for addresses used for a newsletter subscription. Table 7.7 illustrates detailed data about this issue. The service instances, i.e. the names of websites, newsgroups and newsletters, where those e-mail addresses were placed, which attracted most spam e-mails, are listed in Appendix B together with the respective number of spam e-mails received.

Table 7.7: Extent, to which e-mail addresses have been abused

Service	Number of placed e-mail addresses	Number of abused e-mail addresses	Abuse proportion	Number of received spam e-mails				
				Min	Max	Mean	Median	Standard devitation
web	917	399	43.51%	1	829	41.97	9	96.88
newsgroups	390	106	27.15%	1	69	16.06	15.5	12.96
newsletters	848	35	4.13%	1	66	9.77	2	15.78

The development of e-mail addresses' attractiveness for spammers over time (see Fig. 7.12) can be analyzed by regression analysis; weeks without spam e-mails were omitted. We find a negative linear relationship for the service "web sites" with a coefficient of determination r^2 of approximately 0.86. The Pearson coefficient r is approximately -0.93, which strongly indicates a negative linear relationship. Assuming a negative exponential relationship for the service "newsgroups", we get a coefficient of determination of approximately 0.87. Performing a logarithmic transformation of the data, we again look for a negative linear relationship. The Pearson coefficient of the transformed data is approximately −0.96, which, then, finally supports strongly the assumption of a negative exponential relationship of the original data. A regression analysis for the service "newsletter" does not appear to be reasonable due to the low number of spam e-mails received (342 spam e-mails only).

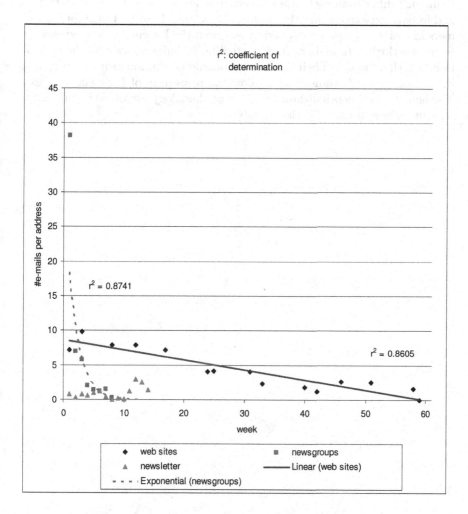

Fig. 7.12: Development of e-mail addresses' effectiveness for spammers over time

The honeypot also allows the checking of the relationship between a spam e-mail's topic and the topic of the location at which the recipient's address was placed. We manually checked 3,500 spam e-mails in "first come first served" order and found only 53 e-mails (1.54%) which shared a topic. Therefore, we suppose that spammers do not send their e-mails in a "context sensitive" manner.

The empirical results of the study presented in this chapter confirm the findings of previous studies, i.e. that particularly web pages and Usenet groups belong to the most vulnerable Internet spots regarding e-mail address harvesting. Although the detected extents to which addresses were misused for spamming differ from each other, Internet locations are still a very attractive and heavily exploited source for address harvesters. In order to hamper spammers in easily procuring e-mail addresses from the Internet at low expense, it seems worthwhile to elaborate on protection techniques, such as those mentioned in this chapter. Their deployment should be continuously accompanied by honeypot-based studies which allow the measuring of their effectiveness. The honeypot conceptualization and the methodology presented in this chapter can serve as a basis for these studies.

8

Summary and outlook

This work is about spam e-mails, which are just one type of spam that we face in electronic communication. Other types are related to SMS, chats, or Internet phone (Spam over IP Telephony), but issues relating to these are beyond the scope of this work.

Although "spam" is a buzzword in today's scientific and other media press, no homogeneous understanding exists of what precisely spam is. We follow the understanding that spam is unsolicited (electronic) bulk e-mail (UBE), which is referred to as unsolicited commercial e-mail (UCE) if the spam features a commercial nature. Most studies share the findings that spam already amounts to more than 50% of all worldwide e-mails, that most spam is relayed by hosts residing in the US or in Asia, and that most spam consists of commercial advertising. However, commercial advertising is just one category of spam; others are related to non-commercial advertising, fraud and phishing, hoaxes and chain e-mails, Joe jobs, and malware.

Spam has crossed the borderline between simply being annoying for private users and causing significant economic harm. The worldwide economic harm caused by spam is estimated at hundreds of billion USD per year. The most significant types of harm are the loss of (employees') productivity, costs for spam-related staff, infrastructure costs, download costs, harm through malicious payload, legal fees, and opportunity costs (for example, the loss of revenue), the loss of reputation, communication and marketing costs, and harm through fraud.

Although many different anti-spam measures have evolved and are currently deployed, they are low-effective, and spammers still manage to bypass anti-spam measures. What is still lacking, is a systematic assessment of the capabilities of single measures. The analysis would also provide support for (the development of) holistic anti-spam measures, which cover all options for sending spam e-mails. Complimentary to this functional-oriented view, we also identify the need for data-oriented research: Valid e-mail addresses are among the most valuable resources for spammers. Although it is known that spammers procure valid e-mail addresses by harvesting the Internet, only little is known about the quantitative properties of e-mail address abuse on the Internet and how to measure this.

This work aims at bridging these gaps by providing

❏ a comprehensive overview of behavioral, legislative, organizational and technological (including economic) anti-spam measures,

❏ a methodological framework for the empirical analysis of the abuse of e-mail addresses and its application for determining the extent of the current abuse,

❏ a methodological framework for the model-driven analysis of (the effectiveness of) technological anti-spam measures and its application for determining the effectiveness of proposed anti-spam measures, and

❏ a technological and organizational infrastructure framework that allows the holistic coverage of spamming options.

A graphical overview of the different parts of this work and their dependencies is given in Fig. 8.1.

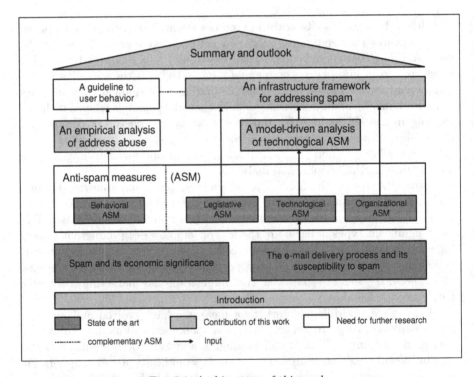

Fig. 8.1: Architecture of this work

We now summarize our findings with regard to the single contributions of our work, which are mentioned above.

Anti-spam measures

Many different anti-spam measures have evolved and are currently deployed. Laws and regulations, organizational approaches implementing different kinds of cooperation, behavioral measures, economic measures, and technological measures provide today's most important anti-spam leverages. They address three conditions: motivation, capability, and permission. Motivation and capability are mandatory for bulk e-mailers. The third condition refers to the legal permission some bulk mailers are grasping at in order to avoid litigation.

The authorities of some countries and federal states have started to address spam by legislation. However, today's world-wide legislative coverage of unsolicited bulk e-mail is heterogeneous, and no legislation information is available for large parts of the world, such as Africa, the Middle East, large parts of Asia, and Latin America. Countries with an anti-spam legislation mainly address commercial e-mails. When comparing the world-wide legislation with those countries that are responsible for more than 50% of all e-mails that were classified as spam, we find that these countries, namely USA, China, Republic of Korea, and Russia, either have a non-restrictive law, such as an opt-out law, or have no anti-spam laws at all. Countries with opt-in rules, such as those that implemented the European Directive 2002/58/EC, were found to play only minor roles in sending spam. This indicates that opt-in laws have a positive effect on spamming whereas opt-out laws are scarcely prohibitive.

Organizational measures comprise abuse systems, which are intended to help the Internet community to report and control network abuse and abusive users. Ideally, spammers are identified and duly prosecuted. Organizational measures also include forms of international cooperation, such as bilateral government-to-government cooperation, cooperation between private sector groups, government-to-private sector cooperation, and multilateral cooperation.

Behavioral measures aim at e-mail users' procedures in using and distributing their e-mail addresses and dealing with any spam e-mails that they receive. Locations and services that seem to deserve protection are newsgroups, mailing lists and newsletters, web pages, chat services and chat rooms, and address books and e-mails residing on users' hosts. For protecting e-mail addresses from being harvested, many approaches have been proposed, including the usage of throw-away e-mail aliases and address obscuring/obfuscating techniques. These approaches may help obscure addresses as long as spammers' harvesters are not trained to deal with the most frequently deployed hiding techniques. However, they are of limited use where e-mail addresses cannot be obscured arbitrarily.

A vast set of technological anti-spam measures, including the implementation of economic measures, has been proposed and deployed. These can be classified according to the stage of the e-mail delivery process at which they are applied, according to whether they can be applied independently of the route the e-mail took through the Internet, functionally, and according to the time and effort their respective deployment takes. This work follows a functional classification, which differentiates between

- ❏ IP blocking (a server decides to accept or reject an e-mail on the basis of the IP address of the e-mail client),
- ❏ filtering (a server classifies an e-mail as spam e-mail or ham e-mail on the basis of e-mail content and/or IP connection data),
- ❏ TCP blocking (blocking of outgoing TCP port 25, to which e-mails are usually directed to),
- ❏ authentication (including SMTP extensions, cryptographic authentication proposals, and path authentication proposals),
- ❏ verification (challenge-response procedures),
- ❏ payment-based approaches (these rely on e-mail systems to create economic disincentives to spam; the mode of payment could be CPU time or memory capacity as well as real-world currencies or virtual currencies),
- ❏ the limitation of outgoing e-mails (rate limits on outbound e-mail traffic),
- ❏ address obscuring techniques (including virtual channels, extended e-mail addresses, and single-purpose addresses), and
- ❏ reputation-based approaches (a server accepts or rejects e-mails on the basis of the reputation of the sender and/or the SO).

A model-driven analysis of the effectiveness of technological anti-spam measures

In order to address the theoretical effectiveness of (route-specific) technological anti-spam approaches, we model the Internet e-mail infrastructure as a directed graph. This graph is used to formally derive – by means of automata theory, including regular expressions – and categorize all existing delivery routes that a spam e-mail may take (spamming options) and that any holistic anti-spam measure would need to cover. The route-specific anti-spam measures are analyzed relative to covering the spamming options (see Table 8.1, in which an "x" indicates effective coverage and a blank space indicates the impossibility thereof).

When summing up the effectiveness of the anti-spam measures, it must be stressed that no anti-spam measure is currently capable of effectively stopping those spam deliveries that take advantage of ESP infrastructures (scenario V). The main problems are third party exploits and that it is all too easy for spammers to set up e-mail accounts automatically. The former is a plague that is becoming more acute as botnets – networks of compromised and remotely controlled machines – flourish among spammers. However, the model-driven analysis of the effectiveness of (route-specific) anti-spam measures gives valuable hints on how to integrate them in a modified e-mail infrastructure that covers all spamming options. We propose such an infrastructure.

Table 8.1: *Effectiveness of (route-specific) anti-spam measures*

Scenario	Regular expression	Nodes involved	IP blocking	TCP blocking	SMTP extensions	Cryptographic authentication	Path authentication	Limitation of outgoing e-mails	Reputation-based
I	d (k ∨ ff*k) ∨ ff*k	MTAs of provider	x						x
II	(d ∨ Λ)(ff*gg*k) ∨ dgg*k	MTA of provider, then relay(s)							
II	(d ∨ Λ)(ff*gg*hH) ∨ dgg*hH	MTA of provider, then relay(s) and gateway(s)							x
II	(d ∨ Λ) (ff*hH) ∨ dhH	MTA of provider, then at least gateway(s)							
III	ak	Local MTA		x			x		x
IV	(a ∨ b) gg*k	Local MTA or MUA, then relay(s)							
IV	(a ∨ b)(gg*hH ∨ hH)	Local MTA or MUA, then relay(s) and gateway(s)	x			x	x		x
IV	cj*i (hH ∨ gg*H ∨ gg*k ∨ k)	Local agent other than MTA or MUA, then at least gateway(s)							
V	(ad ∨ bd ∨ bed)(k ∨ ff*k)	Local MTA or MUA, then MTA(s) of provider	(x)	(x)				(x)	(x)
VI	(ad ∨ bd ∨ bed)(ff*gg*k ∨ gg*k)	Local MTA or MUA, then MTA(s) of provider, then relay(s)							
VI	(ad ∨ bd ∨ bed)(ff*hH ∨ hH)	Local MTA or MUA, then MTA(s) of provider, then at least gateway(s)		(x)			x	(x)	(x)
VI	(ad ∨ bd ∨ bed)(ff*gg*hH ∨ gg*hH)	Local MTA or MUA, then MTA(s) of provider, then relay(s) and gateway(s)							

An infrastructure framework for addressing spam

We propose a technological and organizational infrastructure framework that features a complementary application of several anti-spam measures.

The core ideas of the framework are (1) to limit the number of e-mails that can be sent during a specific time-window and per account, (2) to restrict the automatic set-up of e-mail accounts, and (3) to provide means for controlling this limitation of e-mail traffic by introducing an element of centralism. In order to support these ideas, a new organizational role is introduced: the

Counter Managing & Abuse Authority (CMAA). The framework is intended to include several organizations, each of them taking on the full CMAA role. These organizations are either new and designated ones or established ones, such as trustworthy ESPs. In our framework, in principle, a sending organization (SO), for example an ESP, either directly transmits an e-mail to the receiving organization (RO) or sends the e-mails to a CMAA organization, which then relays the message to the SO. The former option is today's default option for sending e-mails, but is intended to be used in our framework only if the RO trusts the SO with regard to the implementation of effective anti-spam measures. Otherwise, the latter option applies, which means that the CMAA first checks whether the sender would exceed the number of e-mails he or she is allowed to send on one day. Depending on the result, the CMAA would then either bounce the e-mail or relay it to the RO, whereby every CMAA organization offers a relaying service.

This replacement of the direct SMTP connection between the SO and the RO by a relaying procedure represents an element of centralism which allows for controlling and accounting the (volume of) e-mail traffic. This control is intended to enormously reduce the sending of unsolicited bulk e-mail. Solicited bulk e-mail may still be sent if a person or organization accepts (legal) responsibility for its proper usage. The (anti-spam) control is also intended to make additional anti-spam measures undertaken by ROs obsolete. As the control mechanism is unlikely to prevent all spamming, it seems reasonable to complementarily provide a forum for e-mail users' complaints about unsolicited e-mails. Therefore, every CMAA organization is intended to also operate a central anti-spam abuse system. The abuse system and the relaying system are connected to each other in that numerous complaints about the spamming activities on behalf of a specific sender may lead to the blocking of that sender's CMAA account and, thus, to the bouncing of further e-mails from this sender. However, we also have to take privacy concerns into account when e-mail relaying is done by only several central organizations.

An important feature of the framework is the option of the SO to send an e-mail directly to the RO in order to reduce a CMAA's workload. However, whether an e-mail that has not been relayed and counted by a CMAA is accepted by an RO depends on the RO's policy, which could include a dynamic white list of trustworthy SOs. This alternative procedure, which is today's standard in e-mail delivery, makes the framework flexible and scalable in both its operation and deployment.

In order to implement the accountability, on which the framework is based, the SO sets up a record for each sender's e-mail account prior to the user's application for an e-mail account at his/her SO and prior to the first relaying. The records are stored in a database, herein denoted as Counter Database (CDB). As a CMAA is also responsible for the locking of accounts owing to abuse complaints, these complaints are stored in another database, herein denoted as Abuse Database (ADB). A third database, the Organization Database (ODB), serves for the storage of information about those SOs that are registered on the CMAA for the usage of its services. Figure 8.2 illustrates the (simplified) infrastructure framework.

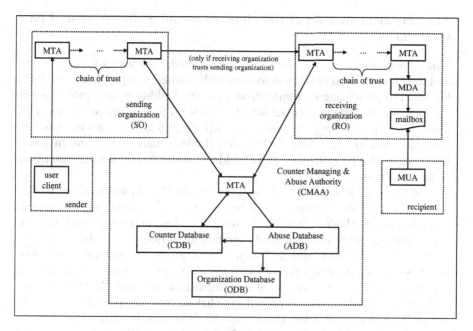

Fig. 8.2: Overview of the infrastructure framework

With regard to the theoretical effectiveness of the proposed framework, we can use the model of the Internet e-mail infrastructure. We show that all derived spamming options are covered effectively by our framework.

An essential precondition for the wide deployment of a new e-mail infrastructure seems to be that its key elements can be introduced smoothly and flexibly, i.e. that the adoption of the infrastructure (additions) can occur evolutionarily. Our infrastructure framework provides for this challenge as follows: The framework is designed to use both a direct e-mail communication and an indirect one by integrating CMAAs. This flexibility means a scalability of the framework that allows the avoidance of a "big bang" at its introduction, but leaves the (time) schedule for using CMAAs to each organization.

The introduction of the proposed infrastructure indicates a limitation of the overall e-mail communication. The degree of limitation will depend on the extent to which the CMAAs will be accepted and used. If the proposed infrastructure is either widely accepted or hardly accepted, then, the limitation is low. A high limitation would result from a balanced distribution.

The implementation of the framework requires both organizational and technological modifications of today's Internet e-mail infrastructure. These modifications have to be propagated by Internet organizations and providers in order to become widely accepted.

The empirical analysis of the abuse of e-mail addresses placed on the Internet

Valid e-mail addresses are among the most valuable resources for spammers, and the identification of address sources and spammers' exploiting procedures is crucial to preventing spammers from procuring addresses and subsequently misusing them. It is widely known that, besides generating addresses with brute force mechanisms and dictionary attacks, spammers procure valid e-mail addresses by harvesting the Internet. However, only little is known about the quantitative properties of e-mail address abuse on the Internet and how to measure these.

For the empirical analysis of the usage of e-mail addresses that are seeded on the Internet, we propose using a honeypot. Using a honeypot, we assume the following methodological issues to be the most important ones: (1) the determination of the analysis' goals, including the questions to be addressed, (2) the selection of appropriate Internet locations as well as e-mail addresses to be seeded, (3) the development of proper data and database models, (4) the conceptualization of the honeypot's IT infrastructure, and (5) the selection and application of evaluation procedures that address the analysis' goals. It is especially items 2 and 3 for which some kinds of generic "frameworks" seem to be appropriate. Therefore, both a framework for seeding e-mail addresses and data(base) models for storing e-mails are proposed. The framework uses the dimensions "service", "language", and "topic" for specifying categories of Internet locations. We present an object-oriented data model, an equivalent relational data model, and a relational database model. The development of these two equivalent data models is driven by the goal of supporting the use of databases that follow one of the two currently most important modeling paradigms: structural modeling and object-oriented modeling. The representation of a relational database model results from the fact that such a model was chosen for storing e-mails in the prototypic implementation of an empirical study.

The prototypic implementation of an empirical study follows the proposed methodology. The study's main objective is to assess, on a quantitative basis, the extent of the current harassment and its development over time with regard to US and German web pages, newsletters, and German-speaking as well as English-speaking Usenet groups (newsgroups). The key findings of the study are:

❑ Web placements attract more than two-thirds (70%) of all honeypot spam e-mails, followed by newsgroup placements (28.6%) and newsletter subscriptions (1.4%). Language-specific proportions do not considerably differ from the proportions in total.

❑ Analyzing the relevance of the e-mail addresses' top-level domain (TLD) to receiving spam, we find that the empirical proportion of spam sent to e-mail addresses which were placed on the Internet follows a discrete uniform distribution. The empirical data regarding spam on e-mail addresses which were not placed on the Internet differ from the data considered above, in that spam e-mails directed to "org" addresses amount to almost 85%. Brute force and dictionary attacks seem to focus on e-mail addresses with the TLD "org".

❑ We find that more than 43% of addresses that were seeded on the web have been abused, whereas about 27% was the case for addresses on newsgroups and only about 4% for addresses used for a newsletter subscription.

❑ The development of e-mail addresses' attractiveness for spammers over time can be analyzed by regression analysis. We find a negative linear relationship for the service "web sites" and a negative exponential relationship for the service "newsgroups". A regression analysis for the service "newsletter" does not appear to be reasonable due to the low number of spam e-mails received.

❑ The honeypot also allows the checking of the relationship between a spam e-mail's topic and the topic of the location at which the recipient's address was placed. We manually checked 3,500 spam e-mails in "first come first served" order and found only 53 e-mails (1.54%) which shared a topic. Therefore, we suppose that spammers do not send their e-mails in a "context sensitive" manner.

Outlook

On the basis of this work, research could continue in the following areas:

❑ Our proposed infrastructure framework includes a new organizational role, the Counter Managing & Abuse Authority (CMAA). The development of business models that the CMAAs underlie is crucial to the deployment of the framework, but business models have not yet been elaborated.

❑ The proposed framework is presented on a conceptual level only. Prototypic implementations of the framework including the adjustment of various framework parameters, such as the precise procedures for manually setting up accounts and for authenticating at the CMAAs, are still lacking.

❑ We have not considered upcoming costs of the proposed infrastructure framework, which occur due to its introduction and operation. These costs also depend on the business model which the Counter Managing & Abuse Authorities underlie. Quantitative analysis of the economic impact of the infrastructure framework is desirable.

❑ Our empirical analysis of address abuse is limited in Internet services and in time. More comprehensive empirical studies, which could follow our proposed method, could amend our findings. Furthermore, our study does not include any analysis of the practical effectiveness of address obscuring techniques. Such experiences and findings are useful in order to develop e-mail user guidelines, which make recommendations on how to use and distribute e-mail addresses.

☐ Beside spam distributed over SMS, chat, or Internet phone, e-mail spam is just one type of spam that we face in electronic communication. We might look for (the world-wide deployment of) integrated solutions, which cover all these harassments. From the author's point of view, the increase of accountability on a personal level may support such solutions in the long run. Particularly, public key infrastructures seem to provide appropriate (technological and organizational) means for implementing this.

A

Process for parsing, classifying, and storing e-mails

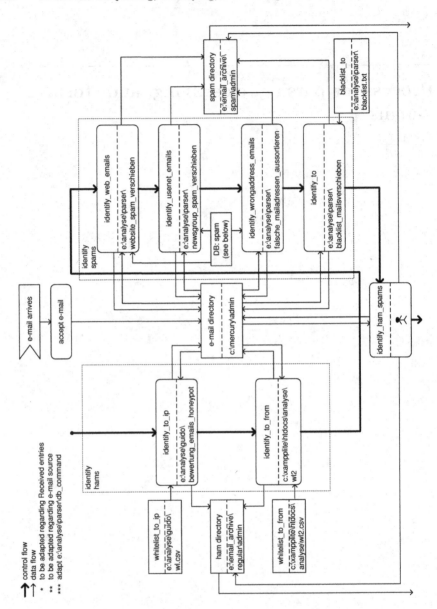

Fig. A.1: UML activity diagram for parsing, classifying, and storing e-mails (1)

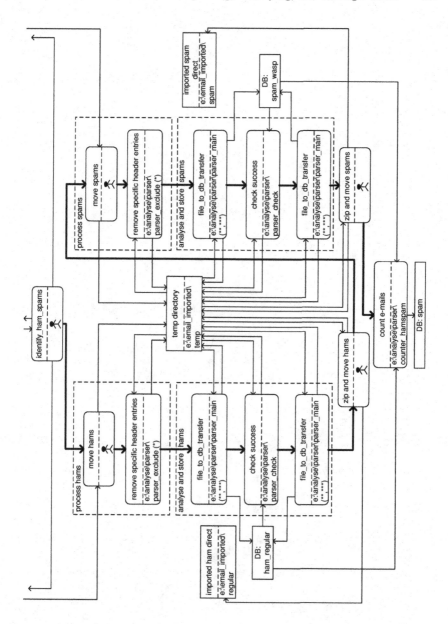

Fig. A.2: UML activity diagram for parsing, classifying, and storing e-mails (2)

B

Locations seeded with addresses that attracted most spam

#spams	web location*
829	http://jeepbrokers.com/jeepbrokers_guestbook.htm
536	http://www.theaterhaus.com/easync/easync_page.php?id=1,4,1&page=forum_geastebuch.htm
534	http://www.theaterhaus.com/easync/easync_page.php?id=1,4,1&page=forum_geastebuch.htm
518	http://www.la-palma24.net/de_visitas/guestbook.php3
510	http://www.la-palma24.net/de_visitas/guestbook.php3
499	http://www.la-palma24.net/de_visitas/guestbook.php3
453	http://www.beaufortrlty.com/guestbook.html
412	http://www.cyber-kitchen.com/cgibin/gbook/guestbook.cgi
396	http://www.germantownnews.com/guestbook
393	http://www.cyber-kitchen.com/cgibin/gbook/guestbook.cgi
383	http://www.kelso.gov/
378	http://www.cyber-kitchen.com/cgibin/gbook/guestbook.cgi
337	http://www.bowlsengland.com/efgbk00.htm
337	http://jeepbrokers.com/jeepbrokers_guestbook.htm
332	http://jeepbrokers.com/jeepbrokers_guestbook.htm
304	http://jeepbrokers.com/jeepbrokers_guestbook.htm
275	http://www.metager.de
253	http://www.ourchurch.com/view/?pageID=111918
237	http://www.radiojamaica.com/guest-book/
222	http://books.dreambook.com/dawsadopt/main.html

*multiple occurrence of web locations refers to the placement of different e-mail addresses on these locations

Fig. B.1: Web locations seeded with addresses that attracted most spam

#spams	newsgroup
69	de.rec.sport.paintball
67	de.rec.tv.buffy
60	alt.drugs
52	de.sci.misc
50	alt.america
41	alt.airports
35	alt.fan.brad-pitt
30	de.rec.sport.misc
29	de.talk.jokes
29	de.org.ccc
28	de.soc.weltanschauung.misc
27	de.rec.tv.technik
26	alt.fan.shania-twain
26	alt.games.microsoft.age-of-empires
26	microsoft.public.microsoft.transaction.server.integration
25	de.etc.selbsthilfe.angst
23	de.talk.jokes.d
23	alt.windows-me
22	alt.off-topic

Fig. B.2: Usegroups seeded with addresses that attracted most spam

#spams	Newsletter*
66	Churchill College, University of Cambridge; http://www.opendays.com/newsletter/
45	Jayde B2B Search Enginge;http://www.jayde.de
44	Jayde B2B Search Enginge;http://www.jayde.de
40	Jayde B2B Search Enginge;http://www.jayde.de
22	Jayde B2B Search Enginge;http://www.jayde.de
21	Churchill College, University of Cambridge; http://www.opendays.com/newsletter/
21	Weisser Ring, http://www.weisser-ring.de/bundesgeschaeftsstelle/newsletter/index.php
16	Central Florida Photography Club, http://www.cflphotoclub.com/home/newsletter_form.htm
6	French Erotic Site; http://www.sexy.legratuit.com
6	Lowell Jaks Welcome Page, http://www.lowelljaks.com/
6	Churchill College, University of Cambridge; http://www.opendays.com/newsletter/
6	French Erotic Site; http://www.sexy.legratuit.com
6	Churchill College, University of Cambridge; http://www.opendays.com/newsletter/
5	French Erotic Site; http://www.sexy.legratuit.com
3	Edvisors.com: International Student Newsletter; http://www.edvisors.com/cgi/page.cgi?p=newsletter
3	Edvisors.com: International Student Newsletter; http://www.edvisors.com/cgi/page.cgi?p=newsletter
3	Lowell Jaks Welcome Page, http://www.lowelljaks.com/
2	Casinomeister, http://www.casinomeister.com/newsletter.html
2	Casino Bielefeld, http://www.casino-bielefeld.de/newsletter.php
2	Edvisors.com: International Student Newsletter; http://www.edvisors.com/cgi/page.cgi?p=newsletter

* multiple occurrence of newsletters refers to multiple subscription to these newsletters (each subscription uses a unique e-mail address)

Fig. B.3: Newsletters seeded with addresses that attracted most spam

References

[1] Abadi, M., Burrows, M., Manasse, M. and Wobber, T.: 2003, Moderately Hard, Memory-Bound Functions, *Proceedings of the 10th Annual Network and Distributed System Security Symposium*, pp. 25–39.

[2] Allman, E.: 2003, Spam, Spam, Spam, Spam, Spam, The FTC and Spam, *ACM queue* 1(6).

[3] Allman, E.: 2003/2004, The economics of spam, *ACM queue* 1(9).

[4] Allman, E., Callas, J., Delany, M., Libbey, M., Fenton, J. and Thomas, M.: 2005, DomainKeys Identified Mail (DKIM), *Internet draft*, IETF Network Working Group.

[5] Androutsopoulos, I., Koutsias, J., Chandrinos, K., Paliouas, G. and Vassilakis, C.: 2000, An Evaluation of Naive Bayesian Anti-Spam Filtering, *in* G. Potamias, V. Moustakis and M. van Sommeren (eds), *Proceedings of the 11th European Conference on Machine Learning*, pp. 9–17.

[6] Androutsopoulos, I., Koutsias, J., Chandrinos, K. and Spyropoulos, C.: 2000, An Experimental Comparison of Naive Bayesian and Keyword-Based Anti-Spam Filtering with Personal E-mail Messages, *in* N. Belkin, P. Inwersen and M. Leong (eds), *Proceedings of the 23rd ACM SIGIR Conference on Research and Development in Information Retrieval (SIGIR 2000)*, p. 160167.

[7] Androutsopoulos, I., Magirou, E. and Vassilakis, D.: 2005, A Game Theoretic Model of Spam E-Mailing, *Proceedings of the 2nd Conference on Email and Anti-Spam (CEAS 2005)*.

[8] Androutsopoulos, I., Paliouras, G., Karkaletsis, V., Sakkis, G., Spyropoulos, C. and Stamatopoulos, P.: 2000, Learning to Filter Spam E-mail: A Comparison of a Naive Bayesian and a Memory-Based Approach, *in* H. Zaragoza, P. Gallinari and M. Rajman (eds), *4th European Conference on Principles and Practice of Knowledge Discovery in Databases (PKDD 2000)*, pp. 1–13.

[9] Anti-Spam Technical Alliance (ASTA): 2004, Anti-spam technical alliance technology and policy report, *Technical report*.

[10] Back, A.: 2002, Hashcash - A Denial of Service Counter-Measure, http://www.hashcash.org/papers/hashcash.pdf.

[11] Balenson, D.: 1993, Privacy Enhancement for Internet Electronic Mail: Part III: Algorithms, Modes, and Identifiers., *RFC 1423*, IETF Network Working Group.

[12] BBC: 2003, E-mail vetting blocks mps' sex debate, http://news.bbc.co.uk/1/hi/uk_politics/2723851.stm.

[13] *BGB*: 2002, Bundesgesetzblatt I S. 42, ber. S. 2909 u. Bundesgesetzblatt 2003 S. 738).

[14] Bless, R., Conrad, M. and Hof, H.-J.: 2005, Spam Protection by using Sender Address Verification Extension (SAVE). http://doc.tm.uka.de/2005/SAVE.pdf.

[15] Böhme, R. and Holz, T.: 2006, The Effect of Stock Spam on Financial Markets, http://weis2006.econinfosec.org. Working paper, presented at the Workshop on the Economics of Information Security (WEIS) 2006, University of Cambridge.

[16] Bradner, S.: 1997, Key words for use in RFCs to Indicate Requirement Levels, *RFC 2119*, IETF Network Working Group.

[17] Brightmail: 2003, The State of Spam Impact & Solutions.

[18] Bundesamt für Sicherheit in der Informationstechnik (BSI): 2005, Antispam - Strategien: Unerwünschte E-mails erkennen und abwehren.

[19] Callas, J., Donnerhacke, L., Finney, H. and Thayer, R.: 1998, OpenPGP Message Format, *RFC 2440*, IETF Network Working Group.

[20] Campbell, K.: 1994, A NET.CONSPIRACY SO IMMENSE...Chatting With Martha Siegel of the Internet's Infamous Canter & Siegel, http://www.eff.org/legal/cases/Canter_Siegel/c-and-s_summary.article.

[21] *CANSPAM Act of 2003*: 2003, PUBLIC LAW 108187DEC. 16, 2003.

[22] Carreras, X. and Mrquez, L.: 2001, Boosting Trees for Anti-Spam Email Filtering, *in* T. Chark (ed.), *Proceedings of the International Conference on Recent Advances in Natural Language Processing*.

[23] CAUBE.AU: 1999, The CAUBE.AU Spam Survey, *Technical report*. http://www.caube.org.au/survey.htm.

[24] Center for Democracy & Technology: 2003, Why Am I Getting All This Spam? Unsolicited Commercial E-mail Research Six Month Report, *Technical report*. http://www.cdt.org/speech/spam/030319spamreport.shtml.

[25] Chhabra, S., Yerazunis, W. and Siefkes, C.: 2004, Spam Filtering using a Markov Random Field Model with Variable Weighting Schemas, *Proceedings of the 4th IEEE International Conference on Data Mining*, pp. 347–350.

[26] Christensen, B.: 2006, WARNING TO ALL DOG OWNERS (Joke), http://www.hoax-slayer.com/warning-dog-owners.html.

[27] *Coding email links to avoid spam*: 2003, http://www.bronze-age.com/nospam/.

[28] Cohen, W.: 1996, Learning rules that classify e-mail, *Papers from the AAAI Spring Syposium on Machine Learning in Information Access*, pp. 18–25.

[29] Commtouch: 2006, Spam statistics, http://www.commtouch.com/Site/ResearchLab/statistics.asp.

[30] Cranor, L. F. and LaMacchia, B. A.: 1998, Spam!, *Communications of the ACM* **41**(9), 74–83.

[31] Crawford, E., Kay, J. and McCreath, E.: 2001, Automatic induction of rules for e-mail classification, *Proceedings of the Sixth Australasian Document Computing Symposium*.

[32] Crispin, M.: 1994, Internet Message Access Protocol - Version 4, *RFC 1730*, IETF Network Working Group.

[33] Crocker, D., Leslie, J. and Otis, D.: 2005, Certified Server Validation (CSV), *Internet draft*, IETF Network Working Group.

[34] Crocker, D. and Overell, P.: 1997, Augmented BNF for Syntax Specifications: ABNF, *RFC 2234*, IETF Network Working Group.

[35] Damiani, E., De Capitani di Vimercati, S., Paraboschi, S. and Samarati, P.: 2004, P2p-based collaborative spam detection and filtering, *Proceedings of the Fourth International Conference on Peer-to-Peer Computing*, pp. 176–183.

[36] Danish, H.: 2004, The RMX DNS RR and method for lightweight SMTP sender authorization, *Internet draft*, IETF Network Working Group.

[37] De Winter, J.: 1996, Smtp Service Extension for Remote Message Queue Starting, *RFC 2818*, IETF Network Working Group.

[38] DECLUDE Internet Security Software: 2005, List of All Known DNS-based Spam Databases, http://www.declude.com/Articles.asp?ID=97.

[39] DeKok, A.: 2004, Lightweight MTA Authentication Protocol (LMAP) Discussion and Applicability Statement, *Internet draft*, IETF Network Working Group.

[40] Delany, M.: 2005, Domain-based Email Authentication Using Public-Keys Advertised in the DNS (DomainKeys), *Internet draft*, IETF Network Working Group.

[41] Denning, P.: 1982, Electronic junk, *Communications of teh ACM* **25**(3), 163165.

[42] *Directive 2002/58/EC*: 2002, Official Journal of the European Communities, L 201/37.

[43] Doll, J.: n.d., Spam Attack, http://www.joes.com/spammed.html.

[44] Doubleclick: 2003, New Research: Spam: The Consumer Perspective, http://www3.doubleclick.com/market/2003/10/dc/email1.htm.

[45] Drawes, R.: 2002, An artificial neural network spam classifier, *Technical report*. www.interstice.com/drewes/cs676/spam-nn/spam-nn.html.

[46] Drucker, H., Wu, D. and Vladimir N. Vapnik: 1999, Support Vector Machines for Spam Categorization, *IEEE Transactions on Neural Networks* **10**(5), 1048–1054.

[47] Dwork, C., Goldberg, A. and Naor, M.: 2003, On Memory-Bound Functions for Fighting Spam, *in* D. Boneh (ed.), *Proceedings of the 23rd Annual International Cryptology Conference (CRYPTO 2003)*, number 2729 in *LNCS*, Springer, pp. 426–444.

[48] Dwork, C. and Naor, M.: 2002, Procing via Processing or Combatting Junk Mail, *in* D. Boneh (ed.), *Proceedings of the 22rd Annual International Cryptology Conference (CRYPTO 2002)*, number 740 in *LNCS*, Springer, pp. 137–147.

[49] Email-policy.com: 2004, Real-time Spam Black Lists (RBL), http://www.email-policy.com/Spam-black-lists.htm.

[50] Email Service Provider Coalition: 2003, Project Lumos: A Solutions Blueprint for Solving the Spam Problem by Establishing Volume Email Sender Accountability, *Technical report*.

[51] EU: 2004, Cooperation Procedure Concerning the Transmission of Complaint Information and Intelligence Relevant to the Enforcement of Article 13 of the Privacy and Electronic Communication Directive 2002/58/EC, or Any Other Applicable National Law Pertaining to the Use of Unsolicited Electronic Communications.

[52] Evett, D.: 2006, Spam Statistics 2006, http://spam-filter-review.toptenreviews.com/spam-statistics.html.

[53] Fahmann, S.: 2002, Selling interrupt rights: A way to control unwanted e-mail and telephone calls, *IBM Systems Journal* **41**(4), 759–766.

[54] Fecyk, G.: 2003, Designated Mailers Protocol, *Internet draft*, IETF Network Working Group.

[55] Fenton, J. and Thomas, M.: 2005, Identified Internet Mail, *J. fenton and m. thomas*, IETF Network Working Group.

[56] Ferris Research: 2005, The Global Economic Impact of Spam, 2005. Report #409.

[57] Fiat, A. and Shamir, A.: 1986, How to proof yourself, *Proceedings of CRYPTO 86*, pp. 641–654.

[58] Freed, N.: 1996, SMTP Service Extension for Returning Enhanced Error Codes, *RFC 2034*, IETF Network Working Group.

[59] Freed, N.: 2000, SMTP Service Extension for Command Pipelining, *RFC 2920*, IETF Network Working Group.

[60] Freed, N. and Borenstein, N.: 1996a, Multipurpose Internet Mail Extensions (MIME) Part Five: Conformance Criteria and Examples, *RFC 2049*, IETF Network Working Group.

[61] Freed, N. and Borenstein, N.: 1996b, Multipurpose Internet Mail Extensions (MIME) Part One: Format of Internet Message Bodies, *RFC 2045*, IETF Network Working Group.

[62] Freed, N. and Borenstein, N.: 1996c, Multipurpose internet mail extensions (mime) part two: Media types, *RFC 2046*, IETF Network Working Group.

[63] Freed, N., Klensin, J. and Postel, J.: 1996, Multipurpose Internet Mail Extensions (MIME) Part Four: Registration Procedures, *RFC 2048*, IETF Network Working Group.

[64] Freier, A. O., Karlton, P. and Kocher, P. C.: 1996, The SSL Protocol Version 3.0, *Internet draft*, IETF Network Working Group.

[65] FTC: 2002, Email Address Harvesting: How Spammers Reap What You Sow, *Technical report*. http://www.ftc.gov/bcp/conline /pubs/alerts/spamalrt.htm.

[66] FTC: 2004, National Do Not Email Registry A Report to Congress, *Technical report*.

[67] FTC: 2005, Email Address Harvesting and the Effectiveness of Anti-Spam Filters, *Technical report*.

[68] Gabber, E., Jakobsson, M., Matias, Y. and Mayer, A. J.: 1998, Curbing Junk E-Mai via Secure Classification, *Proceedings of the Second International Conference on Financial Cryptography*, pp. 198–213.

[69] Garfinkel, S.: 2003, Email-Based Identification and Authentication: An Alternative to PKI?, *IEEE Security & Privacy* 1(6), 20–26.

[70] Gauthronet, S. and Etienne, D.: 2001, Unsolicited Commercial Communications and Data Protection.

[71] Gburzynski, P. and Maitan, J.: 2004, Fighting the spam wars, A remailer approach with restrictive aliasing, *ACM Trans. Inter. Tech.* 4(1), 1–30.

[72] Gellens, R. and Klensin, J.: 1998, Message Submission, *RFC 2476*, IETF Network Working Group.

[73] Gettys, J., Mogul, J., Frystyk, H., Masinter, L. and Leach, P.: 1999, Hypertext Transfer Protocol – HTTP/1.1, *RFC 2616*, IETF Network Working Group.

[74] Gómez Hidalgo, J. and Maña López, M.: 2000, Combining Text and Heuristics for Cost-Sensitive Spam Filtering, *Proceedings of CoNLL-2000 and LLL-2000*, pp. 99–102.

[75] Graham, P.: 2002, A Plan For Spam, http://www.paulgraham.com/spam.html.

[76] Graham, P.: 2003, Better Bayesian Filtering, *Proceedings of the 2003 Spam Conference*.

[77] Hall, R.: 1996, Channels: Avoiding Unwanted Electronic Mail, *Proceedings of the DIMACS Symposium on Network Threats*.

[78] Hoffman, P.: 2002, SMTP Service Extension for Secure SMTP over Transport Layer Security, *RFC 3207*, IETF Network Working Group.

[79] ICANN: 2004, new sTLD RFP Application .mail, Part B. Application Form, *Technical report*.

[80] Ilett, D.: 2004, Most spam generated by botnets, says expert, http://news.zdnet.co.uk/internet/security/0,39020375,39167561,00.htm.

[81] InfoSec: 2004, Email Spamming (include scam), *Technical report*.

[82] Internet Assigned Numbers Authority (IANA): 2002, MIME Media Types. http://www.iana.org/assignments/media-types/index.html.

[83] Ioannidis, J.: 2003, Fighting Spam by Encapsulating Policy in Email Addresses, *The 10th Annual Network and Distributed System Security Symposium Conference Proceedings.*

[84] Ironport: 2006, Internet Email Traffic Emergency: Spam Bounce Messages are Compromising Networks, http://www.ironport.com/bouncereport/.

[85] ITU: 2003, Memorandum of Understanding Between the Korea Information Security Agency and the Australian Communications Authority and the National Office for the Information Economy of Australia Concerning Cooperation in the Regulation of Spam.

[86] ITU: 2005a, A Comparative Analysis of Spam Laws: The Quest for a Model Law, Background Paper for the ITU WSIS Thematic Meeting on Cybersecurity, Geneva, Switzerland, 28 JUNE 1 JULY 2005.

[87] ITU: 2005b, ITU Survey on Anti-spam Legislation Worldwide.

[88] Johansson, E.: n.d., Camram, www.camram.org.

[89] Kaliski, B.: 1993, Privacy Enhancement for Internet Electronic Mail: Part IV: Key Certification and Related Services, *RFC 1424*, IETF Network Working Group.

[90] Kaushik, S., Ammann, P., Wijesekera, D., Winsborough, W. and Ritchey, R.: 2004, A Policy Driven Approach to Email Services, *Proceedings of IEEE 5th International Workshop on Policies for Distributed Systems and Networks (Policy 2004).*

[91] Kent, S.: 1993, Privacy Enhancement for Internet Electronic Mail: Part II: Certificate-Based Key Management, *RFC 1422*, IETF Network Working Group.

[92] Klensin, G., Freed, N., Rose, M., Stefferud, E. and Crocker, D.: 1995, SMTP Service Extensions, *RFC 1893*, IETF Network Working Group.

[93] Klensin, J.: 2001, Simple Mail Transfer Protocol, *RFC 2821*, IETF Network Working Group.

[94] Köcher, J.: 2004, Anti-spam-gesetze, *DFN Mitteilungen* (64 - 3), 29–30.

[95] Leibzon, W.: 2005a, Email Security Anti-Spoofing Protection with Path and Cryptographic Authentication Methods, http://www.metasignatures.org/path_and_cryptographic_authentication.htm.

[96] Leibzon, W.: 2005b, META Signatures (Message Enhancements for Transmission Authorization), *Technical report.* http://www.metasignatures.org/meta_signatures_protocol.htm.

[97] Levine, J., Crocker, D., Silberman, S. and Finch, T.: 2004, Bounce Address Tag Validation (BATV), *Internet draft*, IETF Network Working Group.

[98] Lindberg, G.: 1999, Anti-Spam Recommendations for SMTP MTAs, *RFC 2505*, IETF Network Working Group.

[99] Linke, A.: 2003, Spam oder nicht Spam? E-Mail sortieren mit Bayes-Filtern, *ct* pp. 150–153.

[100] Linn, J.: 1993, Privacy Enhancement for Internet Electronic Mail: Part I: Message Encryption and Authentication Procedures, *RFC 1421*, IETF Network Working Group.

[101] Loder, T., van Alstyne, M. and Walsh, R.: 2004, Information Asymmetry and Thwarting Spam, *Technical report*, University of Michigan.

[102] Lyon, J.: 2005, Purported Responsible Address in E-Mail Messages, *Internet draft*, IETF Network Working Group.

[103] Lyon, J. and Wong, M.: 2005, Sender ID: Authenticating E-Mail, *Internet draft*, IETF Network Working Group.

[104] MessageLabs: 2006,   MessageLabs   Intelligence   Report: Spam   Intercepts   Timeline   May   2006, http://www.messagelabs.com/publishedcontent/publish/threat_watch _dotcom_en/threat_statistics/spam_intercepts/DA_114633.chp.html.

[105] Metzger, J., Schillo, M. and Fischer, K.: 2003, A Multiagent-Based Peer-to-Peer Network in Java for Distributed Spam Filtering, *in* V. Mark, J. Mller and M. Pechoucek (eds), *Proceedings of the 3rd International Workshop of Central and Eastern Europe on Multi-Agent Systems (CEEMAS)*, pp. 616–625.

[106] Microsoft: 2004, Email Postmarks.

[107] Mockapetris, P.: 1987a, Domain names - concepts and facilities, *RFC 1034*, IETF Network Working Group.

[108] Mockapetris, P.: 1987b, Domain names - implementation and specification, *RFC 1035*, IETF Network Working Group.

[109] Moore, K.: 1996, MIME (Multipurpose Internet Mail Extensions) Part Three: Message Header Extensions for Non-ASCII Text, *RFC 2047*, IETF Network Working Group.

[110] Mori, G. and Malik, J.: 2003, Recognizing Objects in Adversarial Clutter – Breaking a Visual CAPTCHA, *Proceedings of the Conference Computer Vision and Pattern Recognition*.

[111] Moustakas, E., Ranganathan, C. and Duquenoy, P.: 2005, Combating Spam through Legislation: A Comparative Analysis of US and European Approaches, *Proceedings of the Second Conference on Email and Anti-Spam(CEAS 2005)*.

[112] Myers, J.: 1996, Local Mail Transfer Protocol, *RFC 2033*, IETF Network Working Group.

[113] Myers, J.: 1997, Simple Authentication and Security Layer (SASL), *RFC 2222*, IETF Network Working Group.

[114] Myers, J.: 1999, SMTP Service Extension for Authentication, *RFC 2554*, IETF Network Working Group.

[115] Myers, J. and Rose, M.: 1996, Post office protocol - version 3, *RFC 1939*, IETF Network Working Group.

[116] Nelson, S. and Parks, C.: 1997, The Model Primary Content Type for Multipurpose Internet Mail Extensions, *RFC 2077*, IETF Network Working Group.

[117] Newman, D.: 2000, Deliver By SMTP Service Extension, *RFC 2852*, IETF Network Working Group.

[118] NOIE: 2002, The Spam Problem and How it Can be Countered An Interim Report by NOIE, *Technical report*.

[119] NOIE: 2003, Final Report of the NOIE Review of the Spam Problem and How It Can Be Countered, *Technical report*.   www.noie.gov.au/publications/NOIE/ spam/final_report/SPAMreport.pdf.

[120] Nucleus Research: 2003, Spam: The Silent ROI Killer.

[121] O'Brien, C. and Vogel, C.: 2003, Spam Filters: Bayes vs. Chi-squared; Letters vs. Words, *Technical Report TCD-CS-2003-13*, Trinity College Dublin.

[122] OECD: 2003, Issues on the Measurement of Unsolicited Electronic Messages.

[123] OECD: 2004a, Background Paper for the OECD Workshop on Spam.

[124] OECD: 2004b, Report of the 2nd OECD Workshop on Spam.

[125] OECD: 2004c, Report on non-OECD Countries' Spam Legislation.

[126] OECD: 2005a, Anti-Spam Law Enforcement Report.

[127] OECD: 2005b, Anti-Spam Regulation.

[128] OECD: 2005c, Spam Issues in Developing Countries.

[129] Otis, D., Crocker, D. and Leslie, J.: 2005, Client SMTP Authorization (CSA), *Internet draft*, IETF Network Working Group.

[130] Palme, J.: 1997, Common Internet Message Headers, *RFC 2076*, IETF Network Working Group.

[131] Palme, J.: 2002, Common Internet Message Header Fields, *Internet draft*, IETF Network Working Group.

[132] Pantel, P. and Lin., D.: 1998, SpamCop - A Spam Classification & Organization Program, *Proceedings of AAAI-98 Workshop on Learning for Text Categorization*.

[133] Partridge, C.: 1986, Mail Routing and the Domain System, *RFC 2183*, IETF Network Working Group.

[134] Postel, J.: 1975, On the Junk Mail Problem, *RFC 706*, IETF Network Working Group.

[135] Postel, J. B.: 1982, Simple Mail Transfer Protocol, *RFC 821*, IETF Network Working Group. obsoleted by RFC 2821.

[136] Prince, M., Holloway, L., Langheinrich, E., Dahl, B. and Keller, A.: 2005, Understanding How Spammers Steal your E-Mail Address: An Analysis of the First Six Month of Data from Project Honey Pot, *Proceedings of the Second Conference on Email and Anti-Spam (CEAS)*. www.ceas.cc/papers-2005/163.pdf.

[137] Provost, J.: 1999, Naive-Bayes vs. Rule-Learning in Classification of Email, *Technical Report AI-TR-99-284*, Department of Computer Science, The University of Texas at Austin.

[138] Rabin, M.: 1979, Digital Signatures and Public Key Functions as Intractable as Factoring, *Technical Report TM-212*, Lab. for Computer Science, MIT.

[139] Ramsdell, B.: 2004, Secure/Multipurpose Internet Mail Extensions (S/MIME) Version 3.1 Message Specification, *RFC 3851*, IETF Network Working Group.

[140] Raz, U.: n.d., How do spammers harvest email addresses, http://www.private.org.il/harvest.html.

[141] Rescorla, E.: 2000, HTTP Over TLS, *RFC 2818*, IETF Network Working Group.

[142] Resnick, P.: 2001, Internet Message Format, *RFC 2822*, IETF Network Working Group.

[143] Sahami, M., Dumais, S., Heckerman, D. and Horvitz, E.: 1998, A Bayesian Approach to Filtering Junk E-Mail, *Proceedings of AAAI-98 Workshop on Learning for Text Categorization*.

[144] Sanders, T.: 2005, Microsoft takes on spamming botnets, http://www.vnunet.com/vnunet/news/2144976/microsoft-takes-spamming.

[145] Sandvine: 2004, Zombie PCs spew out 80% of spam.

[146] Schneider, K.: 2003, A comparison of event models for naive bayes anti-spam e-mail filtering, *Proceedings of the 11th Conference of the European Chapter of the Association for Computational Linguistics (EACL'03)*, pp. 307–314.

[147] Schryen, G.: 2004a, A Scalable and Flexible Infrastructure Framework for Addressing Spam, *Proceedings of IPSI International Conference on Advances in the Internet, Processing, Systems, and Interdisciplinary Research*.

[148] Schryen, G.: 2004b, Approaches addressing spam, *Proceedings of the HHCCII*.

[149] Schryen, G.: 2004c, Effektivität von Lösungsansätzen zur Bekämpfung von Spam, *Wirtschaftsinformatik* 46(4), 281–288.

[150] Schryen, G.: 2004d, Fighting Spam: Motivating an Account-based Approach, *Proceedings of the IADIS International Conference WWW/Internet 2004*, Vol. II, IADIS Press, pp. 937–940.

[151] Schryen, G.: 2005, An e-mail honeypot addressing spammers' behavior in collecting and applying addresses, *Proceedings of the 6th IEEE Information Assurance Workshop*, pp. 37–41.

[152] Schryen, G.: 2006, A formal approach towards assessing the effectiveness of anti-spam procedures, *Proceedings of the 39th Annual Hawaii International Conference on System Sciences*.

[153] Schryen, G.: 2007a, Anti-spam legislation: An analysis of laws and their effectiveness, *Information and Communications Technology Law* 1(16).

[154] Schryen, G.: 2007b, Armed for the spam battle - a technological and organizational infrastructure framework, *Proceedings of the 40th Annual Hawaii International Conference on System Sciences*.

[155] Schryen, G.: 2007c, Do anti-spam measures cover the e-mail communication network? A formal approach, *The Journal of Information Systems Security* . accepted for publication.

[156] Schryen, G.: 2007d, Preventing E-mail Spam: The Conceptualization and the Analysis of an Infrastructure Framework, *Technical Report 07/01*, RWTH Aachen University, Faculty of Business and Economics.

[157] Schryen, G.: 2007e, The Impact that Placing Email Addresses on the Internet has on the Receipt of Spam, *Computers and Security* . accepted for publication.

[158] Schryen, G. and Hoven, R.: 2004, Appropriateness of Lightweight MTA Authentication Protocols for Fighting Spam, *Proceedings of IPSI International Conference on Advances in the Internet, Processing, Systems, and Interdisciplinary Research*.

[159] Sester, P. and Mutschler, S.: 2006, Neue Kooperationen und rechtliche Entwicklungen im Kampf gegen Spam, *Informatik-Spektrum* **29**(1), 14–22.

[160] Sophos: 2005a, CAN-SPAM Act can do better, http://www.sophos.com/pressoffice/news/articles/2005/12/canspam05.html.

[161] Sophos: 2005b, Sophos Security Threat Management Report, http://www.sophos.com/sophos/docs/eng/marketing_material/SophosSecurityReport_2005.pdf.

[162] Sophos: 2006a, Defending networks against rapidly evolving threats, http://www.sophos.com/sophos/docs/eng/papers/sophos-defending-networks-wpus.pdf.

[163] Sophos: 2006b, Sophos report reveals latest 'dirty dozen' spam relaying countries, http://www.sophos.com/pressoffice/news/articles/2006/04/dirtydozapr06.html.

[164] Spamhaus: 2006, Spamhaus Statistics : The Top 10, http://www.spamhaus.org/statistics/countries.lasso.

[165] Spamhaus: n.d., The Definition of Spam, http://www.spamhaus.org/definition.html.

[166] Spammer-X: 2004, *The SPAM Cartel Why Spammers Spam*, Syngress Media.

[167] *Strafgesetzbuch*: 1998, Bundesgetztblatt I S. 3322.

[168] Stumpf, M. and Hoehne, S.: 2005, Marking Mail Transfer Agents in Reverse DNS with TXT RRs, *Internet draft*, IETF Network Working Group.

[169] Symantec: 2006, Spam-Statistiken, http://www.symantec.com/region/de/PressCenter/spam.html.

[170] Tanase, M.: 2003, IP Spoofing: An Introduction, http://www.securityfocus.com/infocus/1674.

[171] Templeton, B.: n.d.a, E-stamps, http://www.templetons.com/brad/spam/estamps.html.

[172] Templeton, B.: n.d.b, Origin of the term "spam" to mean net abuse, http://www.templetons.com/brad/spamterm.html.

[173] Templeton, B.: n.d.c, Reaction to the DEC Spam of 1978, http://www.templetons.com/brad/spamreact.html.

[174] The Government of Hongkong: n.d., Nigerian letters, http://www.info.gov.hk/police/pda/con-tricks/con7.htm.

[175] The Honeynet Project & Research Alliance: 2005, Know your Enemy: Tracking Botnets, *Technical report*.

[176] The New York Times: 2003, We Hate Spam, Congress Says (Except Ours), http://www.nytimes.com.

[177] The Radicati Group: 2003, ANTI-SPAM MARKET TRENDS OVERVIEW 2003-2007.

[178] *THE LONDON ACTION PLAN On International Spam Enforcement Cooperation*: 2004, http://www.londonactionplan.org.

[179] Tompkins, T. and Handley, D.: 2003, Giving E-mail Back to the Users: Using Digital Signatures to Solve the Spam Problem, *FirstMonday* 8(9).

[180] Troost, R., Dorner, S. and Moore, K.: 1997, Communicating Presentation Information in Internet Messages: The Content-Disposition Header Field, *RFC 2183*, IETF Network Working Group.

[181] Turner, D. A. and Havey, D. M.: 2004, Controlling Spam through Lightweight Currency, *Proceedings of the 37th Annual Hawaii International Conference on System Sciences*.

[182] Turner, D. and Ross, K.: 2003, A Lightweight Currency Paradigm for the P2P Resource Market.

[183] United Nations: 2005, List of Member States, http://www.un.org/Overview/ unmember.html.

[184] *UWG*: 2004, Bundesgesetzblatt Jahrgang 2004 Teil I Nr. 32.

[185] Vaudreuil, G.: 1996, Enhanced Mail System Status Codes, *RFC 1893*, IETF Network Working Group.

[186] von Ahn, L., Blum, M., Hopper, N. and Langford, J.: 2003, CAPTCHA: Using hard AI problems for security, *Proceedings of Eurocrypt*, pp. 294–311.

[187] von Ahn, L., Blum, M. and Langford, J.: 2004, Telling Humans and Computers Apart Automatically, *Communications of the ACM* 47(2), 57–60.

[188] W3C: 2003, SOAP Version 1.2 Part 1: Messaging Framework, http://www.w3.org/TR/soap12-part1/.

[189] Wirtz, B.: 2001, *Electronic Business*, 2 edn, Gabler.

[190] Wong, M. and Schlitt, W.: 2005, Sender Policy Framework (SPF) for Authorizing Use of Domains in E-MAIL, version 1, *Internet draft*, IETF Network Working Group.

[191] Zhou, F., Zhuang, L., Zhao, B., Huang, L., Joseph, A. and Kubiatowicz, J.: 2003, Approximate object location and spam filtering on peer-to-peer systems, *Proceedings of ACM/IFIP/USENIX International Middleware Conference*.

Index